The WEIGHT-LOSS DIARIES

COURTNEY RUBIN

McGraw·Hill

New York   Chicago   San Francisco   Lisbon   London   Madrid   Mexico City
Milan   New Delhi   San Juan   Seoul   Singapore   Sydney   Toronto

The McGraw·Hill Companies

Library of Congress Cataloging-in-Publication Data

Rubin, Courtney.
        The weight-loss diaries / Courtney Rubin. — 1st ed.
                p.   cm.
        ISBN 0-07-141623-4 (pbk. : alk. paper)
        1. Weight loss.   I. Title.

    RM222.2 .R79   2003
    613.2′5—dc21   2003014404

3 4 5 6 7 8 9 0 FGR/FGR 3 2 1 0 9 8 7 6 5 4

ISBN 0-07-141623-4

McGraw-Hill books are available at special quantity discounts to use as premiums and sales promotions, or for use in corporate training programs. For more information, please write to the Director of Special Sales, Professional Publishing, McGraw-Hill, Two Penn Plaza, New York, NY 10121-2298. Or contact your local bookstore.

This book is printed on acid-free paper.

For my mother

*In memory of some fine Fines: my grandpa Irving and
my uncle Dennis*

And especially for my grandmother Ruth Fine

Introduction

*I*n the fourteen years since my first successful diet—at age fourteen—I've lost and gained more than 350 pounds.

Some people have tried every kind of diet—Weight Watchers, Atkins, grapefruit, Zone, Sugar Busters—and I have, too. I've usually lasted about three days on each. My big weight losses—thirty-five pounds, forty pounds, fifty pounds—were usually on diets of my own devising: either extremely low calorie or extremely low fat, the latter of which was introduced to me by my freshman-year college roommate. (Emily was also the one who introduced me to the concept of exercise, but we'll get to that later.)

I'm good at starting a diet. I even like it. Actually, it's the prospect of starting that I love, the same way I savor the prospect of a first date. Since he hasn't yet popped a zit at the table, calculated how much of the paella I've eaten and then split the bill accordingly, or just plain not called again, I'm free to daydream about the way things could unfold. The regrets and disappointments of relationships past dissolve in a flurry of what-should-I-wear? and what-if-he-doesn't-show-up? and the possibility that maybe, just maybe, this date might be good.

Usually it isn't. The thrill of the new wears off fast.

The same with starting diets. In my teens I would read every "Lose Ten Pounds with Four Simple Changes" article I could find, reread *The Woman Doctor's Diet for Teenage Girls* (the first diet book I ever owned), page through *Seventeen* magazine dreaming about the clothing I'd finally be able to buy, and make elaborate plans about what I would and wouldn't eat. It was really only about food then, because in those days, the eighties, gym memberships were mostly still for the neighborhood health nuts, and besides, the idea of exercising in public seemed too humiliating. I was always secretive about my plans—for me, my dreams and diets were as delicate and fragile as bubbles, ready to pop at the slightest raise of an eyebrow from anyone. So I'd wake up early (and without an alarm clock) the morning I was going to start— always ravenous, but also brimming with resolve and the pleasure of my secret.

I was never quite sure when I'd start telling people about my diet. Preferably they'd just start noticing as the weight fell away. It didn't matter, though, because I never got that far. I'd make it until after school on Day 1 of the diet and the munchies would start. Or I'd make it through three days and my family would go out to dinner and I'd give in. Or no big diet-busting thing in particular would happen, but by Day 5 or 6 I'd have had it with struggling every hour; thoughts of food blotting out nearly everything else. I'd think about all the days that stretched ahead of me—days without oatmeal-raisin cookies or full-fat cheese—and give up. And of course, I'd start eating everything I'd forbidden myself, thinking: *Tomorrow I'll start. Definitely tomorrow.*

My successful diets worked because they worked relatively fast. I wanted to be thin, and in my typically impatient, nothing-caffeine-and-an-all-nighter-can't-solve mentality, I wanted to get the job done as quickly as possible. So that meant unrealistic, punishing regimens of an hour of exercise and 750 calories a day—regimens that drove me straight to the bakery counter before long. The diet camp I went to at age fourteen—my first successful diet, bankrolled by my grandmother—I'd chosen specifically because its success stories seemed to have lost the most pounds. (I quickly gained back the weight I'd lost when I returned home to unrestricted access to the refrigerator and no enforced aerobics classes.)

For as long as I can remember, I've fought, with varying degrees of success, two battles—one with my weight and the other with my family about my weight. Most people don't have the idealized version of themselves staring them in the face, but I do: I'm half of a set of fraternal twin sisters, and for years Diana could eat so much yet stay so slim that my parents used to joke that she had a hollow leg. For the past five years or so, even she has had to watch herself, but that's not much consolation.

Eating has consumed my life for years. I was bingeing (which differs from plain pigging out or overeating in that it is frantic and frenzied and out of control, and for me usually involved going to at least three stores to buy all the food I wanted because I was too embarrassed to buy it in one). I was starving. I was dieting. I was wishing I could have the willpower to stay on a diet.

Not a day went by that I didn't think life would be better or easier if I were thinner.

My diet pattern—either three days here and three days there, or lose forty pounds, fall off the diet with a spectacular crash, and then gain sixty—changed in the fall of 1998 when I was twenty-three. I began my usual starvation diet in September, right after Yom Kippur, the Jewish Day of Atonement. The day of fasting required by Jewish law was the perfect way to start a diet—or so I'd been hearing all my life from my grandmother. I got a new gym membership card—it had been so long since I'd used mine that I'd lost the old one—and started a rigid regimen of hour-long workouts five days a week.

I got twelve pounds into the diet. I was heavy enough at the time that this was just enough weight for me to feel tantalizingly close to actually *seeing* results, but certainly not enough for anyone else to see them. Then I ate four chocolate-chip cookies at a coworker's birthday party. Ditching the Lean Cuisines and egg-white omelets immediately followed. But a funny thing happened: I decided to keep going to the gym anyway. I was tired of my life—tired of feeling out of control, tired of remembering major events based on what size I wore and what I had or had not eaten, tired of my pants being too tight—and not sure what else to do. Fitting in workouts somehow seemed more manageable than completely revamping my eating, something I'd failed at so miserably so many times. I had a good fifty pounds to lose, so I didn't really expect that I could lose them with a few hours a week of stationary biking or walking around the track. But maybe, just maybe, a miracle would happen.

In a way, it did.

I kept up the gym workouts through November. Some weeks I'd go just once or twice, other weeks four or five times. In retrospect, I realize it was my first success with moderation—I was used to doing all five workouts (all no less than one hour) per week or not doing anything at all. My food—and weight—stayed pretty much the same, though, except occasionally I'd give up a brownie here or there and hope that my minor calorie savings would magically melt away some pounds.

One day in early December 1998—just as I was wondering how I would possibly keep up my exercise routine through the holidays—Leslie Milk called me into her office. You've probably heard of the concept of "office spouses"—well, Leslie is my office mom. She tells me when I look like I haven't gotten enough sleep, warns me when there's an "occasion for sin" (like a birthday cake), and always knows where to shop. A serial dieter for much of her life, Leslie had road tested various regimens on the pages of *Washingtonian*. So of course I'd told her about my gym-going routine. She also wrote occasionally for a fitness magazine called *Shape*, and she knew they had a story idea in search of a young writer—or really, a writer-dieter. They wanted someone who already was motivated on her own to lose weight—someone, Leslie thought, like the already gym-going me.

They wanted this woman to keep a very public weight-loss diary about what the struggle was really like. They also wanted to photograph her.

They were crazy.

Then I stopped to consider. Writing for a magazine—in other words, making a public commitment to losing weight—might give me the push to actually finish what I had started so many times. In the back of my mind, I also hoped that doing this publicly might stop me from bingeing—I'd be way too embarrassed if I ever had to admit in print how much I could sometimes eat.

When the columns began appearing, people wrote or even came up to me on the street to congratulate me and thank me for what they usually called "bravery" in writing about myself and my weight. But it wasn't bravery—it was mostly my own, um, fatheadedness. At the time I agreed to write the columns, I didn't know anyone who read *Shape*, because it wasn't something I admitted *I* did. I'd read the success stories while waiting in line at the grocery store, and—lured by the promises of a "bikini body in four weeks"—I'd shove the magazine under the breakfast cereal and Lean Cuisines as if it were a trashy novel and hope the cashier wouldn't comment: what was a fat girl like me doing buying a magazine like that?

So when *Shape* asked me to write about myself, I figured it could be great. I'd get paid to lose weight and no one would ever have to know.

Ha.

Shape has a circulation of 1.6 million, and I didn't find out until after the first column hit print that even people in my immediate circle of friends read the magazine. I guess I never knew because *Shape* just wasn't something that demanded discussion, like a really great article in last week's *New Yorker*. Either you followed the workouts or you didn't, but unless there was news of a way you could lie on your couch and still get that bikini body in four weeks or less, you rarely needed to bring up what you'd read at lunch the next day.

In the year of writing for *Shape*, I was supposed to become the "after" picture. *Shape* would set me up with a doctor and a nutritionist (but not, as most people assumed, a personal trainer, because a trainer would remove the story from the realm of "you can do this" and into the celebrity realm of "well, I could be thin, too, if I had a low-fat chef and a personal trainer"). And off I'd go to the land of women who never have to worry about whether the Gap's size XL shirt will fit and whether anyone they knew will see them walking into Lane Bryant.

In the beginning, all went according to script. I lost ten pounds the first month, five in the first half of the second. Then it finally happened. I spent so much time worrying and waiting and wondering when it would happen, and it did. "It" being a pig-out nearly two months into the diet. I didn't gain any weight from it, but I didn't escape other consequences. The need to over-eat—to binge—slowly became one I couldn't ignore. Nor could I control it. Before long, I finally gained weight from the bingeing: two pounds. I'd already lost enough that month to show a net loss in print, but I began to panic.

My attempt at damage control did more damage. As a veteran of starva-tion diets, I figured I could easily get rid of the two pounds. So I bumped up the workouts and skimped on a few meals. In doing so, I started a binge/starve cycle that would go on for months as I binged, freaked out that I had a *Shape* photo shoot or column deadline coming up, tried to starve, and then ended up bingeing again.

One of the reasons I had signed on with *Shape* was that I'd hoped the pressure of losing weight in public would help me kick the bingeing habit I'd been fighting all my life. Instead, it kicked it into high gear. I was so ashamed of how much I ate—and so terrified of being seen as a failure—that I couldn't admit my slipups to anyone, much less in print. No one in magazine success stories ever seemed to mess up—they started at the beginning and then didn't stop until suddenly they were at goal weight: a stunning size 6 with abs of steel. No one in success stories went from one day eating grilled chicken and salad to eating, as I did one day in the space of a half hour, two packages of Hostess cupcakes, an iced cinnamon-apple roll, a Chunky bar, a piece of corn bread, one blueberry muffin, one chocolate-chip muffin, and two can-noli. Obviously, I thought, there must be something wrong with me. Besides, *Shape* had already objected that some of my columns were too negative, too depressing, that I was making losing weight sound too difficult. I couldn't imagine what they'd say if I wrote about gaining weight. Talk about a downer.

The binges were occasional at first but soon grew so frequent I couldn't starve or exercise enough to offset them.

Late one night, I finally wrote to my editor about gaining weight, about how terrifying it was to have worked this hard and now to feel myself get-ting fatter by the hour. I sent the e-mail off and spent a sleepless night sitting on my couch, watching the shadows creep across my apartment. I tortured myself with nightmarish scenarios of my being fired, not to mention what sorts of things *Shape* might write in the magazine to explain why they were yanking the column. (Maybe an editors' note where they explained that I'd eaten myself out of a job? Don't think Grandma's going to be passing *that* article around the condominium.) I remembered joking with a journalist friend when I started the project that, given the pathetic success rate of most dieters, it actually would be easier to identify with the story if I didn't lose weight. But I didn't want to be an accurate representation of reality—I just wanted to be thin.

After some debate—and a little toning down of my self-flagellation—*Shape* published what I'd privately dubbed my weight-gain diary. I was overwhelmed by the response. Readers had been pouring out their tales of frustration to me since the beginning, but never like this. My *Shape* e-mail account overflowed in forty-eight hours. People sent cards and words of encouragement and empathy and thanks for "being real," as more than one woman wrote. I had to get caller ID because so many tracked down my home number.

The truth had set me free from everything except the bingeing. The one month where I gained weight became two, then three. My year contract with *Shape* was extended to two. I lost a couple of pounds, then gained them back plus more. I began to cringe at the photos of me appearing in print and wondered if I'd finish the project heavier than when I started. Then suddenly I'd be filled with fresh resolve, and I'd lose some more weight.

Though I often cursed *Shape* for stressing me out about losing weight, the blessing was that when I was finally ready to admit I needed help—serious help—with the bingeing, I knew where to get it. I began consulting with Shari Frishett, a therapist who worked in the office of Dr. Pamela Peeke, the doctor of internal medicine and nutrition researcher *Shape* had set me up with. For about eight months of the second year, my weight yo-yoed crazily while I worked on my head. What I discovered was this: while I'd spent a pile of time learning about carbs and cardio, weight lifting, and planning, what I really needed to know was that being overweight has little to do with food. Of course, food is what packed the pounds on, but when you've got more than fifteen or twenty pounds to take off, the food is being used to replace *something*.

In my case, I ate because I couldn't stand up for myself (eating, for example, out of exhaustion, because I felt I couldn't say no to anyone); because I couldn't tell people (even my family) how I felt; because I didn't really know any way to be nice to myself besides white cake with big buttercream flowers. Being overweight, for me, was about demands that were too high and resources that were too low. Why did I choose to eat instead of, say, drink or smoke or do drugs? I don't remember ever actively choosing eating over anything else, but I was a good kid who followed the rules, and eating was a relatively safe way to escape uncomfortable feelings. I couldn't show up for school or work drunk or stoned, but I could definitely show up full.

When I dreamed of writing a book, it was always a novel or maybe a historical biography, never an account of what I considered some of my darkest secrets: my weight (the actual number), my body image, and my dysfunctional relationship with food. Though my weight consumed my thoughts, there was no evidence of that in my professional life (I'd never written about it before *Shape*) or, I hoped, in my personal life.

Of course, I literally wore the consequences of my obsession—extra weight—but I worked so hard to hide any other evidence: the cupcake wrappers, the predinner dinners so I could eat like a "normal person" in public, the constant mental recalculating of calories to figure out whether I could have another roll at a restaurant.

It was only when some of the more painful columns began to hit print that I found out how good at deception I'd been. After reading a few paragraphs about my fear of restaurant eating, one of my most perceptive friends called and said, "I've never thought of you as anyone but a person who always has someplace important to go and something funny to say. I had no idea that you thought about any of these things as much as you do." She paused and added, "Besides, you're always out. How do you even have time to binge, much less obsess about all this?"

Another friend, one of my closest, said she couldn't believe the divide between the side of myself I presented in public—"someone who really has her shit together"—and the sad, angry, frustrated side she glimpsed in the columns. I didn't know what the traditional image was of someone who had as tortured a relationship with food as I had—maybe someone who sat home every night waiting for the phone to ring or who talked about food all day—but apparently I did not fit it. I wasn't relieved. I had always wondered whether, if my friends knew about the bingeing and the secrecy, we'd have become friends in the first place. After seeing their reactions to the columns, I wondered it more than ever. I found myself asking how well you can ever really know another person. I can be a cynic and a harsh judge, but suddenly I had a fresh sympathy for—and curiosity about—nearly everyone I met. For a while, I would actively wonder: if I had hidden everything so well, what might be hiding under, say, the annoying girl next door's polished but frosty blonde exterior?

I also was shocked by how many people—both friends and (thin) strangers—I had always assumed had a normal relationship with food would venture an offhand comment that they saw bits of themselves in my columns. Maybe not as extreme, but they, too, had thoughts of fishing half-eaten candy bars out of the garbage or watching other people at the table to see if anybody else took a third slice of pizza before doing it themselves. A thin friend called one afternoon, seeming edgy. After a long conversation about nothing in particular, she finally said, "Listen, I need to ask. What is a binge? Is it eating four slices of cake? Because I've definitely done that."

During the two years I wrote for *Shape*, I had the same love-hate relationship with fitness books and magazines I've always had. It's the success stories, especially, that get to me. The smiling faces in their sleeveless tops and slim-fitting pants taunt me. I read every word, yet I don't feel as though I understand anything. I've had a million "I've had it with my fat self" moments, I want to yell at them, so what made the one that kicked you into gear different? Did you ever mess up? How did you not give up hope when you looked at the calendar and saw you had a friend's birthday party and then a weekend away and four lunches out? Did you ever just flat-out want to eat because you were so damn sick of thinking about what you could and couldn't eat that you thought you'd go mad? And did you ever wonder deep down if all of this—planning and calculating and organizing and exercising and denying—was worth the effort?

Shape gave me a page for the column, which translated to about 450 words a month. That was about enough to sketch out a few major themes about planning meals or how crummy it felt to gain weight. It was not enough to do what I really wanted, which was what I'd been looking for and hoping for myself in the hundreds of diet books and articles I'd read over the years. I wanted to read something honest about what it felt like, day in and day out, to try to lose a significant amount of weight. When you're trying to diet, some days you need cheerleading. Other days you need sympathy. Reasons why you shouldn't eat. Reassurance that you're not the only one who's ever felt this way or eaten this much. (And then there are the days you really do need an ice-cream sandwich. You're on your own for that one, though.) I hope this book—call it the uncut version of the journals I kept during the two-year period I wrote for *Shape*—will be all of those things.

Most of all, I wanted to write my journey down—to record it while it's still raw so as not to repeat it, and because I would do anything to keep others from going where I went and seeing what I saw. And if nothing else, to let others know what I learned the hard way: losing weight—and accepting yourself, whether you lose or you don't—doesn't happen in that nice, linear way you read about in magazines and books. It's messy and it's complicated, and you're going to screw up a whole bunch of times before you get it right. That's OK. You're not alone.

The Eve of the Diet

First, Pig Out

*S*hort list of things for which there never seems to be an ideal time:

1. telling your boyfriend you've accidentally forwarded his naughty e-mail on to his mother (with attachments)
2. paying pesky credit-card debt (what is it they say . . . creditors can't get you when you're dead?)
3. telling a coworker he smells like some sort of dead animal
4. starting a diet

I know that a diet—excuse me, change of eating habits, as you're supposed to refer to it—has to be compatible with your life to be successful, but actually starting one seems incompatible with any lifestyle beyond that of a total hermit/loser/person-who-is-allergic-to-all-appetizers-and-party-snacks. Which I am not (allergic to all appetizers, anyway).

This week's reasons (excuses?) why I can't start becoming the New and Improved Me: two lunch interviews (ordering no-sauce this and substitute that always makes me feel like the superpicky Meg Ryan in *When Harry Met Sally*, only not as adorable in my neurosis), a cocktail party, and a friend's birthday party. Oh, yeah—and I have three stories due by Friday, which for me means a lot of afternoon and late-night snacking (depending on the progress of the story, either a reward for job done or a bribe for getting one started). I could start tomorrow—OK, next week—but then I've got a dinner, a handful of bars to review, and another couple of parties. And so on.

At this rate, I'll be better off waiting to wake up looking like Jennifer Aniston than waiting for the ideal week to start a diet. As a kid, I couldn't cram my list of extracurricular activities into the space allotted in the yearbook. Now I'm still the girl who can't say no, except these days my long days and late nights come from freelance assignments and not wanting to miss out on dinners, movies, drinks, or anything else that sounds fun. I'm always afraid I'll miss out on something, and you can't get in on an inside joke after the fact.

So after years of "I'll start tomorrow," obviously I haven't. Now I'm 5'8" and 206 pounds—a good 50 pounds overweight. I'm twenty-three years old and trying to hush my perfectionist inner voice and be patient with myself, because—if all the diet advice I've read and heard over the years is any indication—I'm gonna screw up.

Besides, learning to ease up on myself sure beats the alternative: another year gone by where I'm dissatisfied with my health and energy, not to mention my inability to wear sleeveless clothing. Another year where I go to parties and immediately look around the room for someone, anyone, who's fatter than me. Another year where I hopefully try on the largest sizes at the Gap, give up, creep into Lane Bryant, stand in front of the mirror in a size I cannot stand, and swear it's the last time I'm going to shop there. (And also wish that its bags did not say "Lane Bryant" quite so prominently. The bags might as well say "I AM FAT" in blinking neon. If they're so sympathetic to overweight women, can't they package their stuff in, say, Macy's bags?)

Easing up on myself also beats another year where I dread going to visit my mother and grandmother only because I don't want them to see me so overweight, and sometimes even dread going to work, because I have nothing to wear that fits. Another year where I write things in my journal—as I did last fall on the eve of a diet I never actually started—like: "I feel gross and ugly and fat. Oh, yeah—and too full. And depressed. And like a big blob taking up space. I don't feel like thinking about this, much less writing about it. But I'm hoping writing it down means getting it out of my head for a while, like jotting down at night things I must remember to do the next day. Rule 1: no eating on the run. Rule 2: no eating anything anyone else cannot see me eat. I make myself ill sometimes. Honestly, I can hardly face myself in the mirror."

Sure, I've promised myself a million times to do something about my weight. And if I need any reminder of all my past failures to follow through, all I need to do is call my grandmother, who's been nagging me about my weight all my life. I know that Grandma wants me to be thin because she equates it with having lots of dates, as she did, and with being happy (both from the dates and because I'll be able to wear anything I want). But often, I am happy. I know I'm lucky to have some great friends and a job I love. But even I have to confess that I find it unbelievably ironic that I write the singles columns for the magazine, since some days I feel like the last woman any guy would focus on at a bar.

Grandma's not alone in her idea of "thin equals happy"—most of my friends think so, too—and that bothers me, because I know being thin won't solve other problems in my life (lack of clothing choices excepted).

Still, much as I rail against it on principle, I know deep down that being thin—or at least being fit—could make me happier. As hokey as it sounds, these days—my twenties—are supposed to be the days I'll always remember, and I know they can't be when I feel as though there's something (like about fifty pounds) keeping me from doing things I want to do, however small. I don't think anyone would say my life is lived in a holding pattern, but I hate knowing that I won't take up swing dancing or bike around the monuments in cherry blossom season. I hate feeling too self-conscious to walk up to a guy at a party, and I hate even more that I fall into the trap of letting my weight dictate my confidence. I hate buying outrageous black satin four-inch heels and then tottering around the Grammy Awards wondering if I'm going to break them—or burst out of my dress (and if I do, wondering if there is a single item in all of Los Angeles that will fit me). And I hate the lethargy that comes with being too full, my pants too tight.

Most of all, I hate that I've lost my sense of scale. No, not the bathroom one (I threw that one out years ago), but the one that would keep me from eating a rigid 750 calories for six days and then, the minute I eat a bite more than that, eating heaven knows how many calories for weeks. I hate that bad is good and good is bad, where I'm simultaneously happy to have a hectic professional and social life and then upset that appetizers and drinks and business lunches and late nights seem incompatible with getting thin. Realistically, I know they're not; it's just that I've forgotten—maybe never knew?—what an appropriate portion is, and I haven't learned that food is just food, not anesthesia for stress or boredom or frustration. But I know I need to learn.

The question of the hour, I suppose, is: why (and how) is this time going to be different from any other time? (Besides, of course, that I'm going to be doing it in front of a whole bunch of people, on the pages of a magazine.) I know I can lose weight; to paraphrase Mark Twain, starting a diet is easy—I've done it hundreds of times. It's continuing to lose weight—or at least, not putting on every last pound plus extras—that's always tripped me up.

Dr. Peeke, the diet doctor *Shape* has told me to consult with, says that before I can get started, I've got to put my diet history on paper so she can see what my blind spots are. She also wants a list of "toxic" relationships—people who make my life difficult—and what she calls "stress milestones," major stressors like deaths and illness. I ran Peeke's name through the Lexis-Nexis news database, and it seems her mantra is that stress makes you fat. I hope she isn't going to be one of those doctors who tells you that you really shouldn't work late or take a weekend assignment or some such impossible-in-Washington-if-you're-young-and-trying-to-get-somewhere thing. Like doctors don't have to work late nights and live unhealthy lives to get through med school?

I'm not too eager to regale Dr. Peeke with my diet failures, but I suppose I can't expect this diet to be any different if I don't let her pick through what a dysfunctional relationship I've had with food in the past.

I don't remember exactly when I became conscious of food and weight—I think the feeling was always there. I have a diary I started when I was six, and in it are stars I drew in pink marker for days I didn't eat any more than my twin sister, Diana, did. By the time I was nine, I often vowed to "cut out snacks," but after an afternoon of sucking on ice cubes when I was hungry (a tip I'd picked up from reading my mother's *Family Circle* magazines), I'd give up. In my elementary-school diaries, in between tales of learning to dive and winning a spelling bee, are chronicles of clothes-shopping trips, which invariably ended in tears and then resolutions to diet. What I find amazing is that when I looked at pictures of myself as a kid the other day, I was shocked by how *not* fat I was. I definitely wasn't thin—I weighed more than my sister, and probably more than a child of my height should have—but nor was I the little Oompa Loompa I seem to remember.

I must have imbibed the "I am too fat" mentality by osmosis, because for a long time my mother rarely commented about my size outright. To get her to lose weight, Grandma had nagged her, and her father had tried to inspire her with cash incentives. She always said she didn't want that for me. But somehow I still got the message that everyone would be happier with me if my sister and I really were identical, if I could be the "skinny mini" that Diana was.

Somewhere between fifth and seventh grade, I crossed the line from baby fat to fat. In seventh grade, when I actually was overweight, my diary recorded my fear of ordering what I really wanted in a restaurant. It didn't matter that, unofficially, I was "the smart one" of the Rubin twins. My sister—who did well in school herself—was "the thin one," and I gladly would have traded. No matter how many science fairs and math contests I won, I'd still have to do it in clothes that never seemed to look as good on me as they did on everyone else. And when I walked up onstage to get my awards, the kind of music that accompanies dinosaurs stomping through video games often played in my head.

By the time I started high school, Mom was frequently engaging in what she considered subtle commentary about my weight: raising her eyebrows or narrowing her eyes when I reached for seconds, and an occasional "You don't need that" in a low, dark tone. One summer Grandma got right to the point, asking about a pair of shoes we'd bought together that I no longer wore: "What's the matter? Did your feet get too fat?" Later, Diana oh-so-helpfully reported that Grandma had told her I'd gotten "as big as a house."

I feared being caught eating. The tiles seemed to squeak impossibly loudly between my room and the kitchen, so I often sneaked food into the guest bathroom. When my parents left my sister and me home alone, we both gleefully raided the refrigerator—with its giant "He Who Indulges Bulges" hippo magnet on the door—but she never seemed to gain weight from it.

At the diet camp I went to the summer before tenth grade, I lost thirty-one pounds—the first time I lost a significant amount of weight. The camp recommended kids go to Weight Watchers when we got home. I lasted maybe a month. At the lone meeting that suited my schedule, I was the only person under forty, and I'd sit there feeling resentful that I had to spend an hour in a room of people my parents' age while everyone else I knew was out doing something fun. I also hated having my mother and grandmother—both Weight Watchers veterans—watching every bite that went into my mouth, seemingly waiting for me to fail.

So I'd eat what I wanted to in private. I'd go on an eating jag—"just this once," I'd tell myself, vowing to cut back the next day to make up for it. But inevitably I'd be hungrier than usual the next day, and in my black-and-white world any unplanned bit of food was evidence of my total lack of willpower. So I'd eat more, and pretty soon I'd gained back all the weight I'd lost over the summer, plus a little more.

I lost a lot of weight a handful more times—always on very low-calorie or very low-fat diets—but I'd never get down to my goal. I'd get close to it, but by then the months of deprivation would have me primed for months of bingeing.

The worst the diet-and-binge cycle ever got was two years ago, when I first moved to Washington. I'd just graduated from college and was determined to lose all the weight I had decided was holding me back from the life I dreamed of.

I began on a not-unreasonable 1,400-calories-a-day diet but soon grew frustrated with my plodding progress. So I began cutting out foods until I was down to 700 calories a day. Omelet made of three egg whites plus mushrooms for breakfast, Lean Cuisine frozen entrée for lunch, Pillsbury frozen blueberry pancakes for dinner (250 calories and what seemed to me to be a whopping four grams of fat), and a Weight Watchers 40-calorie chocolate-mousse pop for dessert. I adored packaged foods because I could be absolutely sure exactly how many calories they had. I drank Diet Coke like it was my job.

I've always prided myself on doing unpleasant tasks as quickly as possible, and losing weight was no exception. If some cutting down was good, more was better. By August, I'd replaced both breakfast and lunch with two peaches, often "running errands" at lunch so no one would question what I ate. I'd exercise an hour every day. Anything less was total failure. Some days I was so light-headed and tired, I didn't think I could drag myself up the stairs to my second-floor office, but there was no way I would allow myself to take the elevator.

If I took the Metro, I tried to beat my time running up all 137 steps of the escalator at my stop. (I'd count them as I ran.) When I got home to the studio apartment I was sharing with my (size 10) sister, I'd try on her clothes obsessively, seeing how much closer they were to fitting. I'd fall asleep with my fist pressed into my stomach, feeling—and being inordinately pleased with—how hungry I was.

Come September, I was two sizes smaller than I had been at graduation. I'd lost about forty pounds in just over three months. That's when it all fell apart. I decided to eat half of an Au Bon Pain oatmeal-raisin cookie at an office birthday party, and it was as if a fire alarm went off in my head—loud, insistent, and a little frightening. I ate the other half. And then another one. And then another. When the cookies were gone, I couldn't think about anything except how I was going to get something else to eat. I couldn't turn off the alarm. I couldn't stop eating.

I began making myself pay for a day of bingeing with a day of starving (four peaches and sometimes, if I couldn't concentrate because I was too hungry, a soft pretzel). Except pretty soon I gave up the starving part and just binged.

Those were the days when even seeing the words *all you can eat* terrified me, because I knew I could probably eat a buffet seven times over, and sometimes felt as though I had. I'd start out allowing myself to eat whatever I craved, but I'd grow frustrated trying to choose among all the things I wanted. So I'd get it all—or as much of it as I dared to order—going from bakery to restaurant, ready to snap the head off a cashier who so much as fumbled with my change. I wanted it all, and I wanted it that instant.

When I was done, my skin would feel so tight I'd give anything to rip it off. Several times, I tried to throw up, but my body wouldn't cooperate. I'd lie in bed, my sense of disgust and failure complete. I couldn't even succeed at being bulimic.

I'll never forget what those binges felt like. That "I can't do this/I have to do this/I'm going to hate myself/I do hate myself" tidal wave. That fear that I was a size 10 today but could be a size 16 tomorrow. That struggle to finish whatever I was eating, no matter how full I was, because I wasn't going to eat any of these things again. *I'm absolutely, positively never going to do this again, because I'm starting a diet tomorrow*, I would think. I even thought the diet would be easy, because I was so sure that I'd never again want to feel as horrible as I did at that very moment.

But somehow that was never incentive enough. And there I was again, so full and more disgusted with myself than the last time—a level of disgust I never thought possible.

This time has to be different. I'm tired. And annoyed. And angry. And sad. I think about how much time and energy I've wasted adding up calories, measuring, exercising, berating myself for missing a workout, and generally feeling that I can't leave the house because I hate the way I look.

I'm thinking about how many things I missed—one trip to San Francisco, in particular, where almost all I can remember is how much time I spent worrying about how I was going to exercise and what I might eat if we went to such-and-such restaurant. And finally, I'm thinking about the lies I told, ridiculous ones, to go off and binge or exercise or not eat—whatever my craze was at the moment.

Why can't I just overeat like a normal person? Why does one cookie suddenly have to become six? And why must I torture myself mercilessly after I eat these things? Why can't I just pick up and get on with it? These are the things I know have to change if this weight loss is to be any different from all the other (failed) attempts.

Toxic relationships. I don't want to call my grandmother toxic, exactly, but she does stress me out about my weight, which she never fails to ask about (on the phone) or comment upon (in person). Call her the typical Jewish grandmother: she nags me about weight and at the same time pushes food at me. In a single dinner, she'll tell me I shouldn't eat bread, then insist I have to eat some of her meal because she can't possibly finish it all.

My sister is probably my most difficult relationship. Diana constantly talks about food and weight and what she's craving and is forever talking about how fat she is, which of course she isn't. I know some of that is normal girl—and normal sibling—behavior, but it goes beyond that.

The summer I went to diet camp, she wrote me letters detailing what she'd eaten for dinner or where she'd gone for ice cream. Later, whenever I'd talk about starting a diet, she'd drag me out for cupcakes at a grocery store whose buttercream icing we both loved. The summer I came home from college after losing forty pounds, my mother suggested I try on Diana's clothes, since I didn't have anything to wear. They fit—and I don't think my sister spoke to me for the rest of the evening.

That whole summer Diana kept nagging me: "You're not eating enough. You go to the gym too often. Just this once isn't going to hurt you." When we were home over Thanksgiving this past fall, we shared a car, so I told her not to go to the gym in the morning without me. She went without me anyway. And these days, if we go out to dinner and I order a salad or otherwise don't eat a lot, she snaps at me not to be such a martyr and asks pointedly if I'm starving myself.

Besides looking like my idealized version of myself, Diana is the voice that says aloud every negative thing I've ever privately thought about myself. I can't just ignore her—as more than one person has counseled me to do—because what she says are my deepest fears realized: Fat *is* the first thing people notice about me; I really *can't* leave the house looking like that; it *is* a fluke I have done as well as I have in school or work; I *am* boring; I *am* bitchy; I *am* rude. And so on. No matter how much outside confirmation I might get to the contrary, Diana can negate it in an instant. I hate that I allow her this power, but I do it because I can't help thinking that she's known me my entire life. Maybe it's just taking everyone else I know a while to catch on.

Stress milestone: my mother. For years when I was growing up, no one could figure out what was wrong with her. The battery of doctors she went to always ended up ascribing her fatigue, listlessness, and inability to do much—get out of bed, take a shower, finish a conversation—to Epstein-Barr virus, otherwise known as chronic fatigue syndrome. I was often angry with her. Why didn't she pay any attention to me? Why didn't she seem to care about herself or the house or us or anything? Why did she call my sister and me into her room only to ask us to fetch her something from the table at the foot of her bed? I remember half crying, half screaming at her one afternoon that she wouldn't care if I never came home again, since she never seemed even to speak to me. She gestured limply toward a spot on the bed, as if telling me to have a seat; then she fell asleep.

My sister and I date the beginning of the worst of it to the spring of 1987, just after our bat mitzvah, when we were twelve years old. I couldn't understand how anyone could be so tired from planning a party—the excuse Mom gave—but she took to her bed, seeming to have given up even pretending she cared about anything at all. On the rare times I'd hug her, I'd hold my breath, not wanting to smell her unwashed odor. My father, a doctor and professor of medicine, worked long hours at a hospital. He refused to believe Diana and me—or maybe couldn't let himself believe us—when we told him how bad she was. In English class at age fourteen, for a teacher I'd also had the year before and therefore trusted, I wrote essays about Mom where the emotion was so raw that a few times Ms. Clark said there was no way she could put a grade on them. I wrote about leaving Mom's room one afternoon and standing in the bathroom, listening to the plip-plop of my tears as they fell into the sink: "I force the sharp corners of the counter into my palms, as if hoping for a pain that hurts more than Mom, but a pain I can at least stop when I want."

In the fall of 1990, when I was fifteen, Mom went for an MRI as a last resort. No one was expecting much—at that point it was just another test to cross off the list.

"See anything?" my father asked the technician casually as my mother lay in the tunnel of the machine, fighting claustrophobia.

Yes. A brain tumor. Two of them, in fact. One of them so big that her surgeon later said if it had gone untreated any longer, at some point in the not-too-distant future, my sister and I would have come home from school and found Mom dead.

She had two daylong surgeries, though doctors couldn't remove all of the especially offending tumor because it was too close to the hypothalamus and the optic nerve, which meant a millimeter slip of the knife could blind her—or kill her. I remember going to visit her in the neurosurgery intensive-care unit, where the condition of each patient got worse and worse as you got closer to the nurses' station. Mom was directly in front of their desk.

The whole rest of the year—my junior year of high school—was disjointed, time expanding and contracting at painful intervals. Time at the hospital lasted hours. So did conversations with my father—awkward ones where he tried to catch up on what was going on in my life while he'd been working late the past ten years. "Haven't seen Susie much these days," he'd say, unaware that my friend Susie had moved to Wisconsin two years before. As a fifteen-year-old girl, I found it an awkward time to be left with just my father. One of many cringe-worthy episodes: my sister and I explaining in fits and starts that we had to buy more tampons—that the supply of pantyliners in the closet would not do, because no, you could *not* just use two of them stuck together.

My father's own mother had died of breast cancer when he was sixteen, and in his effort not to keep us in the dark about Mom's condition, as his father had, he explained everything in the sort of excruciating detail that only a professor of medicine could. He told us how the surgery worked and what she might be like afterward and all of the possible complications. I didn't want to hear any of it. I'd sit there concentrating on not crying or otherwise doing anything that might prolong the conversation. I'd nod at him while my mind skipped over his words as if they were a foreign language, my thoughts drifting to the way I'd behaved toward my mother over the past few years—how angry I'd been. When she'd call to ask me to fetch her something, I'd often sigh loudly and stomp across the house. If it wasn't a drink, sometimes I'd throw it at her. Once I snapped that she needed a servant, not a daughter.

I tried not to think about the situation at all. I must have had twenty lines of extracurricular activities next to my picture in the yearbook that year. I stayed late to work on the school newspaper and ran away to debate tournaments on the weekends. I was working at the *Miami Herald* after school twice a week, and I never missed a day. I focused on school and all the things that would, I thought, eventually get me away to college and as far away from my family as possible.

And of course, I ate. Who was going to say anything to me about my weight at a time like that?

At night, I lay awake worrying about my mother—and about myself. I am, as everyone has always said, a carbon copy of her. Pictures of me look so much like my mother that visitors to my grandmother's apartment, upon seeing a picture of my mother as a child, often ask: "Why do you have a picture of Courtney and not of Diana?" I wondered: *What if what my mother has is lying in wait for me?*

I remember when Mom finally came home from rehabilitation in January 1991, her head shaved and a blank, almost mean expression on her face. Diana and I avoided her. We were afraid of her—afraid, I think, of finding out what the next few months might be like. She was alive, and she was home, and for that we should have been grateful. But it was easier to be grateful the less contact we had with her, because we could prolong our ignorance of how different she was. Until she came home from the hospital, the focus had been first on her not dying and then on her slowly regaining basic functions: breathing on her own, brushing her teeth, walking—specific tasks where it was easy to measure her progress and pretend things were returning to normal. But with each interaction—each question she had no idea how to answer, each situation that required an emotion she didn't seem capable of feeling anymore—we felt more acutely that things would never be the same. And each week, my sister—a better, more confident driver than I was, though we both had only learner's permits—drove my mother an hour each way to her radiation treatments, sometimes in awkward silence.

To doctors, my mother was a miracle patient, eventually driving, talking with friends, volunteering with a Jewish women's organization, helping my sister and me pack for college. But I couldn't help focusing on what was missing. Small things, like writing a check, often required what seemed like enormous concentration. She didn't seem to have any emotions besides anger—she never cried or was ecstatic, something my father attributed to the location of one of the tumors affecting the parts of the brain that deal with mood and personality. I could tell at times she was unsure of herself, looking around for cues to the appropriate response to what someone had just said.

"Love you," I said to her one night before going to bed.

She paused. "OK," she finally answered.

I wanted to be grateful for what I had, but I couldn't. I felt as though she'd been gone for so much of my life—lying in bed, listless—and I hated that she still didn't look and act like other people's mothers. She still didn't shower very often. Her clothes were disheveled. Diana and I desperately wished she'd wear her wig, but she complained it was too hot. When her hair grew back, she often didn't comb it, and she still nodded off in the middle of dinners and movies and conversations. Why, I wondered, couldn't I have a mother who got her hair done every week and asked me if I'd done my homework and remembered which of my friends was dating whom?

Outside the house I constantly felt as if I was going to get caught not knowing something I should have known—something my mother should have taught me. My mother wasn't up to talking about makeup or men or even small things, like polishing shoes. I'd visit my friends' houses and watch their mothers fuss over them—whether they needed a haircut or whether their

T-shirt had been washed too many times and ought to be retired—and I'd wonder if I were the one who really needed the tune-up.

Even now, it seems, every day a friend of mine will talk about something she learned from her mother—a special way of folding laundry, an expression, a shortcut—and I'll search my own memory for something similar. I come up empty, and I realize again how awfully little time I really got to spend with her.

That's because, even when she'd recovered from surgery, chunks of her memory and personality were gone. I hear stories about my mother in her twenties and thirties—this smart, capable woman who changed her own tire ("in jeans!" my grandmother says with awe) on Fifth Avenue in the 1950s and was the first person her friends called when they needed to know anything about anything—and I can't help wondering if I ever knew her. I'm supposed to feel lucky that she's around at all, but so many times I feel as if she's here but not really here, and I feel cheated instead. And then I feel guilty.

One of the toughest bits about her illness is knowing how hard my mother worked when I was young to shield me from pain. She knew I was terrified of doctors and dentists and needles and would request that the dentist do whatever needed to be done all in one visit, so I wouldn't have to spend a week or so dreading a filling or having a tooth pulled. When I had to get my tonsils out, she didn't tell me until two days before, so I'd have less than forty-eight hours to worry about it. And in the hospital before my surgery, she got my father to ask that I be given general anesthesia using a mask, so I wouldn't have to feel the IV go into my arm.

I don't know which makes me sadder: that she can't protect me from the pain of watching her or that there's nothing I can do to help her.

My father is almost intimidatingly smart and rarely wrong, but no matter how much he insists that brain tumors are not genetic and that I won't have one, I don't believe him. I don't think about it every day anymore, but when I'm feeling melodramatic, the idea of ending up like my mother adds an extra urgency to a lot of things.

Like many people with whom I went to college, I want to be successful—and if I can be young and successful, so much the better. But I also want not to regret things—and I'm pretty sure that at some point I'm going to regret how angry I've been with myself about my weight and how much time I've wasted feeling that the extra pounds keep me from doing things I want to do. In truth, I end up doing almost everything I want—going to the beach, dancing with friends, ordering dessert—but I do it almost defiantly, my enjoyment tempered by fear and a constant internal voice telling me what an idiot I look like. I'm convinced the voice would shut up—or at least quiet down— if I didn't feel so conspicuous, so *fat*.

So on to the diet, and what I can do to make this one go differently—more successfully—than the ones before it.

For one thing, this time I'm even starting differently. Instead of saying, "I'll start tomorrow" or "next Monday" or "when I get back from vacation" or "January 1," I'm starting now. Which means no night before to pig out and eat everything one last time, swearing that I'm never going to eat these things again. I hate waking up to that sick, full feeling, and I've already got a good fifty pounds to go—so do I really need to pig out and add a couple more pounds to the pile?

Here's another way this time will be different: I'm not starting in a flash of rage or humiliation or disgust.

I've had many bring-on-the-celery-sticks moments over the years: when Bruce the Spruce—one Florida mall's answer to Santa Claus—told me to eat my vegetables so I'd be tall and thin like my sister. When my mother yelled at me for being fat as I dove into the Halloween candy, spilling it all over the kitchen floor. When my grandmother yelled at me for taking a second help-ing in front of an entire table of Passover guests. When a pair of size 18 jeans was too small. When, as I was standing with two friends at a party, two guys walked up to the three of us and treated me as though I were invisible.

But diets that started out of, essentially, revenge haven't worked. A few weeks later, the moments still stung—in fact, they still sting today—but somehow that has never been enough to keep me going. Losing weight is hard enough—painful enough—on its own. Adding the constant mental replay of my most embarrassing moments somehow has always driven me into the arms of something sweet, instead of away from it.

This diet isn't starting from the pit of despair, either. Instead of a flood of tears and a flash of "I must do something now," this diet has its roots in a gradual realization: I'm tired of feeling out of control. As I reread old jour-nals one dark afternoon last week, I was struck by how much my weight fig-ured into everything I thought and did. No matter what else I was writing about, somehow I'd end up writing about weight.

Me writing about a party where I drank far too much: "I have a hang-over this morning, which would be a more than fair price to pay if something fabulous happened, but nothing did. And it isn't that I don't remember it, either. Being drunk may loosen everyone else's inhibitions, but unfortunately it does nothing to rid me of this terrible self-consciousness of being fat. When you're fat, it all just hangs out."

On looking for a new job: "More than plowing through piles of awful clips or trying to come up with ridiculous action-verb synonyms for *wrote* (*penned*? ick) for my résumé, the thing that always stops me from getting too far is the idea of having to find something to wear. I need a black pantsuit, and I hate the idea that probably the only one I'll be able to find will have an elasticized waist."

On a concert: "One of these days, I will find the perfect pair of shoes to wear to the 9:30 Club. The bottoms of my feet always hurt after concerts there—you have to stand the whole time. Is this a fat thing or does this happen to everybody? I know, I know—I should just wear sneakers. But every time I go to put on sneakers with normal clothes, I can't help thinking about this one very fat woman I read about who *had* to wear sneakers everywhere— her feet were too fat for normal shoes."

I read page after page, horrified by what I had become. I felt trapped by my own body, literally weighed down by it. I was saddened by the things I wrote: my (somewhat sick) wishes that if everyone has his or her way of dealing with stress, why oh why couldn't mine be smoking or *not* eating? My disgust with myself that although I was fat enough that losing all the weight I wanted to lose would take seemingly forever, somehow I still wasn't fat enough for a gastric bypass, aka the stomach-shrinking surgery, which required you to be 100 pounds overweight. There were times when I went so far as to wonder if it wouldn't just be easier to gain the weight needed for the surgery than to try to lose all I had to lose.

Other people, I realized as I read my journals, marked their lives with birthdays or graduations or major purchases (cars, apartments). I marked mine with weight. Anyplace I went—restaurant, city, whatever—I could remember what size I wore (I usually avoided the scale) when I was there last. Holiday memories were divided into ones where I ate whatever I wanted (nasty comments and sharp looks from family members be damned), ones where I ate exactly what Diana ate but then ended up late at night in the kitchen eating everything I hadn't eaten earlier, and ones where I was so restrained and "good" that I was cranky and grumpy the whole time.

So here goes nothing. Tonight I'm off to go grocery shopping for the first half of the week. I know it would be more efficient to buy for the whole week, but the idea of a refrigerator that full . . . I can't handle that right now.

I must be the only person on the planet who—out of lack of cookies or crackers or pretzels—could manage to pig out on low-fat string cheese and nonfat yogurt and raspberry preserves, but if that's the way I am, I might as well recognize it.

I'm also going to buy—I admit it—my usual pile of fitness magazines. Their "lose five pounds with these five easy changes" articles always appear to be geared for those people who need to lose only five pounds yet somehow still regularly drink whole milk ("substitute skim!" the mags tell us oh-so-wisely) and eat fried chicken ("substitute grilled chicken"). Who are these people, and if they eat so much fried chicken for these changes to add up, how is it they have only five pounds to lose, anyway?

But I digress. Paging through the magazines often keeps me from stuffing my face (at least for one night), so if the tips actually worked for me, I guess I'd have to consider that a special bonus.

Anyway, enough. I'm off.

Day 1

*T*he first day of a diet is unpleasant—*unpleasant* being a euphemism for the sort of word my editor would say can't be printed in a family magazine. The thrill of starting something new lasts for maybe four minutes, which leaves me approximately twenty-three hours and fifty-six minutes to wonder (a) how long until my next meal, (b) how long I can keep this up, (c) whether one chocolate-chip cookie would do that much damage, (d) how much weight I can lose in a week, and (e) whether I possibly can be a size smaller in time for my friend Kate's party in three weeks.

I was never one to fill the margins of my high school notebooks with my name plus the last name of my current crush, but this morning I was being equally ridiculous, scribbling calorie counts for hypothetical meals all over my *Washington Post*. It's worse than trying to use up store credit—my attempt to not let a single calorie of my 600 calories per meal go to waste is resulting in some ludicrous-sounding repasts:

Lunch: one Lean Cuisine macaroni and cheese (280 calories); three peaches (120); one fat-free, sugar-free Fudgsicle (45); three Hershey's Kisses (72). Which still leaves 83 calories. Note to self: must find website that lets you search for foods by very specific number of calories.

And of course, all the calculating of possibilities made me hungry for every one. Consider the snack options: a can of Progresso rotini in chicken broth (160 calories, three grams of fat) or a can of Progresso tortellini (140 calories, four grams of fat)? String cheese or yogurt? Peach or nectarine? (Well, that one's easy: peach—it has half the calories of a nectarine, so I can have two.) I wanted them all, and I'd just had breakfast.

It's all about options, and having options is what gets me into trouble. Reduced to its simplest terms, more food options equals more eating. Period.

Fewer options equals less wondering what to snack on, which equals staying within calorie count, which equals losing weight . . . I hope. But once I get into the penne-versus-peach debate, it's all over. If the can of rotini is 120 calories more than a peach, and I choose the peach over the rotini every day this week, that's 120 calories times seven. Which equals a savings of 840 calories. Which is equal to a dinner and a half, or a little over a third of one day's calories. In a month I could lose an extra pound. Big deal.

So I started thinking about more dramatic calorie savings. Which brought up more options. Then started to think I really wanted the rotini anyway, which is twenty calories more than the tortellini. And if I did that every day, that's twenty times seven. . . .

It's been said that math is supposed to be sense. This is nonsense. I know that, and still I can't help it.

To make things worse, I've started on the day after Christmas, an idea that seemed like less and less of a good one as the minutes passed. Not only is my family in town, which means we eat every meal in a restaurant, but everywhere there are Christmas leftovers and half-price Christmas chocolates. But I figured if I didn't start today I'd eat like mad until they left in two days. Then somehow I'd use those two days of eating to justify putting off starting until New Year's or, more likely, January 2, since there's still plenty of eating and drinking to be done in the wee hours of New Year's Day. . . .

I had my carefully measured cup of Special K with one-half cup of skim milk and one medium banana for breakfast, but I was still hungry. The idea of two restaurant meals looming later already made me want to give up and go buy one of those Godzilla-sized chocolate-chip muffins. I know from experience that no matter how plain I try to order my food in a restaurant, I still get frustrated by not being able to know *exactly* how my chicken or fish is being prepared (how much butter is really in there?). I don't dare order pasta—no way can I deal with trying to figure out what depressingly small bit I'll be allowed of the Mount Saint Pasta I'll no doubt be served as a portion.

If I were a smoker—and there are so many times when I can't help wishing, despite my pulmonary-doctor-father's best scare tactics, that cigarettes were my vice—I'd be the sort who could quit only by going cold turkey. Since I can't give up food completely, I feel this need to be as perfect as possible in the beginning of a diet, if only because I figure I'm just going to get sloppier as time goes on. And if I start out sloppy, that leaves that much less space for margin of error (translation: times I can screw up and still have the scale go down).

I don't have much margin of error. I'm already counting the weeks to a friend's wedding in April and figuring that even if I lose two pounds a week— a weight loss that I know perfectly well can't happen every week—I still will be lucky to be a size 14 in time. Which seems like such unbearably plodding progress. . . .

One of the many pickles of dieting—excuse me, changing one's eating habits—is that you want to be thin the minute you start. Heck, you feel like with this amount of denial and deprivation, you *deserve* to be thin. But you catch sight of yourself in the bathroom mirror at some point during the day and you make a face. Even though you haven't eaten—let's make a list here— the extra piece of cheese at breakfast, the rest of the rice at lunch, the half a cookie left in the office kitchen, you're still fat. And it all just seems like more effort than you can stand—how much easier it would be to go back to what you know, which is food. And then you think: if you can barely make it through this one day, how are you going to make it through the days and days that stretch ahead? It seems hopeless, so you might as well just eat.

A perceptive friend once ventured that I had a fear of success with dieting, and I can't help wondering if she was right. Yes, it's just food, but it's so much a part of the way I live my life. It's a bit like trying to change in an open dressing room—you've got your own clothes half off and you're desperately trying to yank on whatever it is you're trying on so you're not standing there naked. Without food to reach for automatically, I feel, if not defenseless, then definitely vulnerable and unsure of what to do with myself.

It's scary to think that I'll probably never put anything in my mouth again without thinking about it and mentally calculating how many fat grams and calories are in it and whether I can have any more. It sounds so ridiculous, but what will fill my brain? I feel as if I'm about to end a long-term relationship and am desperately looking for things to do on a Saturday night. What will replace the Kozy Shack rice pudding and two plastic spoons during rambling conversations with Kara about men? I know the pizza place my friends hit at 4:00 A.M. after a late night most definitely does not serve salad. And let's not forget all the calories in the liquor that has us out until all hours in the first place—does this mean I'm going to have to stay in, at least in the beginning, until I get more used to things? I so resent the idea of food keeping me home on a Saturday night—it seems so unfair. Hasn't food already done enough damage?

We—Mom, Dad, Diana, and I—passed the whole morning sitting around my sister's apartment, which happens to be in the same building as mine but on a different floor. Dad was being incredibly high maintenance in his effort to be low maintenance, and Mom was keeping quiet—her standard (but usually unsuccessful) attempt to avoid an argument with him. Dad said he'd do whatever Diana and I wanted, but the minute we suggested something, out came the qualifiers. Essentially, he wanted to do whatever is the coolest thing in D.C., but he didn't want to have to wait on line for it. Sure, Dad.

By 11:30, I was getting antsy. I had eaten breakfast at 9:30 (tried to sleep in so more of Day 1 would disappear, but no such luck). If we first decided what to do at 11:30, by the time we all got moving and actually got there, I knew we wouldn't end up eating lunch for hours. Which normally would be OK—I'd just grab a snack. But I didn't want to end up eating an extra snack today. I wanted Day 1 to be perfect.

Dad likes to go only to restaurants he hasn't been to before, and ones that serve "interesting" food. (Chinese, Mexican, and other American-ethnic staples don't qualify.) So it wasn't totally self-serving when I pointed out that once we were in the vicinity of all the museums, there wasn't going to be anything but food carts and Starbucks.

"Didn't you want to try Teaism?" I asked. It's a Dupont Circle teahouse that serves Indian and Japanese food. I conveniently forgot that it also serves salty oat cookies, which are so good (and portable) that former Washingtonians often ask you to bring them some when you visit.

Diana glared at me. She's got a sixth sense for all things diet-related, and she wasn't pleased.

"Can't we just go and eat lunch later?" she asked.

I knew then that if the argument/discussion went anything like the zillions that had come before it, Dad would say he was stuffed from breakfast, even though he hadn't eaten any, and Mom would say we had to "get a bite to eat." Dad would protest and Mom would insist that "the kids"—that's Diana and I, though we're twenty-three years old—had to eat, though really it was *she* who wanted to eat. Deadlock would ensue, and eventually we'd go eat, quite possibly because everyone would be forced to behave in a public place. Or maybe it's because food seems to have the same effect on all of us that free chocolate-chip cookies at the grocery store have on toddlers—it makes the whole ordeal that much more bearable.

Anyway, that's indeed what happened: we headed out for food. And to think I wonder how I got so fat in the first place.

Another problem with starting a diet: facing the idea that maybe weight isn't the problem I think it is. I know that sounds contrary to everything I've said so far, but consider that everyone seems to think being thin is the answer to all my problems.

I wonder if it's easy to focus on losing weight as the cure-all because it seems like such an obvious problem with a relatively straightforward (though not easy) solution. It's like women constantly changing their hairstyle because it's something they can actually have some control over, unlike height or complexion. There's so much that I blame on weight—I don't know that I want to find out that something much harder to fix (my personality, *me*) is really the problem.

As a child I associated happiness exclusively with going out to eat. Inside our house, resentment rippled beneath the surface, occasionally breaking through. To me it all seemed to stem from my parents' marrying the idea of what the other was supposed to become, instead of who they were at the time.

"I thought you were going to be in private practice," my mother—who had worked to help put my father through medical school—would occasionally mutter.

"I thought *you* were going to work after the kids were born," my father would say. It was his answer—sometimes said aloud, sometimes not—to everything. Why he worked the long hours he did (a constant source of tension). Why he chose to spend Saturday night puttering around the garage instead of spending time with my mother. (He worked hard all week, and he was going to do what he wanted.) Why he wouldn't let her call someone to fix the dishwasher. (He could do it himself, when he had time, so it irked him to pay someone to do a job he was sure wouldn't be done to his exacting standards.)

My sister and I never had to cringe at the sight of our parents holding hands or kissing—I don't remember ever seeing it happen. Anger—yelling—seemed the only legitimate emotion. Crying was not tolerated well—the stock responses were: "Be a big girl," or "I'll give you something to cry about," or just plain, "Don't cry." Boredom also wasn't accepted: "Mom, I'm bored" was met with "I'll give you something to do," or "Go play with your sister. You girls have built-in playmates."

If we had anything to celebrate—birthdays, awards—we celebrated by going out to dinner. I remember that even the prospect of going out could make a whole day seem brighter. The actual dinners were rarely the shimmering moments I envisioned, but I loved the anticipation of them the way I'd later love starting diets. There was the prospect of perfection, of food mellowing us the way alcohol mellowed others, creating what felt like connection among the four of us. There was the prospect of being—if only until the entrées were cleared—the way I imagined other people's families were. And of course, there was the prospect of something else we rarely had at home because none of us "needed it" (my parents' words): dessert.

For the record, for lunch on Day 1 I had a grilled-chicken kebab with the best estimate I could make of a half a cup of rice. I also had a quarter of a salty oat cookie—Diana had insisted Mom and Dad try one and, of course, continually called attention to the fact that I hadn't had so much as a bite. So finally I did. The guilt was overwhelming. When the cookies were gone, all I could think about was how to get another one. I had eaten only one-quarter of one measly cookie, but in my mind I had already screwed up. Big time.

I was a crumb away from ditching the diet, eating whatever I wanted in the afternoon, and then going ahead and eating dinner as if it were the Last Supper because, hey, I'll just start tomorrow. But I didn't, partly because I couldn't figure out how I was going to sneak away to buy another cookie. But mostly, I didn't quit because I'm tired of all the years of false starts. Yes, it's a long road to looking the way I want, but it's not going to get any shorter until I get moving.

I've read so many articles and books about diets over the years that there's a twenty-car pileup of words in my head. I feel as if I could justify any food as being on some diet somewhere. You know, start out the day with eggs and bacon—an Atkins diet day. Then at lunch decide I want pasta and rationalize that I've switched to a low-fat diet (and just happened to have used up my day's allotted fat grams at breakfast). Chocolate in the afternoon? Well, isn't it total number of calories in a day that matters, so I'll just subtract this Twix bar from the total. And so on. To top it off, the two experts *Shape* sent me to consult with have dueling eating plans, which means I'm constantly second-guessing myself. Should I be trying the other plan? Would the other one work better—or faster?

The two couldn't be more opposite in terms of what and how much I'm eating. Dr. Peeke doesn't have me counting calories—she's given me what amounts to a modified Atkins diet—high protein and controlled carbs (none at dinner and no refined carbs—like white rice or white bread—at all). From her, I have a template that calls for me to eat essentially the same thing every day.

Breakfast: oatmeal or cereal with milk or egg-white omelet with vegetables, plus fruit. Midmorning snack: fruit (but not if you're eating lunch exactly three hours after breakfast, in which case skip the snack).

Lunch: high-fiber bread with lots of green things and 3 ounces of turkey, chicken, or fish or two Boca Burgers, plus fruit. Snack: soup with six to ten low-fat crackers or nonfat yogurt with Grape-Nuts or cottage cheese and vegetables. I'm allowed to eat as many vegetables as I want—woo-hoo, go crazy!

Dinner: giant salad with about six low-fat croutons (yes, she really did say "about six") with diet dressing or balsamic vinegar and a tablespoon of olive oil, plus vegetables—I can eat a whole package of frozen ones if I want—plus, again, 3 ounces of chicken, turkey, or fish or two more Boca Burgers or an egg-white omelet with lots of veggies.

I'm supposed to have eaten the bulk of my calories by 5:00 P.M. so I'm not overloading my body with calories right when my metabolism is slowing down for the night. And I'm supposed to avoid pasta and bread at dinner, since I don't need the kind of energy that carbs provide as I'm getting ready to go to bed. Hoping for some slight relaxing of the rules, I tried to protest that I don't go to bed before at least midnight, but bed at 10:00, bed at midnight—they're the same, Peeke says. Unless I'm running marathons after dinner.

Peeke says that obviously I'm not going to eat like this every day for the rest of my life but that this is a start for someone like me who's on the run and doesn't love to cook. Things will get added and changed in a couple of months, she promises.

Nancy Clark is a sports nutritionist, which means the first thing I told her is that I'm about as athletic as an anemic slug. She laughed and said not to worry, that she considers activity level when creating eating plans and that just breathing for the day entitles me to a couple of thousand calories. She says that while Peeke's plan sounded fine, she's worried I may be cutting back too far, since Peeke's plan works out to about 1,600 calories per day and she thinks I need to be eating something like 2,300 a day. Nancy's breakdown:

roughly 600 calories for breakfast, 600 for lunch, 500 for a snack, and 600 for dinner.

Nancy's plan is more Weight Watchers style, where supposedly nothing is off-limits. For example, she says I can eat a bagel with peanut butter, whereas Peeke says I can't have any bagels at all, that I "don't know how to eat them." Translation: I don't know how to incorporate them into my diet—to eat a proper size bagel (which is *not* the kind of size they sell at bagel shops) and not load it up with all sorts of high-fat accoutrements. And I don't know how to—here's Peekespeak for you—"taste and savor, not gulp and consume."

The two plans are appealing to me for different reasons. I like Peeke's because of the sheer lack of choice—I don't have to think about food, which is good, because once I get started on that route, I can't stop. But I also look at Peeke's and think: *How can I possibly eat this every day?* Nancy's I like because it sounds so damn reasonable. Five hundred calories for a snack is *a lot* of food: it's a couple of candy bars. Or *two* Lean Cuisines, which would be more than I eat for dinner when I've been on one of my starvation diets. But the addict in me thinks: *How could I possibly lose any weight eating this much?* It will take *forever* for me to lose weight this way, and I know from experience that if I don't see results soon, I won't be motivated to keep going. After all, sometimes feeling better is not enough of an incentive. Carrots do not taste better than chocolate, and sometimes carrots just won't do.

So I decided to follow Peeke's plan. But I'm following Nancy's for the couple of days my parents are here, just because Peeke's doesn't seem restaurant-friendly. In fact, Peeke—not Nancy the sports nutritionist, which I would have expected—is so firmly in the food-as-fuel camp (in other words, taste shouldn't matter) that she'd probably tell me to eat *before* we got to the restaurant, or to bring my own food and insist on eating it there, something I can imagine only some high-maintenance celebrity doing.

Back to the idyllic family tableau. We spent the afternoon trekking around the museums. I've already seen most of the exhibits, but I think it's more because I didn't want to be there—and because Diana, as is typical, kept up a constant chatter about all the things she'd like to eat—that I noticed food all day. Kids with their Ziploc bags of Cheerios. Snack kiosks. People eating hot dogs and popcorn. The Air and Space Museum is filled with chocolate coins and other edible souvenirs, and I knew I was going over the edge when even the freeze-dried ice cream looked appealing.

Everywhere I looked there was enticement to indulge: *You deserve a break today. Bet you can't eat just one.* And it's true—I can't. Later, when I stopped by the drugstore to buy contact-lens solution, I spent an inordinate amount of time in the snack aisle, examining labels and debating. Hmmm, vanilla Hostess cupcakes are 130 calories apiece. That's not much more than a banana. Maybe I could just substitute. It seems so reasonable, so *normal.* That's just the problem. The desire to overeat—and to binge—creeps up quietly, cunningly. One minute I want a vanilla cupcake, and then I can't choose between vanilla and chocolate, and the cinnamon roll suddenly looks pretty good, too, and then I have to have it all: the cupcakes, the cinnamon roll, and anything else that crosses my line of vision. It's impossible to go back to the diet from there—I'm a total failure. I can't even make it through one *day.*

My problem is that I think too much. What I wouldn't give to be able to cut my head off and throw it across the room.

I looked at the food in the drugstore, a collection of fat grams so large it seemed impossible that all of them could be shoved into things as small and innocent looking as a cupcake I could eat in five bites. In a surge of decisiveness I didn't buy any of it. *I will not fail on Day 1,* I thought. *Maybe today I'll break my silent vows not to fight with my sister or snap at my parents, but at least I will get the food right.*

Dinner at *another* restaurant, and I was grumpy and hungry by the time we finally agreed on where to go. I had a grilled-veggie platter that was suspiciously greasy with what I judged to be two-thirds of a cup of mashed potatoes, an awfully buttery-tasting piece of corn bread, and a small salad with vinaigrette. I know I should have eaten protein (more filling), but this looked like the least damaging option, not to mention the easiest to order without having to make a scene about how it was cooked.

Of course, Diana made a pile of nasty comments ("What kind of crazy diet are you on today?" and—as a hiss—"You know we eat out when Mom and Dad are here. Can't you just start tomorrow?"). She kept everyone at the table informed about precisely what I was and was not eating. Only a couple more days of these family meals, thankfully. Of course, I'm sure Mom will tell Grandma it looks like I'm on another diet again, which means Grandma will ask me about it, no doubt at the worst possible moment, like on a day I happen to have pigged out. I'll lie to her or fudge or change the subject, hate myself for failing and being caught at it, and then eat more.

I wish I could disappear for six months and reappear slim. I know my life fat, and I can imagine how it would be slim, but getting from one to the other . . . I close my eyes and can't picture a thing.

An hour before bed. I spent it calling friends (not on a cordless phone, so I couldn't end up near the fridge) and reading every peppy motivational magazine article I could find until it was time to go to sleep.

I feel as though I've spent the entire day just trying to get through it, literally living from one meal to the next. I hate it. And I can't help wondering how it's going to be when I have to go to work tomorrow—how can I write about anything else when my head is filled with food?

The Rest of Week 1

AKA How Many More Hours Until I Can Eat Again?

I fell asleep last night calculating how much weight I could possibly lose—what size I could possibly be and whether I could pull off something sleeveless—by the time of Brent's wedding in April. Four weeks in a month times four months—thirty-two pounds if I lose two pounds every single week, which I know from diets past is completely unrealistic. But there is the extra water weight you lose in the beginning, so maybe I could lose, say, twenty-five? Whatever the number, it's not enough. But even I am not self-destructive enough to get out of bed and eat over that.

Today, Day 2, I was so proud of myself for making it through Day 1 that I practically leaped out of bed to get to the gym, where even a glimpse in the mirror of the lumps of uncooked dough that are my arms didn't ruin my mood. The high lasted all morning. I smiled at people on my way to work, sang out hello to every last coworker, made myself a to-do list, and happily began attacking it.

Unfortunately, the week between Christmas and New Year's is hardly known for inspiring record attendance at work. Because my job depends a lot on other people actually returning my calls, I ended up popping out of my office every ten minutes to see who was around to chat. Bad news, because in popping out I discovered that practically every restaurant in town had sent us a holiday gift basket. There were endless gaily wrapped tins of chocolate and nuts—it seemed so natural to grab a few on each trip past the lunch table, which happens to be in the center of the office, right by the printer and impossible to avoid on the way to the bathroom or the supply closet or out the door. But I didn't.

It was like something out of a cartoon—I could practically hear the food calling to me. I decided to try to clean my office, but that required multiple trips to the supply closet (translation: past the table). I also tried to drink water, but the water is right by the table, too. I'm always amazed by how small things like that can make me feel like everyone and everything is conspiring against my success, so I was inordinately pleased with myself when I finally went out and bought a giant water bottle to save myself trips past the table to refill my cup. Foiled again, because I still had to contend with trips to the bathroom, which is also past the table.

I was disgusting even myself with how much time I spent thinking about food. I felt like I was just marking time between meals, passing minutes until I could eat again. I was doing things (cleaning a desk drawer, organizing files on my computer), thinking about how long each task would take and how close it might be to lunchtime or snack time when I finished.

If food is a drug—and I've certainly used it as such—then these first few days of a diet are withdrawal. Not a process I want to have to repeat, so I hung on until 6:00 P.M. today, Day 2, feeling the siren call from the panettone (love, love, love bread) grow slightly fainter as I sailed by it on my way out the door.

Day 3 of the diet, Day 2 of the diet at the office, no doubt Day 1 of something else diet-related if I think about it long enough: the baskets of chocolates and nuts and other "edible press releases," as we call them, continued to arrive. But I didn't have any. Of course, I want some kind of award for that. It's like when I save the company money by, say, taking the Metro instead of a cab and think: *Can that be added to my salary, please?* Here I think: *Can those extra calories somehow be credited directly to my account, so that I lose pounds just for not having consumed them?*

On top of all the tins of easily grabbable things, there was an office farewell party, which meant trays of cookies. I was hungry—the party was at 4:00 P.M., my snack time—but felt too silly to pull out my cottage cheese in the middle of the festivities. I tried ducking back into my office, but I couldn't—I got stopped in conversation, and the whole time I kept looking for a way to escape to go eat my cottage cheese. (I don't really like cottage cheese, but Peeke says cottage cheese, so cottage cheese it is.) I know I can't take so much as one bite of a cookie. Even though they're never that great, I know I'll still want to finish.

When I was a child, one of my favorite books starred a strong-willed little girl named Ramona Quimby, whose older sister, Beezus, one day found her in the basement surrounded by apples, each with a single bite missing. When Beezus demanded to know what was going on, Ramona replied innocently, "The first bite always tastes the best."

I was about six years old when I read that for the first time. I remember being struck by it and trying for the next few meals to notice how the first bite of whatever I was eating tasted. It did taste good, but to me, so did the second bite and the third bite and beyond. Even if confronted with a whole pile of apples, I wondered if I'd be able to casually toss as much of each apple aside as Ramona had. Even at age six, I doubted it.

I hate feeling caged, which is how I felt today—raging internally about a situation I felt I couldn't escape and becoming as cranky as a tired child because I couldn't get what I needed. Or really, because I couldn't make myself ask for it.

Today I decided to go along with Diana and her friend Jill to IKEA—which is in a mall I can't otherwise get to easily because it requires a car, which I don't have. I'm not stupid enough to go to a mall with my sister—who always points out foods I love and says things like, "Wouldn't an Auntie Anne's pretzel be good right about now?"—without ammunition. So I've brought a container of yogurt and deliberately dug out a larger handbag to hide it—I'm not supposed to go more than three hours without eating, Peeke says, because that's how I get too hungry and then overeat. I also brought a plastic spoon, because—as ludicrous as it sounds—I was pretty sure I'd be ducking into the bathroom to eat. I don't like conflict, particularly with my sister, and I knew she'd say something diet-related that's snide if I whipped out the yogurt in front of her. Some days it makes me laugh that I'm supposed to be the writer in the family, because Diana definitely has a way with words—a way to make them hurt more than anybody I know.

Instead of going to the bathroom, I ended up claiming I was going off to look at lamps. The little white lie set off a spin cycle in my head: lying is what I'm used to doing when I want to sneak off and buy French fries at the food court—not when I want to eat a 100-calorie nonfat yogurt. I ate my yogurt in about four big gulps, feeling as if there was a giant spotlight on me even as I tried to look inconspicuous.

Next problem: I should have guessed that Diana and Jill wouldn't be ready to eat dinner anywhere near the time I'd want to. On this diet I'm inexplicably hungry about an hour after my afternoon snack, though I try to delay eating dinner for as long as I possibly can—after all, once dinner's over, I'm not supposed to eat the rest of the night. When I eat at 5:00 or 6:00, I panic that I won't make it through until breakfast, and even though I know eating a piece of fruit won't make the difference between my losing and gaining in a given week, my mind still sticks to just one formula: extra calories equals failure. And I'm pretty sure that if I give in and eat something extra, I'm not going to stop with just a piece of fruit.

By 6:30 P.M., I was becoming antsy. I was counting down the minutes until we'd leave. It didn't help that I had zero interest in eighty-five-dollar bathroom storage units, which Diana and Jill were debating with a graveness I don't think I'll even have if and when I buy a house. Bored, I had nothing to do but think about the fact that I was hungry—something I will never say aloud unless someone else does first—and wonder what sort of argument would ensue about where we'd eat.

At 8:30, we ended up at a Chinese buffet restaurant at Diana's insistence. It's an understatement to say I have a bad relationship with buffets. I tend to spend the entire time looking at other people's plates, trying to guess what an appropriate portion is and how much food I can take without attracting attention.

I spotted a menu and decided to skip the buffet altogether. There was no way I could handle endless trays of food when I was that hungry. The plates coming back from the buffet didn't bother me as much as I would have thought, though I did wish Diana and Jill would stop being so polite and telling me to help myself from their plates.

Jill offered once. Diana kept offering. You don't start fights with your sister in front of friends, so when Jill went to the bathroom, I told Diana to please stop.

"It's rude not to offer," she told me in a tone that teetered on patronizing. For some reason, Diana has always taken it upon herself to lecture me on manners. In high school she used to snap at me if I didn't immediately say, "Bless you," when she sneezed.

"I think it's rude to offer when someone's already told you they're not eating that," I said.

She muttered something I couldn't hear. When she returned from her next trip to the buffet, she offered me a fried dough ball dipped in sugar.

The rest of Week 1 veered crazily between I-can-do-this (cue *Rocky* theme) and this-totally-sucks (no soundtrack, just intense desire for food). Call me a teensy bit impatient, but there were moments when I thought it was taking forever for anything to happen. I spent a lot of the week hating being fat, hating worrying about everything I put in my mouth. I hated that I couldn't even go out with friends and have a drink without figuring out what has the fewest calories, or else ordering Diet Cokes. My friends aren't alcoholics, but give them a couple of drinks apiece and the dynamics *do* change—and being the only totally sober person in a roomful of drunk people is not fun.

At other moments—such as after I passed up some food I'd normally eat or after I finished a workout—I could practically feel my jeans getting a tiny bit looser. Of course it was my imagination—if you really could lose weight that fast, would so many people have trouble sticking to diets? But at least for a few minutes, I could convince myself that just *feeling* thinner was enough, that pretty soon it would be real.

Sunday was the worst day of Week 1, and I think it probably always will be the worst day of the diet week. That's because Sundays bring the prospect of brunch and movies and mall food courts and other activities and places that involve snacks or meals out, plus the nagging sense that you shouldn't be doing anything fun—you should be doing all the errands and chores you've meant to do all week. I don't have a car and have to walk everywhere, so if the weather's anything less than my ideal (sixties and crisp, which it is about two weeks a year), I never feel much like schlepping around. Just the thought of loads of errands on freezing, rainy, or sweltering days usually makes me want to use eating as a delay tactic. As my grandmother would say, I have to eat, don't I? So as long as I'm eating, I don't have to do anything else.

If I don't have to work—and often, even when I do—I'll spend hours with the Sunday *New York Times*. I usually sit in the Xando coffee bar two blocks away and read it, often looking over at the muffin and cake display cases, considering having something and usually wanting everything. I envy the ease with which other people seem to linger over their coffee and cake, apparently forgetting about the cake for entire sections of the paper. I rarely manage to put my fork down unless there's nothing left.

Sunday is also my evening for catching up on phone calls, always to my grandmother and then to my parents. Unlike my sister, who is frequently accused of making snap decisions and then regretting them, my parents seem to think I have it all together. Diana often cries when frustrated, now admits she chose her college almost randomly, and has had the more typical twenty-something's career trajectory—job hopping while she figures out what she really wants to do.

While in high school, I started working at our hometown newspaper, plugging away at my dream of being a writer. Maybe because I've done things my parents might not have chosen for me—gone far away from home to college, then decided against graduate school and instead headed for a decidedly nonlucrative, nonacademic career—I've always worked hard to edit my tales of what's going on. "I know exactly what I'm doing" is the message I'm trying to get across—that and "You don't understand." Apparently, I've been such a ruthless editor—done such a good job of convincing them—that they rarely question my choices anymore, which makes me feel more like an imposter and more alone than ever. When I venture that I might be floundering at any number of things in my life, my parents don't seem to know what to say. Now they really *don't* understand. For them, my problems seem to be a surprise ending for which they've had not a hint of foreshadowing. They give me the verbal equivalent of a pat on the head and tell me how well I've done in the past and that they never worry about me because of that. Nice, but not helpful.

Since my father isn't often home and rarely answers the phone when he is, mostly it's my mother I talk to when I call, and maybe that's why I get so upset. You'd think after all these years I could accept that she's never going to be the sort of mother you call at least once a day to report on anything and everything, or even the sort of mother you call to ask what you should wear to dinner at so-and-so's house or what you should write on a condolence card. But I can't. Since the surgeries, my mother's attention span has gotten shorter and shorter, to the point where these days conversations with her last ten minutes, maximum. She tells me what she's watching on television, and I try not to get annoyed and frustrated by her second-by-second update of the latest Danielle-Steele-book-turned-Lifetime-movie. I try desperately to think of something we can talk about for more than thirty seconds, but for the most part my mother doesn't participate in normal conversational give-and-take. She waits for me to finish speaking, then says something unrelated, or nothing at all. It isn't that she's rude—only that she can't concentrate.

Still, it's my instinct to call my mother when something goes horribly wrong or wonderfully right, times when I want my mother—want *a* mother. My pre-call hope that maybe this once I'll get what I want—what I need—from her is what makes these conversations even worse than they might be. She won't be excited, and I'll feel deflated. Or she won't be upset or outraged, and I'll become more so.

By some bizarre quirk of brain or scalpel, there are a few stories in my mother's long-term memory that have been left intact, like the one house on a block left unscathed after a tornado has turned all the others to rubble. At least one Sunday a month, when I feel like I really, really need her but deep down can admit that I'm probably not going to get what I want from her, I try to get her to tell a few stories from her childhood that I know she likes and remembers. How as kids, she and her brother, my uncle, used to make a fuss when my grandmother made fish for dinner, sailing up the stairs making a big production of holding their noses. Or how she and Uncle Dennis got my grandparents out of the house so they could get things ready for a surprise anniversary party. I know these stories by heart, but I want to hear her tell them. What I love to hear is the sound of her voice—more animated than I seem to have ever known it, as if she's remembering not just the event but once again feeling the feelings that went with it. I cocoon myself in her voice, shutting out the knowledge that she's anything less than fine, for as long as the story lasts.

But the second she finishes, the spell is broken. Though I've felt it a zillion times before, there's a fresh sensation of missing her, and I inevitably get off the phone feeling worse than ever.

Lost four pounds this first week, which I, Ms. Glass Is Half Empty, have somehow managed to turn into a negative. In diets past, I've lost seven and eight pounds the first week, so four pounds is a major disappointment. After all this effort, I want more. I feel I deserve it. And it makes me cranky to think that this is probably the most I'll ever lose in a week—soon it will trickle down to half a pound, then nothing, then maybe even a gain.

Four pounds is not enough, nor is the fact that I've gotten through one week. It's not long enough for my new eating habits to be automatic, not long enough for the kinds of stunning results that would give me resolve of steel— and just long enough to feel as though all my effort is going to go up in flames (or cheesecake) any minute, the way it always has in the past.

It's not that I haven't been successful—I have, at least according to the scale. But one of the greatest ironies about trying to lose weight is that after all these years of fixating on the numbers, all of a sudden they don't matter much. What I really want is to look in the mirror and see the difference, and I don't. Not yet.

The Rest of Month 1 (January)

*T*here's something about dieting that makes your body public property, the way I'm told it is when you're pregnant. Everyone has nutrition advice, and the bag of baby carrots always open on my desk seems to be a neon orange sign that announces I'm dying to hear every last well-meaning-if-often-annoying word. This friend did the Atkins diet. That one swore off French fries. This crony of somebody's mother gave up everything white—no flour, no sugar, no mayonnaise. And surely I must know that a red-carpet pileup of celebrities swear by the Zone?

If I had my choice, I wouldn't tell anyone I'm on a diet. But you can't suddenly begin eating radically differently than you have in the past and expect no one—particularly when your friends and colleagues are journalists—to ask. So I've just been saying I'm trying to eat healthy, and avoiding the words *weight* and *diet* because both always seem to be a cue for women to start talking about how fat they are, which is very annoying when nearly all of them definitely are not. "Eating healthy" doesn't seem to flip quite the same conversation switches, yet most everyone understands that it translates as "losing weight," the way women understand that when a man says, "I'll call you," he means "How's never? Does never work for you?"

I'm just over two weeks into this diet—um, eating healthy—thing, and the scale says I've lost weight: six pounds (four pounds the first week and two the second). But I want so badly to *look* like I have that it seems all I do is second-guess myself. Am I doing enough exercise? Have I misread a serving size and therefore accidentally been eating too much? Would I lose weight faster if I left the carefully measured teaspoon of olive oil off my salad and just used balsamic vinegar? Is the Zone really the way to go—should I maybe attempt to follow it while still following Peeke's *and* Nancy's advice? Heck, is that even possible?

At one point, I'm so stressed out by whether I'm doing enough and whether the nutritional advice I'm listening to at the moment is the one I should be listening to—not to mention stressed by a bunch of deadlines—that I nearly cram a chocolate-caramel cluster into my mouth without thinking. The fierceness of my reflex to eat one—and then another two or three—is so intense that I literally catch my breath. For some reason I think of a postcard I once saw on one of those free-card kiosks: "A moment of hesitation is all it takes to miss the boat." If I could just pause for a moment, maybe this urge to eat would pass.

But how to pause—to shut my brain off from the endless debate of whether and what and how much I should eat, or what I can eat without anyone commenting? I know it sounds hokey, but I take a deep breath and try to figure out what I really want, chocolate-caramel cluster aside. In this case, it's someone to do the crummy parts of my job, leaving me just the good bits. It comes to me in what feels like a brilliant, lucid flash: *I want to eat because I don't feel like doing what I have to do today and the rest of this week.* It seems so self-evident that I can't believe it's taken this long to occur to me. But how could it have? I was always too busy stuffing down unpleasant or scary thoughts—do I need a new job? what if I can't find one? what if I'm totally unsuited to this profession and just haven't figured it out?—by eating.

To complicate matters, I also want to eat because I might eat later. No kidding. This is the problem with planning—this endless thinking about what food problems might come up over the next day or week makes me feel as though I'm constantly about to fail. I picture myself on a racetrack knocking over hurdles instead of sailing gracefully over them, except in my mind the hurdles aren't made of wood—they're just giant treats à la Willy Wonka's Chocolate Factory. This week's problem-that-I-have-to-think-about-yet-don't-want-to is that I have to do all these sports bar reviews, and bars are hardly diet friendly. Even if I sit around drinking Diet Coke, I'm still going to have to at least look at the menu. How else am I going to be able to go back to the office and write up the bars with cringe-inducing sentences like, "If your team is losing, the Fred Flintstone–sized plate of nachos ($5.95) is a good distraction"? And looking at the menu means contemplating the options, which means . . . well, usually not anything good.

More alien to me than regular exercise or sandwiches stuffed with Boca Burgers and vegetables (which I'm already getting sick of) is all the planning required in making these lifestyle changes. After all, I'm the kind of person who pulls all-nighters and then ends up on vacation without toothpaste or underwear because I've packed fifteen minutes before heading to the airport. But now I've got challenges that caffeine and convenience stores won't solve, since you can't leave five workouts to do until Sunday night or hope to make a healthy dinner out of cupcakes from the CVS snack aisle. Now I go to the grocery store once a week—me, whose refrigerator once held only leftover Chinese food, if that—and sketch out my meals for the week on Sunday mornings. I make a huge salad and keep it in a plastic container so it's the first thing I grab when I get home, starving, at 9:00 P.M. I pack lunches the night before.

And I hate it. I hate thinking about dinner when I haven't even had breakfast. I hate thinking about whether there will be appropriate snack food at a meeting, or whether the meeting will run late, and whether I should eat beforehand. Thinking, thinking, thinking—all this thinking about food. Will I ever be one of those people who push their leftover chicken idly around their plate with a fork, not thinking about it? Not feeling proud that I've left something over nor barely able to restrain myself from finishing it?

I don't want to eat out very much because I can't tell exactly what's been put in my food, and I worry that I'll be tempted by too many choices or too much after-dinner lingering with leftovers still in front of me. I find myself lying to friends to avoid having to go out to eat—I'll say I'm not sure when I'll be off work, or I'll ask if I can meet up with them for drinks (in my case, a Diet Coke) later. On days when I am eating out, I panic all day about what will happen if I become too hungry before dinner or if someone's really late and we can't eat when we're supposed to. I know I could eat an extra snack, but that makes me panic about having fewer calories available for dinner.

Sometimes I find myself doing a cost-benefit analysis of going out: is whoever will be there or might be there worth the chance that I might screw up my diet? The way the math works out, it almost never is. Birthday dinner of a not-very-good friend whose friends I'm not crazy about—I probably won't go because (a) you always eat and drink more at birthday dinners than at normal ones, and (b) I might eat even more than the regular old birthday indulgence because I'm bored with who I'm sitting next to or because, say, we've gone somewhere family style and I feel totally not in control of what I'm eating. My good friends will be my friends whether I eat out or not, or so I hope, so I don't have to go out to eat with them. The only people who end up making the eating-out cut are people I might not see for months and months if I don't see them for dinner. And even then, sometimes I'll still try to find a way around it.

I e-mailed Shari Frishett, the licensed clinical social worker who works with Peeke, that I was scared that I was becoming obsessed—that I feared restaurants and parties and meetings that ran late and just about anything that might throw off my meal schedule. She pointed out that I needed to restructure my sentences (and my thinking). Why was it, she asked, that I think of what I'm doing as obsessing instead of as "being vigilant about self-care"? And instead of thinking I'm crazy for not wanting to go certain places, she said, why not think of it as not putting myself in situations that compromise me emotionally?

I can't accept this way of thinking—at least, not yet. Thinking as Shari does makes me feel like food is still running my life, except instead of being obsessed with how to get it, I'm obsessed with how to avoid it.

And once I start thinking along these (cranky) lines, there's no stopping how far I'll go. Tonight at the gym I caught sight of myself in the mirror and was unable to stop thinking about how far I have to go. Usually, that's my cue to throw in the towel, but this time I also couldn't stop thinking: *What good would* that *do?*

The magazine I work for is supposed to help readers find the best of Washington, but sometimes, at least behind the scenes, we are embarrassingly undiscriminating. Catch us at 3:00 in the afternoon and some of us might even eat three-day-old cheddar-cheese-flavored popcorn if it's sitting out on the table.

For the past couple of weeks, it's been an active struggle for me not to eat whatever's sitting there—and yes, some of it actually has been worth eating. But today there was a giant box of chocolate truffles, and I wasn't even especially tempted. Victory! Usually I would have spent the entire time I was at the lunch table thinking about them, and then I would have ended up having two or three, or as many as I thought I could take without being particularly obvious about it. Or I'd try to escape from the table as quickly as possible.

Victory two: I had half a glass of Merlot and one sip of a martini—not bad when you consider I spent six hours at four different bars for a story. (After the Merlot, my strategy was to order drinks I loathe—like dirty martinis—so I could walk around with a drink but not feel tempted to sip it.) Yes, alcohol is not technically part of the Peeke plan. She says it preferentially stores fat on the stomach, which I definitely do not need. I'm to stay completely clear of hard liquor—it has too many calories and "really disinhibits," known to the rest of us as getting tipsy and then eating too much without thinking. If I absolutely have to drink something, I'm supposed to nurse a glass of wine (100 calories). "Taste and savor, not gulp and consume," Peeke says.

It is virtually impossible to write about nightlife and not drink anything at all. Peeke says I should ask for a different assignment, but I can't. Writing about nightlife is part of my job, and I can't suddenly announce I won't do it anymore. Cue which-is-more-important-in-my-life argument from Peeke. But I want it all: I want to be successful *and* I want to be thin. Do I have to choose?

Craving 2 percent cottage cheese, maybe because it's the most fattening-tasting thing I'm allowed to eat.

Today I told Peeke I was having major trouble with being hungry about an hour after lunch. She e-mailed back an explanation of the difference between hunger and appetite. Appetite is "I want," and hunger is "I need." If I'm really and truly hungry, she said, I'd have hunger pangs or be shaky or have a headache. Besides, she can't believe I'm actually hungry if I've eaten the lunch I'm supposed to eat: two Boca Burgers on two pieces of bran bread with a haystack of lettuce, plus a piece of fruit.

So I called her—because I didn't really want an explanation, I wanted a solution. Peeke's was to whip out the baby carrots or—this always kills me—recognize what I'm feeling as appetite and walk away. When Peeke said that, in this voice that ought to be on a motivational tape, it all sounded so reasonable. But when I got off the phone and thought about it, I realized that if I could do what she said, chances are I would never have gained this much weight in the first place.

I felt like an idiot—the reporter who has nabbed five minutes with a very important source, then not managed to ask the essential question. So I called her back.

"How do I accept that it's appetite and move on?" I asked.

"Don't think—do," she said. "Women think too much."

Well, that clears it up.

I should have known tonight was not going to be good, Diana-wise.

It began when I had to go downstairs to her apartment to get some mail of mine she'd accidentally taken. We hadn't seen each other since last week, and she was in fighting mode the minute I walked in the door.

"New jeans?" she asked. They weren't, and I didn't want to prolong the line of questioning by asking her why she'd asked in the first place, so I didn't say anything.

"Awfully interested in clothes now that you're losing weight?" she said.

"No," I said.

"I don't recognize that sweater." It sounded like a challenge.

"You were with me when I bought it three weeks ago, remember?"

"You just keep showing up in all these things I've never seen before." Another challenge. I wasn't in the mood to point out that it's very cold outside, and I'm considerably fatter than I've been in a while, therefore I've had to pull out winter clothes from college, which of course she's never seen—we went to different colleges, and when we were home in Florida, we never needed to bring sweaters.

My attempt to discontinue that line of questioning only served to open me up to equally unpleasant ones. Where have I been for the past week? (On deadline.) Why do I only seem to call her when I have nothing to do? (I don't, but we have this argument all the time.) Why didn't I come to brunch with her and her friends this morning? (I didn't want to tell her that brunch is the stuff of which my diet nightmares are made. Should I eat breakfast first since I can't wait to first eat until 11:00 or noon? Should I count it as lunch? Breakfast and lunch combined? And is there a single healthy thing one can eat for brunch at Tabard Inn, land of cream and beignets?)

All of my answers seemed to annoy her—as did my refusal to go to the grocery store with her. I'd already gone, and even if I hadn't, I couldn't think of a more miserable way to spend an hour than to have her pick up every unhealthy thing in the store and talk about how much she wanted to eat it and how fat she was feeling.

Feeling guilty because I'd blown off her brunch invitation and the grocery store, I invited her to come to a movie tonight with my friends Mary and Robin. Afterward, we went to Xando, where I managed not to touch the s'mores that had been ordered. I just sipped my vanilla tea and tried to tune out Diana's full-scale offensive: "Don't you want any?" "Aren't you going to have any?" "They're really good."

As we were walking home, I told her I'd gotten the official green light from *Shape* to start the columns—they'd wanted to see how things went for a few weeks before any contracts were signed. The whole project is "really dumb," she said, since it "wasn't like they actually motivated someone to lose weight." I didn't say anything. I know the prospect that I might succeed drives her crazy, but I hope I don't let her drive *me* crazy in the process.

It happened. I'd been wanting chocolate for days, and when I walked past these chocolates on the lunch table midmorning, I gave in.

In a panic, I nearly ran back to my office, my pants already feeling tighter. *Omigod, omigod. This is it. I'm going to go out there, eat more chocolate, then decide to eat whatever I want today, which of course means I'll be unable to decide what to eat first, and that'll be the end of three weeks of dieting.* I sat in my office, already dreading having to write down what I ate. Unable to focus on my work, I tried to guesstimate how many calories were in a chocolate, not wanting to go see if there was a calorie count on the box because I was afraid I'd just use that as an excuse to eat more. As in, I've already consumed five billion calories, so what's a few more?

I find it almost unbelievable that an innocent piece of chocolate can set off such a chain of thoughts in my head. And I definitely thought about them for a while as I tried to reason myself out of the very feelings of guilt and failure that all the diet advice I'd ever read or heard said I had no reason to have. Still, just as I'm not going to wake up thin, I'm not going to wake up with an instantly reprogrammed brain, which is hard for me to accept. As I've said before, patience has never been one of my greatest virtues.

I go to synagogue maybe twice a year—on the Jewish High Holidays—but today I felt like someone was looking out for me. When I finally left my office, the chocolates were gone.

I passed the Great Bar Challenge—as I nicknamed my sports bar blitz—thanks to lots of Diet Coke. But the disaster of the week happened when I wasn't quite expecting it. It's like the Ms. Pac Man game I loved as a kid—you gobble down three ghosts, duck into a tunnel, and sigh with relief, only to reach the other end and get clobbered by another enemy.

I was out in the Virginia countryside with a friend, and we had plans to try a new sushi place. I'd even asked Peeke for the rules on eating sushi (six to eight pieces—yikes! I normally eat at least twice as much). Sarah and I were supposed to eat at 6:30 P.M., and I'd done fine leading up to the dinner—ate a very filling snack at 4:00 (low-fat cottage cheese with lots of raw vegetables). But we got very lost, and by 8:30 P.M. I knew I was literally hungry, not just thinking I was. I hadn't eaten in more than four hours. Because the options were limited, I didn't protest when she pulled into a Mexican restaurant at 9:00 P.M. I felt almost smug as I quickly revised my dinner plan, thinking maybe I would order fajitas.

Then we sat down, and I realized that maybe you can never be too rich or too thin, but you can definitely be too helpful. Sarah knew about the diet, so when the waitress set down the basket of tortilla chips, Sarah promptly moved it out of my reach. She picked up a chip, nibbled at it daintily, and said, "You're not missing anything."

Suddenly those chips seemed like the only thing in the world I wanted.

She opened the menu, suggesting items and then saying, "Oh, you can't eat that." I thought darkly about Nancy's saying that there's a diet portion of everything. I scanned the menu for fajitas and, once I saw them, closed my menu and announced that's what I was having, hoping to preempt further discussion.

She ordered mini empanadas as an appetizer, and by the time they arrived I was so hungry and so annoyed with her that I ended up having three. And was that a slightly disapproving look I caught from her? It was almost enough to make me grab the basket of tortilla chips. Which did not bode well for my navigation of the rest of the meal.

All during my fajitas, I tortured myself with the fact that I'd eaten three fried things (the empanadas). I couldn't stop thinking: *No matter how good I am the rest of the night, I still screwed up.* It was like realizing toward the end of the semester that even if you got 100 on the last two exams, you still weren't going to end up with the grade you needed, so why bother studying at all?

I had half of Sarah's flan for dessert. By the time I got home—and even though I'd eaten much less, and much more healthily, than I'd normally eat at a Mexican restaurant—my pants felt ridiculously tight. I knew it was scientifically impossible for me to have gained back all the weight I'd lost, but I lay on my couch trying to prepare for the worst. The math again: what is the absolute *most* number of extra calories I could have consumed? What is the absolute highest the scale could creep?

It didn't. I actually still lost two pounds, for a grand total of eight these first three weeks, and I got off the scale feeling as though I'd gotten away with something. And the scale was below 200—I am never ever ever ever writing a "2" as the first digit of my weight again. As if they knew, people kept commenting on how good I looked today. It's funny to watch the divide, though: the women all said I looked like I'd lost weight. (I don't think I do. It's just that if women want to compliment other women on something nonspecific—as opposed to shoes or handbags—"You've lost weight" is a default, as automatic as saying "Bless you" when someone sneezes.) The men just complimented me on my outfit, an (unremarkable) eggplant-colored suit.

All the compliments made me so happy I wanted to eat, of all things. I shouldn't have been as surprised as I was. "Happy" to me automatically flashes back to happy-going-out-to-dinner, as though the two are completely indivisible. Besides, when I'm happy I think: *Life is great. I guess I don't need to lose weight to be happy.*

Some people's entire lives are spent feeling that all would be perfect if they could just lose ten pounds. As of this week, I have lost that and it doesn't make a shred of difference.

I did get those compliments the other day, but I can't help thinking it was my turn or something—like the day I got them happened to be the one day of the year everyone I know decided to start the "Let's try to say one nice thing every day" program. You know, make someone's day and all that.

Tonight I was trying on clothes before going to a party and I couldn't stop thinking about how fat I still am, and how many pounds I have to go before I'm even in the realm of normal, which I define variously as being a size 12 or having my weight not be the first thing someone might notice about me. I steel myself before I look in the mirror, and just at the sight of myself sometimes—like tonight—I feel my throat tighten as if I'm going to throw up. Instinctively, I suck in my stomach, wishing I could pull the entire fatness of me inside every portion of my body and retreat, retreat, retreat from anyone ever looking at me again.

So of course in this frame of mind nothing I put on looks good. I want to stay home tonight, partly because I don't want anyone to look at me and partly because it's at times like this that alcohol and party snacks are especially lethal. It's not because my friends and I are setting out to get drunk tonight. It's because when I'm feeling crummy, I don't handle alcohol well. Booze makes me a more intense version of myself: if I'm happy when I drink, I become louder and sillier—myself in caricature. But if I'm feeling at all bad, some ridiculously small thing (a raised eyebrow, a perceived slight) can make me have to blink back tears.

I know this, and still I keep trying, keep hoping that alcohol will dissolve the feeling that I need to stand defensively at a party, arms across my chest, the phrase "Don't look at me" running through my head like a news ticker, making it hard to concentrate. I picture the alcohol seeping into my brain cells, washing away my incessant examination of all the women around me, stopping me from wishing I looked like any one of them but me. Sometimes I think I can almost feel the seeping, the way you can practically feel a candy bar rotting your teeth—but the alcohol never really works.

Tonight I tried on a bunch of pants that I wore last month, and they're not much looser. I really hope I haven't gained weight from the margaritas at a friend's birthday . . . and I'm panicked that not going to the gym today means I won't lose any weight this week. And what if those two margaritas I drank at the birthday were 300 calories a pop as opposed to the 200 apiece I was estimating? What's more, what if every drink I had this week (a lot of parties) was 300 calories instead of 200? That would be something like 1,500 extra calories total, instead of 1,000. I did do an extra thirty-five minutes of cardio this week to balance things out, but there's no way that was 1,500 calories' worth. So, 1,500 extra calories would mean that I gain half a pound. Or should mean it.

I'm terrified that trying to lose weight is turning me into a cranky, boring person. It's not like I used to think about literature or symphonies or rocket science twenty-four hours a day before, but now I fear that food and calorie counts and when and how I'm going to get to the gym and whether I've lost any weight and when a smaller size will fit is all I think about. I hope it's not all I talk about. It reminds me of a book I once read as a kid, about this little boy who was trying to become the perfect person. After lots of sipping of lukewarm tea (recommended by a book he found on how to be the perfect person), he discovered that perfect people are boring. If losing weight is supposed to make my life perfect, does it follow that it will also make me boring?

By definition, people who are significantly overweight do not trust their gut. And I'm not talking just about ignoring—or being unable to interpret—signals that I'm full. Because for so long I've eaten to blot out every strong feeling (anxiety, sadness, boredom), each bite takes me further and further away from myself, the voices inside me becoming ever fainter until I'm not even sure I've heard them at all. The dissociation shakes me from my bearings, making it impossible to know what I want and need on the most basic level, making it impossible to trust myself.

I thought I shouldn't have gone to the party tonight, but I went anyway. It was the party of a work friend of Mary's, and I just didn't have it in me to chitchat with people I didn't know. The only people I knew at the party were getting tipsy and then dancing, neither of which I felt like doing. So I stood there, not drinking anything except Diet Coke and feeling cranky and edgy and . . . separate from everyone at the party, as though trying to connect with them through a film of Saran Wrap. My cue to go home should have been when my friends started to irritate me—when they seemed so loud and happy that I couldn't stand it. But I didn't. I never want to leave parties until everyone else does. What if something interesting happens after I've already left?

In my less morose moments, I can almost laugh about the unexpected fringe benefits of dieting. Sometimes I feel like the diet makes it hard to have a social life, and it often makes me resent all the things I usually love about my job—that I have to go out a lot. But planning not to be caught hungry at various events is turning out to be quite good for my professional life. One night at a dinner I had to attend, I literally met everyone in the room because I was so busy trying to concentrate on the people and not the Southern buffet of fried chicken, dripping corn bread, and peanut brittle. (I knew the fried chicken was coming, so I'd eaten beforehand.) As an added bonus, at most after-work events—where there are usually greasy appetizers—not eating anything at all means I never get caught in midbite, or in that awkward position of juggling plate and drink so I can shake someone's hand. Nor do I have to worry about spinach in my teeth. Aren't I positively Ms. Glass Is Half Full?

Month 2 (February)

*Y*ou always read in magazines and diet books about volunteering to bring vegetables or a fruit dessert or something else you can eat when you go to someone else's house, but I couldn't imagine actually doing it or, frankly, that anyone else actually did it.

But I tried the bringing-something routine, and I'm here to report that it was easier than I'd thought. I called Alexy to ask if she needed anything for her annual Super Bowl party. But instead of waiting for her to say she had everything covered or to tell me to bring some soda or chips, I followed up my "Can I bring you something?" with "Like maybe some veggies and dip?"

She said, "Oh, that's a good idea. I don't have a single healthy thing planned."

Just as I'd suspected.

I brought a big platter of mushrooms, cherry tomatoes, carrots, and broccoli, and I ate them. So did everyone else—in between pizza, chips, and chocolate.

Not that everything was perfect. I had invited Diana, and after twenty minutes I was beginning to wish I'd swallowed my guilt that she had nowhere to go and left her home. She kept making cracks—which I tried to ignore—about how I was being a martyr by not eating the high-fat dips. She didn't look pleased when my friend Amy started making a fuss about how thin I looked. When I got up to go to the bathroom, I was sure I'd return to find Diana had dipped my vegetables in batter and fried them.

When I was in college, I had a friend who, instead of giving up something for Lent, would commit to doing something good for forty days. Volunteer. Recycle. Call her mother more often.

Other friends used to tease her that her approach was only to make herself feel better because there was no way she could give up the corn fritters she loved from the pizza place down the road. But I always think of her when I try to explain why I'd rather exercise than diet. I'd rather *do* something than deny, deny, deny.

It didn't used to be this way. It's practically a cliché of the overweight to say how much you hated gym class as a child, but of course I did. It was nerve-racking enough to get graded on how many times I could serve the volleyball over the net (A for five times, B for four times, and so on), but then there was the comparing of myself with all the other girls. In regular clothes, I could possibly convince myself my flaws were camouflaged. But not in a gym uniform. Before I left the locker room, I'd lock myself in a bathroom stall, pull my knees to my chest, and stretch my T-shirt over them, hoping to make the shirt big enough to hide me. Later, sitting on the scuffed gymnasium floor, I'd cross my arms over my thighs, hoping to make myself smaller, if not invisible. When I forgot my uniform, the dread that possibly none of the spare maroon shorts and T-shirts would fit sometimes gave me a stomachache. It wasn't that I was so fat in middle school—I wasn't. But I knew that even if the uniform didn't fit because it was, say, an extra-small, I wouldn't be able to laugh it off the way the other girls did.

There were plenty of other kids who weren't very good at volleyball or softball, but that never seemed to matter when it was my turn. I don't remember anyone calling me fat in class or otherwise attributing my complete lack of sports aptitude to that, but I was sure that was what everyone was thinking. When I was standing around waiting for my turn, I did plenty of whispering about all sorts of things that had nothing to do with gym class, but when other people whispered when I was at bat, I was sure they were laughing at me. Which of course never did anything to improve my sporting abilities.

Before I got too self-conscious—which I date around age six, when we moved to Florida from New Jersey—I loved to swim. One of my few memories of my grandfather—he died just before we moved—is of going to the pool with him. Years later—when I wouldn't jump in the deep end because I was afraid my body would make too large a splash—I used to yearn for those days at the pool with Grandpa. Back then, I wouldn't jump for what now seems like such a sweet, childlike, *normal* reason: I was too afraid.

I also remember swimming at a New Jersey pool where a family friend was a member. I must have been about five, trying to earn a red ankle bracelet that qualified you for what, I can't remember. My sister and I swam well for our age; we were considered young to take the test. I failed; I'm pretty sure Diana did, too. Unlike the years that followed, from which I can recall every cringe-worthy detail about every cringe-worthy bathing suit I ever owned and the cringe-worthy way it fit, I can't remember what I wore that day. Nor can I remember why I didn't pass. I couldn't know then it was to be the last time I didn't ascribe a sports-related failure to being fat—and the last time I wouldn't spend the week afterward loathing myself for both the failure and the weight.

In Florida, instead of sending your little girl to ballet class, you send her for tennis lessons. Not Diana and me. My parents weren't fans of any sport, and neither of them liked the outdoors. I can imagine my mother wrinkling her nose when she learned that tennis lessons were the after-school activity of choice. Running around chasing after a ball in the heat?

In the first house I remember, on Long Island, we lived on a cul-de-sac, the sort of storybook place where kids played kick the can and chased Charlie, the neighbor's black Lab, without fear of cars. In Cherry Hill, New Jersey, we also lived on a kid-friendly street—where all the backyards between our street and the one behind us created one huge green space. Diana and I had a jungle gym that was the envy of the neighborhood, and we played on it every summer night. Later, we'd hurtle ourselves across the lawn, trying to trap fireflies in a special lantern. To this day, my enduring image of childhood summers is this: I'm five years old and wearing orange shorts (my mother's favorite color), giggling hysterically as I somersault and slide across the cool grass.

In Florida, we lived on a busy road, and no one had a backyard. Everyone had pools and fences. Our own pool required a lot of upkeep—some of it Diana and I could do (and didn't), and some of it we couldn't—so we rarely used it. I remember my mother taking us to the park on Tuesday afternoons, but on other days I often read. Intellectual pursuits were always encouraged, so I can't remember anyone ever telling me to take my nose out of a book and go play.

Right about that time was when my mother and grandmother started to nag me about my weight and what I ate. It was the early eighties, when tuna fish, celery, and Tab were still the answers to extra pounds. Exercise? I don't remember hearing about it.

As I grew older, I dabbled in exercise, always in secret. At the time I don't think I acknowledged why I didn't want anyone to know—I didn't want to discuss my body and what was wrong with it, since I already heard enough about that. All I remember is that I was insistent on privacy—a rare commodity when you have a twin sister.

About age ten, I found a pamphlet on the bookshelves in my father's study. It outlined a calisthenics regime used by the Royal Canadian Mounted Police. I tried it, squeezed between the two twin beds in my room, the rough brown carpet I hated burning my knees when I did push-ups. After a few days nothing seemed to be happening. I decided I probably wasn't doing the exercises right, but didn't want to ask for help, so I gave up.

Later, I read about walking programs in the *Family Circle* magazines my mother had piled in her bathroom. They nearly always advertised "Drop Five Pounds by Next Month," while simultaneously putting an "easy, luscious" chocolate cake on the cover. Walking around the neighborhood was out of the question; having anyone see me would be too embarrassing. So I'd walk around and around our open kitchen and den, making precise right angles on the square cream-colored tiles. I would decide to start with 100 times around, but someone would nearly always come in in the middle—usually to open the refrigerator—so I'd have to stop and pretend to be wandering idly. That, too, got old.

At some point, my brain turned the vague idea that exercise without diet was pointless into hard fact. Exercise alone wouldn't do anything very quickly, maybe not anything at all. So the summer after high school, when my sister joined a gym to get in shape for college, I didn't go with her. I couldn't seem to diet, and I was sure that even if I went to the gym every day, I still wouldn't lose enough weight to start college thin.

While my sister dashed off to the gym five times a week, I glowered. For years I had daydreamed about a fresh start, about going off to college—and in my dreams I was always thin. But now the moment was upon me and I wasn't.

In the spring of my freshman year at Cornell, I got a new roommate—a thin one who arrived with a stationary exercise bike for our tiny room, one who knew a lot about nutrition. Feeling depressed during the cold winter and adrift at a huge university, somehow I ended up asking her for diet help. Emily was the first person to teach me about low-fat diets—in her world, any food was fair game as long as it didn't have fat. She was also the first person to impress upon me the importance of exercise along with diet.

I hated the stationary bike, so under Emily's tutelage I began jogging in place in our room. I don't think I told her I was too embarrassed to exercise in public, and I can't remember if her suggestion sounded as bizarre to me as it does now. All I remember was the overwhelming relief of putting someone else in charge of cleaning up at least one area of my life—weight—and feeling that my secret was safe with her. So whatever she said, I was ready to do.

First I jogged for fifteen minutes. Then sixteen. Then seventeen. Then a big jump to twenty-five. No matter how late I got home—and some nights I got home from the newspaper at 3:00 A.M.—Emily told me I had to exercise every day. She didn't mind if I jogged while she slept; if she woke up, she smiled and gave me a thumbs-up. She taught me some leg and ab exercises I could do if I was too tired when I got home to do anything else.

Exercise appealed to the competitive, overachieving perfectionist in me. I loved tracing the unbroken chain of days I'd exercised, as if they were pearls on a string. I never wanted to skip a day because once I did, no matter how many days I exercised after that, I was sure the one day I didn't would mock me, ruining my perfect necklace.

I also loved the challenge: nearly every day, I tried to jog at least a minute longer. Usually I'd coax myself into going even longer than that. I listened to music and daydreamed. If that didn't work, I'd stare at the red digits of my clock, calculating, say, that I was one-fifteenth of the way done, then two-fifteenths, then one-fifth, and so on. I'd figure the percentages, dividing the bottom number into the top, so my brain never had too long to pause and consider stopping. After two months, I was up to thirty-five minutes. In three months of diet and exercise, I lost thirty-nine pounds.

I had never exercised if I wasn't dieting, so when I lost control of food again—somewhere in the beginning of my sophomore year—I reverted to my sedentary ways. Every few months I'd start a new diet, and with it a new exercise program. But I had a new problem: I knew what my body felt like lighter and fitter. Instead of challenging me, the fact that I could no longer jog for an hour—heck, I could barely go for ten minutes—was just another reminder of what a failure I was.

I didn't exercise without dieting until a few months ago—the fall of 1998—when I began my usual starvation diet, got twelve pounds into it, binged, but decided to keep going to the Y anyway. And now there's the *Shape* project, which allows me—as I did with Emily—to feel like I'm putting someone else in charge. It gives me someone to please with the results. I do what I'm told, plus some. After all, I've always been a good student.

Until the *Shape* project, I'd been walking three miles in forty-five minutes on the track, occasionally throwing in a few minutes of jogging. So I e-mailed that to Shari Frishett, the therapist (and certified personal trainer) who works with Peeke. Shari has encouraged me to e-mail her daily with a workout report. After a week's worth of missives about what I euphemistically called my walk-jogging routine (because I actually had to report it, I was jogging more than usual, but still not very much), Shari suggested I increase speed by setting a distance goal: say, 3.5 miles in forty-five minutes. "If you find you're coming up on forty minutes and you're nowhere near 3.5," she e-mailed, "then that's your cue to start running some more or running faster."

Besides Shari, *Shape* asked Dr. Daniel Kosich, a Colorado fitness consultant, to talk with me. I had a few phone conversations with him in the early days of the project, and he told me that a handful of times during my workout, I'm supposed to speed up my jogging until I feel like I can't go any faster, then slow down to a more comfortable pace. I laughed at this, since I'm already sweaty and breathing hard from the effort of turning my walk into a jog. But speed play, as he calls it—or interval training, as magazines usually call it—does double duty, improving cardiovascular fitness and incinerating fat, so again I've been doing as I'm told. Speed play also appeals to my competitive side. At first I struggled to make myself move any faster than I already was, but speed play is fast becoming my favorite part of the workout. Every time I try it I think: *How fast can I go?*

I'm going to visit a friend in Nashville next month, and I'm wanting to eat now because—get this—I might eat a lot a month from now.

I'm dreading the visit the way I dread doctors and dentists and anything that requires me to wear shorts in public. I fear the loss of control and worrying about food all weekend. I'll have someone watching what I eat twenty-four hours a day, which always makes me want to eat in secret, like Scarlett O'Hara eating before the ball so she can pick daintily in public. And what if Nicole wants to know things I can't really answer, like why I don't eat more lunch if I really do think I'm hungry an hour later? (I can't—that would be more calories. Besides, Peeke says it's impossible that I'm really hungry.) And most friends and restaurants don't serve perfectly measured-out cereal with milk for breakfast, Boca Burgers for lunch, and salads and an egg-white omelet with vegetables and one ounce of Healthy Choice low-fat cheese made in a nonstick pan for dinner. I can just about handle one meal out without freaking about what unseen (and fattening) ingredients are in my food, but every meal of every day for two days?

Peeke doesn't think what I'm thinking is quite as crazy as I do. I have to "re-create a user-friendly environment within which you will be safe to do your self-care." In the Peeke universe—the more I learn about it, the more parallel to mine it seems—I'm supposed to call Nicole and tell her I'm preparing to do a few 5K races and that I need lots of fruits, vegetables, and good protein options for my "training." Peeke does this all the time, she says, and people respect her for it. Well, yeah, but she's a diet doctor.

This is another diet-doctor solution that sounds not unthinkable when someone's saying it (or has written it), but when I stop and actually consider it, I can't imagine doing it. When you're overweight, the last thing you want to do is issue a pile of special instructions—to friends or restaurants—because the last thing you want to do is attract attention to (a) yourself and (b) the fact that you are, um, *eating*. Which is totally ridiculous, because unless you have a rare disease, it's not like you got fat by any other way *but* eating. Yet somehow I persist in thinking it really matters what I eat in public.

Part of me thinks Nicole won't care if I tell her what I need, but another part is worrying about her thinking I'm annoying and high-maintenance and not fun, the way a handful of us snicker over a friend who makes the world's hugest fuss about her wheat-free diet. (I confess to dashing off some wheat-free haiku after a particularly torturous lunch with her and then e-mailing the poems out to a few friends: "I'll tell you why I/cannot eat a bit of wheat/It'll take just five hours.")

I wish there were a way to mention what I need and to have that be the end of the conversation, but I can't imagine it will be. Maybe it's because my mother and grandmother have always been so oversolicitous when they know I'm on a diet—worrying so much about whether there's stuff around for me to eat that I want to eat a box of chocolate just to show them I'm not going to die from it—that I expect anyone else I tell to be the same way. I don't want to spend a weekend having someone ask every five seconds if such-and-such restaurant will be OK. I just want everything to be normal.

As I did during my freshman-year-of-college exercise regimen, I've begun racking up the mileage. Distance goals appeal to me even more than time goals—I ran three miles, I can imagine myself casually dropping into a conversation one day. But not yet. I've done 3.51 miles in forty-five minutes, then 3.57, then 3.66. I usually walk the first two-thirds of a mile or so, then jog a while (up to ten minutes, if I can), then walk for a bit, then see how energetic I'm feeling before jogging anymore. I'm actually starting to enjoy the sweating, the being out of breath—tangible proof that I've done something, that something is happening.

But the first fifteen minutes of my workout are the worst. Sometimes I have to bully myself through it: *You're going to spend the whole forty-five minutes here. Now, are you going to stand here fixing your ponytail, or are you actu-*

ally going to work out? Other days, only out-and-out bribery works, like buying myself a new CD. Once I get going, I always manage to finish. The perfectionist strikes again.

By the beginning of this month, Month 2 of the diet, I had a new goal, courtesy of Shari. It's to go four miles in fifty minutes. I like this part—the cardio part—of my workout so much more than the strength training, which I'm supposed to do two days a week. I have a simple routine: some dips, some crunches, some bicep and tricep curls. But unlike the walking/jogging, where I can zone out, I have to focus on the lifting. People tell me I'll like it more when I see results, but right now I just think it's incredibly boring, and I resent doing it when there are a million other things I'd rather do with the time.

I look for things not to like, the way I do when I've decided instantly upon meeting someone that I don't like him or her: no headphones are allowed in the weight room, so I'm stuck listening to the gym's crummy music. I can't speed through the weights—that just defeats the point. I also dislike looking in the mirror while I lift, watching the fat on my body shift as I move through the routine. On the track I'm mostly left alone, but in the weight room there are always a few trainers—big, burly guys—and I feel like they're constantly watching me, waiting to dash over and tell me how poor my form is. In a roomful of people wearing weight-lifting gloves, moving purposefully from one exercise to the next, I feel tentative and uncertain and, yes, fatter than ever.

Fat Tuesday, and a very Fat Tuesday it was. It started with my hovering around the office lunch table in my size 16 jeans (better than 18s, but not enough), eyeing the Mardi Gras king cake, this Danish-y cake topped with a sickly sweet frosting I could practically taste. I'd been feeling as though all I'd done for days was resist things I wanted to eat. Yes, it is working—I *am* losing weight—but this was lost on me in the moment. I thought: *I want cake. Now.*

They say that when you feel the urge to overeat, you should stop and think about what's making you feel the compulsion, recognize the thoughts and emotions that lead you to find comfort in food. Fat chance. I *wish* I could point a finger at something specific—stress or frustration, maybe. But I'm not sure what it was. I left the table and started walking back to my office, pretending I had a phone interview to do. But before I got halfway down the hall, I turned and strode purposefully back to the table. After days of eating much the same thing because I don't want to think about it, of avoiding restaurants and happy hours and dinner at other people's houses, I still can't avoid all the possibilities of things I could eat. Though Peeke keeps telling me it's not that I'll never be able to eat chocolate again—that I'll be able to eat it someday, when I "learn how"—I'm tired of waiting. I'm tired of thinking about sneaking in a little bit of what I want—do I really have to tell Peeke if I eat a Hershey bar instead of two Boca Burgers, since they have almost the same number of calories? I'll feel gross—or "feel foul," as my friend Mary would say—if I eat the Hershey bar and not the Boca Burgers. But what if I had one Boca Burger and half a chocolate bar—could I eat half a chocolate bar? Could I eat . . . ?

I was so sick of the endless calculating and thinking that I finally stopped thinking entirely—shoved calories and diets and food out of my mind and grabbed a piece of cake. Because it was there. Because I haven't been able to have anything else I wanted for the past six weeks. Because. Because. Because.

I started with a Courtney-sized sliver, which I'm not sure is anyone else's idea of a sliver but is definitely a much smaller piece of cake than I would have taken in the past. I eventually moved on to three, maybe four servings, not that these things come with preprinted portion sizes.

I felt sick. I wished I had a long shirt on, because after I finished the cake I was afraid to sit down—my pants felt so tight they might split. *Is it possible to gain that much weight in less than five minutes?* I wondered. I've spent the past couple of weeks worrying about when I might really screw up—worrying and waiting and wondering when it would happen—and today I finally did.

It was only 11:30 in the morning, and I wasn't sure how to get through the day. This wasn't one piece of chocolate or a couple of drinks. This was enough cake for me to wonder if anyone had seen me—enough for me to feel ashamed and fat and guilty. Having eaten that much—and knowing that tomorrow is my weekly weigh-in day and it's pretty obvious I'm going to show a gain—I wanted to eat everything I've been wanting to eat for the past six weeks. Every last muffin, bowl of pasta shells and cheese, and chocolate truffle.

For a half hour, I couldn't think about anything else. I surfed the Web, looking at cyberdiet.com and other websites with calorie charts, getting annoyed that all the numbers weren't the same and trying to figure out both what the maximum number of calories I could have consumed was and how many hours I might have to exercise to burn them off. I'm not sure whether I was more bothered by the numbers or by the fact that no matter what figure I came up with and how long I walk/jog later, there's no way I'm going to get on the scale tomorrow and not see a gain. Will I be depressed or determined when I see the number? I wish I could say for sure.

I e-mailed Shari, not telling her quite how much cake I ate but admitting that I had more than I should have. She told me to go ahead and eat my lunch anyway, since the last thing I needed was to deprive myself and then be starving in the middle of the afternoon. I couldn't bring myself to admit to her how much eating the cake had upset me, but I felt better just having told her I'd eaten it and making a concrete plan for what I'm going to do for the rest of the day (get back on plan ASAP). Yes, I've read diet advice like that before, but there was something about telling it to someone directly, and knowing that person would probably ask about it tomorrow, that helped. This, I guess, is why having a diet buddy is supposed to be so great. But I've never had one, because I've never had any friends with anywhere near as much weight to lose as I have. Besides, it always seems to be the one friend who doesn't really need to lose any weight at all who's the person who volunteers.

If I had a bathroom scale at home, I'd be on and off it every fifteen minutes. Shari is always telling me weight is just a number, and "you is what you is." Much as I want to believe her, I can't. How can I explain that I just *know* I looked thinner at 199 than I did at 200, and thinner at 189 than at 190?

I weigh myself only once a week, and only at the gym. Unfortunately, today—approximately nineteen hours A.C., or After Cake—was my weekly weigh-in day.

I got on the scale, telling myself I had to have gained at least two pounds, yet hoping desperately I was wrong.

I couldn't believe it. I hadn't gained a thing.

I got off and on the scale, double-checking, triple-checking, quadruple-checking. No gain. I felt like I'd gotten away with something.

I wondered if the gain could possibly show up later, like sometime next week. Then even I had to laugh at myself for being so paranoid. I couldn't just be happy that I hadn't gained any weight, though—I next had to start thinking about the fact that I hadn't lost any, mentally readjusting my "if I lost one pound a week" pre-wedding timetable (though I'm ahead of schedule, thanks to losing more than one pound a week in Month 1).

All day I considered whether I should try to cut back a little this week so I could lose more by my next weigh-in—make up for lost time—but I knew I shouldn't go there. Besides, if I eat exactly as I'm told, that's at least one less thing to think about. I'll still think about my weight, but at least I won't be sitting around coming up with twenty-seven options for dinner.

Today was one of those days where the weights at the gym feel heavier than usual. I suppose that beats the days my body itself feels heavier and I have to struggle through my walk/jog. My mantra is: *If I did it before, I can do it again.* I don't often love the workout, but I love the feeling of *having* worked out. Another gold star.

I'm especially pleased with myself because I've been going to the gym before work. I'm not a morning person—for important interviews, I have to have friends call me to make sure I'm out of bed. But it's before work or never—after work, there are always so many other things to do. Besides, I definitely love the virtuous feeling of sitting at work, knowing that I've already checked one thing off my list.

The aren't-I-great feeling usually helps inspire me to work on my other activity-related project. That's small changes in my routine. Dr. Kosich says that if you watch the average amount of television and use a remote control to change the channel, that's ten calories a day your body isn't using up. Big deal, right? In a year, that's a pound. Of course, I could get myself crazy—and bore my friends to pieces—making little calculations like that, so I try to add the extra activity slowly and keep it to myself. I take the stairs to my fourth-floor apartment at least once a day. I aim for inefficiency at work, walking back and forth to the supply closet and mail room, instead of saving it all for one big trip. I can never write without taking lots of little breaks anyway, so a trip to get an envelope is a perfect excuse. Sure, sometimes I'm just procrastinating, but at least I'm accomplishing something else.

Month 3 (March)

*A*fter weeks when all the foods I can't or shouldn't and—if some diet experts had their way—may never eat again seem to pop out at me in luminescent colors as if under a black light, suddenly they recede. Tonight I got home from dinner with friends, sat down to write my food diary, and realized I'd thought about food exactly once during the whole meal: when it was time to order. Considering that I normally think about the rolls (can I have more than one without looking like a pig?) and dessert (will anyone order any?) and what's on everyone else's plate relative to his or her size (how unfair it is that so-and-so can eat fried chicken and be so tiny), I felt like calling someone to brag. But I couldn't think of anyone who would quite be able to share my glee over *not* thinking about food, so here I am alternately writing about it and wondering how long it will last.

At the restaurant tonight I got Mary to split a turkey burger with me, since the menu said they were a half pound—more than two times a "serving size" of three ounces. I ignored the roll and fries. I didn't think about them or consider having just one or wonder if I should pour a ton of salt on them (a trick my mother picked up years ago at Weight Watchers) to keep from picking at them. It was as if the entire link in my brain that used to send my hand out automatically to grab them was broken, as was the link that shrieks, "Oooh. Fries. Must have some."

Trying to describe how I managed this is like trying to describe how you learn a foreign language. You memorize all these random vocabulary words and silly dialogues about passing Katya the caviar (if, say, you're learning Russian, as I did), and every time anyone asks you a question in Russian, you realize you can't give the answer you'd like to give because it's just too complicated. But then after a few weeks of feeling like maybe you're not meant to speak Russian, one day someone asks you a question and an answer pops out instantly, unbidden and perfectly formed. Something has snapped into place.

And just as quickly, the link is functioning again, allowing me to consider eating all the things I know I shouldn't. This afternoon at work was bad, bad, bad. I couldn't stop thinking about food. It was a struggle all day—some days are like that. Today's obsessions included chocolate-chip cookies that had been on the table for hours. Then there was lunch out where there's no way to measure food or know precisely what's in my dish, and where even when I manage to divide my portion (as I did today), I debate picking at the edges of the "forbidden" bit. And then there were the Hershey's Kisses that a (thin) coworker keeps in her desk drawer. I can't imagine keeping candy in my desk. In a Camryn Manheim interview I once read, brass at "The Practice" wanted her character to have a bowl of something sweet on her desk. She said no fat person would do that, but if they wanted, she'd look longingly at a bowl on someone else's desk. That's what I did today: thought longingly about what I can't have, especially because everybody knows I'm on a diet and I didn't feel like getting The Look and/or the quasi-sympathetic comments.

You know The Look—the gaze that says, "I know you're eating something you shouldn't be, and I'm not going to say anything, but how can you expect to lose weight if you eat like *that*?" And the quasi-sympathetic comments, usually including things like, "I heard there was a diet where you can eat a candy bar a day—is that the one you're doing?" Or worse: "Oh, but you're doing so well. I couldn't have lasted more than an hour with what you're doing" (this usually from the slimmest girl you know—the one who eats like a football player yet saves sweating exclusively for sex).

After literally twenty minutes of back-and-forthing about whether I could have anything to snack on—and I wonder why some days it takes me half a day to write a few paragraphs—I ended up making low-cal hot cocoa from packets in the kitchen. I knew I had to have something and didn't think I'd be able to hold myself to one piece of chocolate just then, so I didn't want to get started.

By 6:00 P.M., I felt like I'd spent all day resisting the urge to eat, nearly counting the minutes as they passed, every cell in my body screaming for something to eat. Could I eat that? Should I eat that? What if I had just one? Could I exercise it off? And what am I going to tell people at the happy hour later, when I'm not drinking? What can I say to avoid the diet commentary? "I'm on medication"? The voices in my head got louder, and the potential problems grew more numerous until finally, in an instant, I shook them out of my head and just did it—I gave in and consumed extra calories.

I drank at happy hour. Two gin and tonics.

Aaah, I thought after the first sip, sinking into the drink. But the peace didn't last longer than that first sip, the same way it rarely does past a first bite. It's as if that first bit of whatever's forbidden sets something loose deep inside me and sends bubbles up to the surface, demanding everything I've thought about eating in the past few hours, plus everything I've passed up over the past few weeks.

Except before I could finish plotting the excuse I'd use to sneak off and do a drive-by grab of the buffet, a friend who was meeting us at happy hour showed up and whispered: "From far off it took me a minute to realize who was standing here, because there's definitely less of you."

Fight with Diana tonight. She started in on me that my "crazy" food behaviors—like no carbs at dinner—are annoying. Then she berated me for being "less fun" when I'm watching what I eat.

"You sit there like a martyr during dinner," she said. "You make everyone else feel guilty about what they're eating."

Her big complaint: I don't do big pig-outs with her anymore.

"Can't we have fun without doing food stuff?" I asked. (A direct quote. I'd better watch it or I'm going to turn into Peeke.)

"It's winter," Diana said flatly. "What else is there to do?"

This morning I woke up late, and instead of dashing around, I just lay there not wanting to get up, not wanting to go to the gym, not wanting to go to work—not wanting to do anything except lie in bed, read the newspaper, and eat. When I finally got myself to the gym, I had time for only a twenty-minute workout. Since I didn't feel like moving in the first place, pushing myself harder (because I've got only twenty minutes instead of my usual fifty) was out of the question. Which made me feel grouchy. I walked to work, trying to remember that twenty minutes is better than nothing—and that for once I have not taken the all-or-nothing route, every last minute of the workout or none at all. I did *something*. Rah-rah for me. Honestly, losing weight makes me feel like I'm in the middle of some feel-good brainstorming session where everyone's playing by the rules and finding something positive to say about every idea, no matter how ludicrous.

I wonder if this is why I'm so bad at losing weight—because the feel-good mind-set is so alien to me. It requires finding something positive—no matter how minuscule—in everything, and my brain doesn't work that way. So you ate two pieces of chocolate cake? Well, at least you didn't eat your usual four. So you didn't get in a whole workout? At least you got in part of one. I'm not used to being this forgiving of myself. I'm the person who gets an A on the exam but still can't forget that I've missed some incredibly stupid question.

Bought a pair of size 14 jeans! Thankfully, I had a mission—finding jeans to wear to my friend Rebecca's party tonight—otherwise I might have just stood there, not sure where to look first. No worrying about whether the XL will fit or whether I'm part of the "all" club that one size always fits. No plus-size department. In any store there are a zillion things I can try on.

I was practically hugging myself all night long, thinking, *I'm wearing size 14 jeans.* And it wasn't the dressing-room mirror playing tricks on me: I *did* look much slimmer in the smaller jeans. From the moment I walked in the door, everyone I knew at the party was telling me how great I looked—including my friends' boyfriends. The attention was sweet, if a little unsettling. It's not that I'm usually the wallflower type, just that if life were a movie, I'd have the overweight and/or not-beautiful sidekick role. Janeane Garofalo in *The Truth About Cats and Dogs.* The funny one. So when there's attention focused on me that doesn't involve telling a story, I'm not sure how to handle it.

When I got there, Rebecca and I started talking, and she said, "I don't know how to say this, but, um"—she paused, and I looked down to see if my fly was unzipped and wondered if I had something unsavory hanging out of my nose—"you look smaller."

"Yeah," said her fiancé.

Then another friend's boyfriend started quizzing me about what I was doing—what I was eating and how much and what sort of exercise I did. Soon a little knot of us—men *and* women—were discussing exercise and diets. A size 2 friend confessed that throwing out half a candy bar never solved the problem of eating the whole thing—eventually she'd fish it out of the garbage can. One of the guys said he wouldn't let his girlfriend bring ice cream into the house, because he'd eat the whole tub, no matter the size. Who knew that other people—thin people, male people—ever thought about food the way I do?

Diana immediately pounced on the fact that I was wearing new jeans today. "What size are they? You must be losing a ton of weight if you got new jeans."

I shrugged. "Are you under two hundred pounds?" she asked.

I tried to change the subject.

"Are you under two hundred?" she asked again.

"Yes," I said.

"A lot?" she asked.

"What movie do you want to see?" I asked. The "let's not talk about this" technique doesn't work; I've tried it. So I tried ignoring her questions politely—by changing the subject—which held her off for a little while. Then, when I broke out the single-serving cottage cheese in the movie theater, she rolled her eyes and sighed loudly.

Another episode in the Courtney and Diana show(down). Or maybe I should call it a rerun, since every fight we have I feel like we've had a million times before. The flash point this time: clothes that *Shape* sent for my first photo shoot. She saw there was a big box waiting for me at the front desk of our building, and she came upstairs to find out what it was.

"How did they know what size to send?" she asked.

"I told them."

"Well, how come they sent 14s when you told me you were still wearing 16s?"

"The last time you asked about my jeans, I told you what size they were."

"This is the stupidest thing I've ever heard of. Why are they sending you clothes? Is this your 'after' picture? How much weight have you lost?" All in nasty, rapid-fire succession.

"I'd rather not discuss it," I said, straining to sound calm. At the beginning of every fight, I vow not to lose my temper and start yelling. I think I've managed about four times out of the past hundred. She always knows exactly how to get to me, and now I'm so primed for battle with her that the slightest thing sets me off anyway.

"Why don't you want to discuss it? What's the matter? Have you lost too much weight?"

On the way out she accidentally-on-purpose stomped on a white shirt that had fallen on the floor, rendering it unwearable for the shoot.

I've lost twenty-three pounds, and *Shape* is just now shooting my "before" picture because they didn't get around to shooting it in December. Personally, I'm convinced they didn't want to waste the money to shoot me earlier in case I flamed out on the diet, but never mind about that. What worries me is that I'm going to look like an idiot. As much as I don't want to see an unflattering picture of myself—which "before" shots always are—in glossy full color, I think I would've preferred having the "before" picture taken in the beginning. Now, with a twenty-three-pound head start, I'm afraid that even if I lose five pounds this month, my next photo won't show much difference.

I loathe having my picture taken. I'm the person who always brings the camera so that I can be the one taking the pictures instead of having to be in them. In group shots I try to stand in the back, my head peeking over someone's shoulder, my body hidden. I wear black, which *Shape* won't allow. They want something nice and bright.

The chat with the fashion editor—who clearly isn't used to dealing with anyone who isn't a sample size—did nothing to reassure me. I didn't want to be rude, but I felt like I had to keep reminding her that not only am I a 14/16 (even I know that in certain styles a 14 won't fit me, and this is one time where it is not to my advantage to lie about my size), but I am not a trim 14/16. In other words, no sleeveless outfits. And please, please, please—nothing too fitted.

"We want to see your body shape," she told me.

That's exactly what I was afraid of.

So I ended up with a box of the sort of clothes I would never wear. Fitted shirts. A pair of very slim-cut pants. And not only are the clothes bright, but in what seems to be a not-very-good omen of how this photo shoot will go, the things I need a 16 in I've gotten in a 14, and the things I need a 14 in are size 16.

On a scale of not-fun-ness, with one being unpacking after moving and ten being three simultaneous root canals, I'd say the photo shoot was about a six. It snowed yesterday, and it was still freezing today, but because this photo is appearing in the September issue (which, in the weird world of magazine dates, hits the stands at the end of July), I wasn't allowed to wear a winter jacket. Molly (the photographer) and I also had to run around hunting for places where there wasn't snow on the ground.

Molly didn't make me feel any better about the clothes.

"I think you should wear your own clothes," she said.

Too bad most of my clothes are black. Besides, since we're still in winter, I don't really have fall clothes that fit properly—all of mine from last fall are now at least a size too big(!). So I chose the least objectionable *Shape* outfit: a long black skirt with buttons down the front, plus a deep-blue button-down shirt over a white T-shirt.

I thought about calling a friend to come over and advise, but I don't want to discuss the *Shape* project too much with anyone. It's a bit like not wanting to tell anyone you're pregnant until the third month—until it's more of a sure thing. The whole project still seems so unreal to me—maybe because it won't appear in print for months—so best to keep quiet for now.

So off Molly and I went. Unfortunately, Molly decided she liked the brick steps and the light outside my apartment building, so I had to walk up and down the steps, pretending I was heading to work. Molly thought I looked too serious, so she insisted I start skipping, which made me feel even more ridiculous and conspicuous, if that's possible. There were more skipping sessions in a couple of spots where there was (a) no snow visible and (b) views of the Washington Monument—magazines always insist on that sort of background for D.C. shoots. Whatever. I stopped minding the skipping—I was freezing.

Molly had this idea that she wanted me frolicking in the Dupont Circle fountain, à la the "Friends" opening sequence. But even on a blustery March day, there were loads of people in the Circle. I tried to talk her out of it by pointing out that no one frolics in a fountain on the way to work, but reality shalt not get in the way of a good photo.

As I was skipping around the edge of the fountain, trying not to trip on my skirt and fall in (but thinking that in the scheme of embarrassing things that could happen, I'd prefer that scenario to having anyone I knew see me), a guy paused to listen to Molly urge me to smile and look happy.

"What do you think you are, a model?" he yelled and started to laugh. "Girl, you're no model."

My new size 14 jeans and I are preparing to wing our way to Nashville to visit a friend. It's supposed to be fun, but I've been worrying about it for days. This is the first trip I've been on since starting this diet, and trips are usually where I, um, trip up.

First there's the airport and the anonymity it provides—the anonymity I so dearly love. You could eat your way across the airport—cinnamon buns, chocolate, muffins—and the chances are very small that anyone will have any idea how much you've consumed. Then you can eat on the plane. And on the other end if you want to, since just about the first thing anyone asks when you've gotten off a plane is, "Have you eaten?"

But the airport problem seems small in comparison to the idea of more than forty-eight hours with the same person. The idea of someone being able to see everything I eat and when I eat it terrifies me. What if the amounts and things I want to eat aren't normal? What if she's not hungry when I am? I don't know that I can explain—or want to—the urgency with which I sometimes need food, how frustrated and cranky I can get. I can't make myself call Nicole and tell her I'm training for some 5Ks, as Peeke suggested, so I'm packing granola bars, fruit, and baby carrots in case Nicole doesn't have anything or in case I wake up early, starving, and don't feel I can rummage through her refrigerator. It makes me feel a little obsessed to do this—I've spent several days worrying about the food options and how much I'll have to explain myself. What makes it worse is that Nicole is my friend with the best attitude toward food I've ever seen. I've never heard her talk about calories or diets or how full she feels—she just eats. And, it appears, enjoys. Instead of thinking I can take a lesson from her, the last thing I want to do is talk about this with her. If she's as free of all this worrying about food as she seems to be, I don't want to be the one who makes her self-conscious.

I'm so convinced I might screw up that tonight I packed two lunches for the office refrigerator—one, of course, for tomorrow (Friday) and one for Monday, so that even if I eat poorly all weekend, I'll have no excuse to continue doing so once I get back to work.

Yes, I'm planning for the fact that I may just pig out—and though pig-outs are hardly cause for celebration, the fact that I'm starting to recognize that the diet can and *will* go on after a pig-out definitely is worth celebrating. Maybe it's because I've already slipped up—the king cake, the chocolate, the gin and tonics—and I'm still here and still losing weight. Maybe it's because I'm starting not to want to pig out or binge, not just because I might gain weight but because nothing tastes as good as feeling in control—or feeling more in control than usual—feels.

Nicole didn't have a single healthy thing in her apartment, so I'm glad I brought a stash. She looked at me a little funny when I pulled it out but didn't say anything.

Sunday she didn't get up for hours. Thank God for the apple. Have to eat before I jog/walk or I feel sick. Felt sick—in the head—when I was out exercising, since everybody else appeared to be en route to church. Me? I worship at the altar of thinness.

Nicole insisted on the Waffle House for breakfast. There wasn't a single healthy option: no egg whites, nothing that wasn't fried, buttered, or battered. And can you imagine telling them at the Waffle House to go easy on the grease? I was just about to give in and order something I craved—I was lingering over the menu like it was a love letter—when I spied two ancient-looking single-serving-sized boxes of Special K. The Waffle House didn't have skim milk, but I figured whole milk was better than waffles and hash browns with cheese. Still, it made me a little cranky to consume calories I didn't want to consume, the way I hate having to spend paychecks on boring practical things like a new vacuum cleaner when there are so many things I'd rather have.

That evening my stomach was still growling after my shrimp fajitas made with nonfat tortillas and low-fat cheese. When Nicole suggested dessert, I was tired of resisting—I'd been resisting things all weekend. So we split a chocolate empanada. Never mind that half a dessert is less than I'd usually eat. I felt this impending sense of doom before the waiter brought it over. What was I getting myself into? Was this the beginning of the end of this diet? This was the first time since I started this diet three months ago that I had actually requested that anything I shouldn't eat be put in front of me—all the other slipups had occurred when I was confronted with food, when it was already there.

I knew I should try to enjoy the dessert—to eat it slowly and savor it, as Peeke would say, and to eat it as though I had a right to eat it, instead of in the furtive way I usually do with things like it. But I couldn't. I ate like someone was going to take the empanada away from me, like I was going to get caught. I felt like I was eating it ridiculously fast, so I tried to come up with an excuse but failed. Normally I'd probably lie—say something about how I hadn't eaten much dinner or didn't eat lunch, but those lines wouldn't work on someone who'd seen everything I'd eaten for the past forty-eight hours. Nicole put her fork down after several bites, saying she was full. I was just relieved she didn't say the dessert didn't taste that good anyway, because there was no way I was going to be able to stop eating it.

As I got down to the last bit, my forkfuls got smaller and smaller. I didn't want to stop eating, and I was afraid of what I might want to have when the empanada was gone. I felt guilty and disgusted—I hadn't come anywhere near the pig-outs I thought I might indulge in this weekend, but why did I have to ruin a nearly perfect forty-eight hours with this stupid chocolate empanada? I had done so well—why did I have to screw up? When I finally finished eating, I racked my brain for a way to escape Nicole and go binge. But it was late on Sunday night, and there was no place I could plausibly need to go—no "errand" I could run—that she wouldn't have to accompany me to. I tried to calm down. Back at her apartment, I debated eating granola bars—the need to eat something else was that strong. I lay in bed waiting for Nicole to fall asleep so I could get up and eat, but I must have fallen asleep first. The next thing I knew, it was morning.

At a party tonight, Mary—who is not a die-hard runner—started talking about doing a marathon. I'm not even sure how long a marathon is. That it requires running for hours is all I know. And that it's for serious athletes— who else could run for that long?

I've known Mary for only six months, though we've spent so much time together it feels like longer. But if she really had known me longer, she would never ask me about running a race; I'm sure of it. I suddenly realized she's never seen me at my heaviest and most slothful—she knows me only as someone who gets up and exercises every morning. It's so bizarre that *anyone* would think of me as someone to do something athletic with. To try someplace new to go out or to go to a movie with—yes. But a marathon?

I wanted to explain patiently to Mary that she really doesn't know me at all. I wanted to explain that making new friends is like dating. You think you know the guy after a couple of months of dating, and suddenly you find he's got a frightening temper or a fiancée. I wanted to say to her: *You know how when you're on a website and you put the arrow on, say, a picture of a prince and it suddenly, unexpectedly, flips into a frog? That's me. For the past few months— the months that you've known me—I may have looked like someone who has a few healthy habits. But at any moment I could flip back into my unhealthy (fatter) self.*

The whole marathon idea sounds insane, but I told her it sounded interesting. There are lots of outrageous ideas that gain momentum at parties, and you never hear about them again. This has to be one of them.

Month 4 (April)

*T*ell your friends your clothes don't fit—and not because they're too tight—and you won't get a whole lot of sympathy. At least I didn't. I'm definitely detecting some resentment—some people are about as subtle as a marquee. One friend snaps that I'm "wasting away" and that if she didn't see me eat from time to time, she wouldn't even believe that I do. Another accidentally forwards me an e-mail that includes a catty remark about "whether Courtney's gym schedule will allow her time off for a movie."

I never imagined that the very personal decision of what to put in my mouth could change the social landscape of my life, but somehow it does. I'm no longer the friend always willing to go for 3:00 A.M. nachos after a night out (it's not the same for everyone if I go but don't eat—women always feel less crummy about what they eat if someone is sharing with them). Not too long ago, anyone could call me past midnight on a weeknight, but now I don't stay up as late because I know I have to get up for the gym. And—especially in the case of friends who have been "meaning" to get to the gym or to start eating more healthfully—sometimes I'm treated as if my decision to order a salad or skip dessert is a silent critique of someone else's higher-fat selection. Sometimes I can't help thinking how much easier it was to be fat.

Diana tells me all the time that I'm no fun anymore, as if the only fun we've ever had together was raiding the refrigerator when my parents were out and sneaking to the grocery store for cupcakes with buttercream frosting. Even Diana can't eat like that anymore—pig-outs in recent years are mostly restricted to a box of low-fat Nilla Wafers and nonfat whipped cream. But now I'm "psycho" because I won't join her even for those.

Maybe she's right. Am I crazy—either eating everything in sight or sticking rigidly to a diet? Nancy says that when you lose weight you're still the same person, there's just less of you, but I'm not sure I believe her. Suddenly I spend loads of time thumbing through magazines, dog-earing pages of clothes I now could actually wear. I shop too much, I spend too much, I look in the mirror too much, and I'm a lot more critical of other people's weight and what they're wearing.

I'm pickier about men, often judging them the way I'm sure many of them have judged me. I'm not as grateful for any attention as I was when I was heavier. I agreed to go out with a guy who's a good three inches shorter than I am and didn't think: *Hey, I'm on a date,* or *If he's willing to look past the fact that I'm overweight, I should be willing to overlook that he's short.* I spent the whole dinner looking for reasons not to like him. He picked a restaurant—an Indian place in Georgetown—that I think last had customers seven years ago. He ordered carrot juice, which in my mind I turned into an anecdote ("What's up, Doc?" in my best Bugs Bunny voice) before the date was even over.

"A doorknob would make better conversation than he did," I imagined myself telling my friends in the postdate report. "And he seems to have sprung from the womb at age forty."

There will be no second date.

Sometimes the hardest part of losing weight is recognizing what's going to be really lethal for you, and I'm not talking about fettuccine Alfredo. I'm talking about the party weekend where you're going to spend the whole time thinking about how you're the heaviest girl there or the dinner with a "friend" who always makes you want to dash home to your other friends, Ben & Jerry.

Sure, you can't avoid the world and stay home, swathed in a cloud of cotton, eating bagged salad with balsamic vinegar and one carefully measured tablespoon of olive oil. But I've been learning from Shari Frishett that a big part of taking care of myself—besides eating healthfully and exercising—is not putting myself into situations that make me feel unsafe emotionally. I should quit searching for the way to steel myself to get through certain situations, she says, and instead just take myself out of them completely. I shouldn't make overeating the only way I'm nice to myself.

I told Shari I had to spend a birthday weekend with some slightly wild friends where it was virtually guaranteed that I would eat poorly, have a bunch of drinks, and not exercise—all of which would make me feel crummy about myself. I wouldn't budge on the idea that I *had* to go, so she suggested I come up with options. Could I find a way to exercise one day? Even just a walk? (Not sure—depends on whether I feel like I'll be missing out if I go off by myself.) Could I arrive late or leave early? (No, I don't have a car, and the bus isn't a viable option.) She asked what would happen if I didn't go. (My friends might be insulted and I'd feel loserish and left out and otherwise controlled by my diet.) And then she told me to think about the fact that I was choosing other people's needs over my own and at my own risk.

That's the crux of this whole weight problem, isn't it? It's constantly choosing other people's needs over my own or at least being unwilling to ask for what I need and feeling secure enough that I'll get it or that life will indeed go on if I don't. I've always admired Mary's ability to announce at the last minute that she needs a breather on a Friday night to sit home, paint her toenails, and then watch crummy television with her cat. It rarely matters what's going on—if she doesn't want to go, she usually doesn't. I can't do that so easily—it's those "What if I miss something or don't get invited again?" fears. I also have a problem announcing that I want to go to such-and-such restaurant or that I need to eat by such-and-forth time. I don't want to call attention to myself or my diet. I just want everything to be normal, and it isn't.

As for the party weekend, I went anyway, but with a game plan I promptly failed to follow. And I did indeed feel crummy. Cranky, too. I would have felt controlled by my diet if I'd stayed home, but I was equally controlled by it away—my entire outlook seemingly determined by what I put in my mouth. I couldn't stop wondering how much butter had been used to cook my fish, whether everyone thought I was being annoying, and whether I'd gain weight from this excursion even though I wasn't really having fun. I hated feeling like I perpetually was waiting for the next meal, then either breathing sighs of relief for having jumped hurdles or kicking myself for falling. I hated feeling like I was getting through the weekend instead of living it, enjoying it.

Today Mary came shopping with me for a dress to wear to Brent's wedding. The shopping experience wasn't perfect, but it was so much better than it would have been if I were my old size. Of course, if I were that, I probably would have gone shopping alone, because I wouldn't have wanted anyone to come with me to the plus-size department, and I would have gone at the absolute last minute and grabbed whatever fit.

Now that I can fit into a size 14, I found myself avoiding dresses that were cut small and would require me to take the next size up—a 16. I know no one knows the size except me, but honestly, I feel fatter in the size 16s. Dave

Barry once wrote a column about how all clothes should come with the label of a size 6 to make women feel better about themselves. He was definitely onto something.

Because I loathe the sight of my arms, I ended up buying two dresses. One of them, an Ann Taylor dress, is sleeveless. I bought it first, when it looked like there might not be a single wedding-appropriate dress in the Washington area that had sleeves and didn't look like something a mother would wear. I like it better than the other dress I bought, an ice-blue short-sleeved one, but there is the arm problem. Got home and tried on the sleeveless one with a cardigan, but it looked wrong, like gym socks with a prom gown. I was feeling annoyed that I've lost nearly thirty pounds (way more than the eighteen to twenty I estimated I'd have lost by now) and been lifting weights religiously—and my arms still look as big, white, doughy, and grandmotherly as they did three and a half months ago. So of course, then the one-woman cheerleading squad arrived.

When I was in the bathroom, Diana tried on the Ann Taylor dress. She had asked to try on my jeans when she came in, but I'd said no. Anyway, the dress looked better on her, but who cares? We're about the same size! Highly doubt she's as excited about it as I am. Before she left, she knocked the pale blue dress off the hanger while "looking at it." I'm sure it was only the size on the label she wanted to see.

Tonight at dinner I finished a bottle of balsamic vinegar—the first time I've ever been almost proud to have finished any type of food. To me, the empty bottle is a trophy: it means I've eaten dozens of salads with balsamic vinegar and olive oil. I can't remember how many times I've gone out and bought healthy things because I planned to start eating right, used them once, then let them sit in the refrigerator until they went bad.

Just when I really felt like I was making progress, something—rather, someone—came along to remind me how far I had to go.

Emboldened by my ever-progressing exercise routine (I can run on the treadmill for a half hour straight at six miles per hour) plus my newly developed ability to make it through an advanced step class, I got a little overambitious and signed up for a boxing class. During the second class, in the middle of jabs and hooks, the instructor told me I needed to lose weight. Just like that.

I felt like clobbering him.

I also felt like ripping off my gloves and plunking myself on the couch with a just-beginning-to-melt pint of Ben & Jerry's chocolate-chip-cookie-dough ice cream. At the same time, I felt like shrieking, "I've lost twenty-eight pounds, you insensitive [string of unprintable words here]. I'm *working* on it. Why do you think I'm here? You actually think I'm here to learn to box? Everything I do is a ploy to lose weight. Hello, you're talking to the girl who took a writing job solely because she thought it would force her to lose weight."

Instead I stood there, stung. The room got a little blurry as I concentrated on trying not to cry. When I got home, I tried on the contents of half my closet to remind myself that I had indeed lost weight. It wasn't enough. Yes, my friends have commented about how good I look, but it hurts to realize that they mean in comparison to how I used to look. I still don't look good, period—good, no qualifier needed.

As the heaviest person in the class—yes, I can't help noting these things—I'd already felt a little self-conscious. Maybe it was my imagination, but even before his unsolicited "advice," I was sure the instructor was watching me carefully and noting, with disapproval, when I stopped for a breather. On the first day, I thought I saw him raise his eyebrows when I walked in, thinking, I was sure, *That fat girl isn't going to last five minutes in my class.*

Of course I know, as the friend I've finally managed to share this with (Alexy) has pointed out, that I shouldn't care what some guy who knows nothing about me—and who isn't exactly svelte himself—thinks. But the fact is, his voice is drowning out all the others, all the weeks I so joyfully recorded that Mary said I was looking very thin or that I'm overwhelmed by clothing choices in "normal" stores. Whereas before I could look in the mirror and be sure I saw the results, all of a sudden I see a me who is, if not heavier than ever, certainly a long way from where I want to/need to/should be. Sure, I'm being irrational, but this is one of the times when no amount of reasoning with myself seems to work. The only consolation is that I haven't cheered myself up with fudge brownies from Marvelous Market. At least not yet.

At work the morning after boxing class, a coworker and I discussed afternoon snacks, which inevitably led to a discussion about weight. I said all I wanted right now was to be at the point where the first thing people noticed about me was not that I was overweight.

"But you're there," Leslie said.

I wish I could believe her.

Midmorning I decided I had to get out of my office—away from myself and all the thinking about what I could and couldn't eat and about how much I wanted something to take the edge off. I headed for Borders, hoping maybe a quick flip through some fitness magazines would inspire me to keep going. Why I thought this would work I don't know—these days those magazines just frustrate me. I'm doing everything they say—drinking water, exercising, eating more vegetables, keeping a food diary, not letting myself get too hungry (though it seems that even after a meal, I'm still a little hungry). I'm so drowning in diet advice already that what are the chances of my finding one little tip I haven't already heard that makes a huge difference? But still I have to look.

Today was not my lucky day. The first magazine I flipped through had a success story from a woman who started out at 5' 8½" and 180 pounds (essentially what I am now, except I'm half an inch shorter). She went on about how overweight she was. Depressing. She lost 50 pounds and now weighs 130. Getting that low seems an impossible task.

Of course, then my mind—and my gaze—drifted over to the café section of Borders. *Why not?* I thought. *I'm never going to weigh 130 pounds—I've never weighed that in my entire adult life. In college I couldn't get below 168, no matter how hard I tried.*

But I can't give up now, I thought. *If I can't lose weight with the publication pressure of a column on me, when am I going to do this? If I can't do this now, I'll never be able to do it*, I thought—*and I'm not ready to concede that yet.*

I reminded myself that just as no one knows what size clothing you have on once it's on your body, no one knows exactly what you weigh, and the numbers can be surprising. Last year, in a rare moment of openness, Diana told me what she'd weighed at her thinnest in high school—when she was small enough to shop in a 5-7-9 store. It was forty pounds more than I'd thought. Which was only twenty-five pounds less than I weighed at the time—and back then I was sure the number was more like a hundred. If only I had known. In high school, losing sixty-five pounds seemed so hopeless I figured I might as well eat. But twenty-five pounds—that would have been a different story.

Month 5 (May)

*T*he fear of food and of losing control is gnawing at me. I had a choco-late truffle today, and a Hershey's Kiss yesterday, and I know I probably shouldn't have had either. This, I know from experience, is how I go crazy. I have "just a bite" here and "just a bite" there, and I think I'm OK with it. But then the bites get larger and more frequent, until suddenly—maybe not the first or second day but soon—they become a binge. Who *are* those people who can eat a Hershey's Kiss or a mini Snickers bar every day to keep from pigging out on chocolate? For me, one bite is too much and a million are not enough.

Certain foods, chocolate among them, seem to set off a chemical reac-tion in me. I have one piece, and no matter what the circumstances—feeling guilty, not feeling guilty, feeling full, hungry, whatever—I immediately have this urge to eat more. It's a sharp urge, with a trajectory like an unexpected burst of pain: very intense, then a slow recession. Like pain, the urge leaves behind a desire to probe and pick at what hurts, plus a nagging fear that the pain can and will resurface at any moment.

As if poking my tongue at a sore spot in my mouth, I kept pausing in the middle of writing, thinking: *Is that twinge in my stomach hunger? What do I want to eat?*

Woke up this morning thinking about how on this day seven years ago I was exactly two months into the Emily diet—the very-low-fat diet my freshman year roommate devised. I remember how excited I was to start and how relieved. One problem I'm working at, I thought happily when I started. The diet was something to focus on in an otherwise dark and gloomy second semester.

I lost forty-one pounds on the Emily diet, and I still get twinges thinking about all the energy and effort it vacuumed up. My obsession affected my grades—nothing mattered as long as I lost weight.

I frequently stayed until 2:00 or 3:00 A.M. at the college newspaper, where the deadlines distracted me from food. So at 3:00 A.M., when I finally sat down to study, I'd be so hungry that I couldn't concentrate on what I was reading. But I refused to have so much as an extra caramel-flavored rice cake. I didn't realize it at the time, but I craved control. I couldn't control what grade I'd get on a paper—or whether I'd meet anyone at the frat party we went to—but I could control what went in my mouth.

I remember getting home in May, my jeans so loose I could pull them off without unbuttoning them. That night, before my family went out to dinner, Mom insisted I try on Diana's size 10 jeans. They looked so impossibly small, but they fit. I looked at myself in the full-length bathroom mirror—the first time I'd looked at my entire body in several years. *The scale will only go down from here,* I vowed.

Periods of extreme control followed by periods of no control at all. Within a few months, I put all the weight back on—all that energy and effort, seemingly for nothing. Six months later, at Thanksgiving, squeezed into size 14 jeans I was afraid to wash for fear they'd shrink and I'd have to find out I was really a 16 or 18, again I stood in front of the mirror—this time afraid to look. I wondered: *How many times am I going to do this to myself—blow up and shrink as rapidly as Alice in Wonderland?*

I lay around this morning rehashing all my failures. Despite my vows and my certainty that this time is different, is it really? I'm so very tired of remembering chunks of my life by little more than whether I was eating or not eating, whether I could find anything to wear, whether I wanted to leave the house. I remember days when I couldn't seem to drag myself out of bed—I was often still full from the night before and so dreading facing my closet and having to admit that only one pair of pants still fit.

The memory of failures past didn't do much for my already flagging resolve to get up and go to the gym. As the minutes passed and it became clear I wouldn't be able to put in a full fifty-minute workout before heading to the office, I grew more and more frantic. Somehow—in the space of an hour—I'd managed to turn today into a referendum about whether I'd succeed at this diet.

I knew the fact that I wasn't going to get in a full workout today would be constantly gnawing at me. Every time I put something in my mouth, I'd think about whether I could or should leave a little over, to make up for my missing gym time. I'd pick over the day's schedule, wondering if I could fit in the rest of the workout somewhere. And I'd think about my less than half a workout, wondering if it would be the beginning of my excusing myself for missing five minutes here, ten minutes there . . . then not going to the gym for days in a row. I wished I could think of someone to talk about this with, to stop its cartoon-monster-like looming in my head. But I knew what everyone would say: *Stop being ridiculous; it's just one workout.*

I knew that, and yet I continued obsessing—in fact, am still obsessing. How am I supposed to relax and think about the big picture—it's how I eat and exercise day in and day out that matters—when the world is seemingly filled with information about how small things make a big difference? How can I not panic about five minutes off my workout or an extra Hershey's Kiss when there are articles to read about how just three extra bites a day can pack on a pound a month? Yesterday I saw statistics about how sending e-mail instead of taking a two-minute walk down the hall can cause a weight gain of a pound a year, and extra telephone extensions, which mean we don't have to run to grab the phone, add two to three pounds a year.

It makes me want to fidget constantly—the fitness magazines I love to hate report that a Mayo Clinic study showed you can fidget away up to 850 calories a day, or the equivalent of a good eight-and-a-half-mile walk.

It's crazy. *I'm* crazy. Maybe my addiction isn't so much to food but to addiction itself. I fixate on something to fixate on.

Diana interlude. As if I could go more than a few days without one.

Today was my day off from the gym, but I was feeling edgy, so I decided to take a walk. (Long pause to appreciate that I was not only choosing something instead of eating but choosing something that might be construed as exercise.)

Diana and I had been leaving messages for each other all week. We kept missing each other. Today I was having a surge of that springtime let's-clean-everything-including-relationships feeling I get when life seems pretty good. (Am I *looking* for something to mess things up? Is that why I call her?) And because Peeke has been after me to think of ways to catch up with my sister that don't involve food, I called to see if Diana wanted to join me on my walk. She suggested I come with her to pick up something from her office and we'd walk back to Dupont Circle from Bethesda, a rambling eight miles that's mostly downhill.

So . . . we did, except every five minutes she kept talking about the food she wanted to eat along the way, trying to convince me to eat at Cactus Cantina, this Tex-Mex place where it's virtually impossible not to overeat, and she kept up a nonstop patter about how fat she is.

I started wishing I'd taken a walk with only my portable CD player for company. Except that wasn't possible—or at least not particularly advisable—in the middle of Washington, D.C., after dark. But I didn't lose my temper. Instead I played reporter with Diana, asking her about one of her favorite topics: her job.

Every once in a while, my curiosity about Diana trumps my annoyance. Four years at college—except for summers, only sporadic contact—away from each other and from our identities as one-half of the Rubin twins seems to have turned us both into someone the other doesn't recognize. Growing up, I used to take all of my going-out cues from her, so she's not used to me as nightlife reporter—the idea that even though she went to college in D.C., in my two years here I already have been more places than she has. The Diana I knew growing up didn't have any special aptitude for computers and cried when she had to stay up late to finish particularly difficult math homework, so I don't know this Diana who's a driven technology whiz—who can fix her own computer and who works until 8:00 or 9:00 every night.

So today I asked loads of questions about her new job, Internet marketing. Essentially, she surfs the Web for a living, telling clients where and how to advertise, putting together complicated reports using a bunch of programs and a pile of data. I have to admire that she's so obviously good at what she does, and I'd tell her more often if giving her a compliment weren't such an infuriating experience. You have to repeat it at least seven times, and she'll call later and bring it up out of nowhere, just to have you say it one more time.

The scary thing is that I think I might do exactly the same thing when it comes to accepting compliments. What is it they say about our hating in other people the things we hate most in ourselves?

I'm sifting through the rubble of today, piecing it together the way you do when an apparently stable wall collapses.

This morning I felt hungry the minute I finished my banana and Grape-Nuts Flakes with skim milk. By the time I left the gym, I was already wondering how I was going to make it through the morning. And by the time I left for work, I was considering options. Carrot sticks sounded disgusting at 9:30 A.M. An apple? Not appealing.

I walked into work, and there on the table was a platter of leftover muffins from this bakery down the street that I love. The interns, who sit right by the table, were at a meeting. No one was around. My brain shut down. I grabbed a chocolate-chocolate-chip muffin the size of a baseball and ate it in about four bites. I've been craving chocolate for days. I ate another. Then I hovered, picking at a banana muffin and a carrot muffin and—just in case anyone walked by—pretending I was waiting for the printer to spit out an article. I swiped another muffin, stuffed it into my bag, and headed to my office. Then I went back, hovered around the printer again, and grabbed one more.

I could feel the muffins clogging my insides from my stomach all the way up to the back of my throat. I wasn't sure how to get through the rest of the day. I was torn between wanting to eat everything and wanting to starve myself until breakfast tomorrow. I reasoned that I'd better eat the lunch I packed for myself anyway, because if I didn't, I'd almost definitely binge in mid- or late afternoon.

After lunch I felt full and exhausted. It's a feeling I once had daily, but until now I'd almost forgotten how awful it is.

I spent the afternoon alternately working on a story and wondering if I should give up my afternoon snack—and being grateful that nobody could see inside my head to what it is I was worried about. I know there are millions of more important things in the world to think about—AIDS, Third World debt, someone else besides myself? Thinking about myself thinking about calories and weight and muffins and what I would have for dinner made me feel more fat and self-indulgent than ever. But it didn't stop me from thinking about it.

The afternoon passed by agonizingly slowly. Why can't time creep like that when I have a deadline to meet? At 4:00 P.M., just as I was contemplating whether I needed the cottage cheese and carrot sticks I've stashed in the office fridge, there was a call for a birthday party. So I ate chocolate cake. Three pieces, plus extra frosting from around the sides. I'm not sure whether to cry or scream. Things were going so well until today—why did I have to screw things up? Is it that I've been relatively happy these days, and since I usually blame my weight for my unhappiness, I'm not sure what to do when I start considering, even for a moment, that my weight may not be totally to blame for it?

The thought scares me. Though publicly I've scoffed at the notion that losing weight solves all problems, parroting the "I'm still the same person" line, privately I know I've clung to the idea. Sure, losing weight might not get me a promotion or more money (though there are those studies about overweight people being paid less than their thin counterparts), but being thin would, I think, put an end to so much of what makes me unhappy on a day-to-day basis. Namely, looking in the mirror every morning and hating the reflection, not wanting to leave my apartment and face anyone looking the way I do.

Sometimes I think that being overweight is muffling the person I want to be (or is it the person I am?), like hearing a radio from the office next door. At parties, especially, there are people—not just men—I want to speak to but don't feel like I can lumber up to (and that's the way I am in my mind, *lumbering* up to them). At the office I censor myself. I make plenty of sarcastic comments privately, but at meetings I keep quiet, just because I don't want anyone to look in my direction.

A quarter to five. I'm suddenly acutely aware that in fifteen minutes Mr. Lee's, the stand on the first floor of our building that sells snacks, will be closed. If I can hang on for fifteen minutes, I can avoid the danger. At the same time, I'm becoming pretty sure that once Mr. Lee's closes, I'm going to decide I must have food, and I'll be so impatient and frustrated that it may lead to an all-out binge. I'm not sure which is worse. I want cake with icing and cookies that are soft, neither of which Mr. Lee sells (Famous Amos—which Mr. Lee does sell—will not do in a pinch). Besides, Mr. Lee has sold me a giant Diet Pepsi every morning for the past four months and watched me examine the calorie counts on nearly every candy bar, then put each one back. Can't imagine he won't say anything if I suddenly buy something besides diet soda.

Five minutes before he closes, I run downstairs and buy a bag of pretzels. I'm not sure why. They're not even remotely what I want to eat, but I buy them because they're a snack I haven't had in more than four months, and one that isn't a diet disaster.

Five o'clock. Finished the pretzels, which do not do the trick. Mr. Lee's is now closed, but the café in the Borders next door is not. Crumb cake topped with an inch of sugar. Chocolate-covered graham crackers. I realize I have a good six or seven hours before I go to sleep tonight, and there's no telling how much damage to my diet I could do in that time.

What I usually do when I binge when I'm supposed to be on a diet is call someone to go out to dinner. Usually it's my sister, because I can be frantic in front of her—impatient for the food to come the way an alcoholic is impatient for a waitress to show up and take the drink orders. And even though

I can't eat everything I want in front of Diana, I can eat an awful lot. I can order sides that don't seem to go with my main—French fries, candied sweet potatoes, macaroni and cheese even if I've ordered, say, an omelet. Dessert—maybe even a couple of desserts—is a given.

At some point she will stop eating, but I will not. I'll be antsy for the bill to arrive, literally tapping my foot with impatience (and nearly crying when it occurs to me that I'm burning off about a whole four calories from the millions I've consumed) because during the meal I've compiled a mental list of all the other foods I now want to eat. In a rare moment of closeness I once told Diana about the bingeing, and she said that though she often has cravings for cake and chocolate, she could never buy them (much less eat them) in public. She'd be too embarrassed. What I couldn't seem to make her understand was that I feel the same way: though I hate myself for buying these foods and imagine that everyone is laughing at me as I do, my need for the food somehow is stronger even than the guilt and shame, and at that moment I don't care about anything except how I'm going to get what I want, what I *need*.

I'll pretend I'm going home or to run an errand, occasionally being rude or abrupt with her. ("Can we finish talking about this later? I really have to get this call in to Los Angeles tonight.") I'll know I'm being rude and abrupt with her, and I'll know I should consider trying to stick out the conversation, because then maybe I won't binge. But I can't pay attention, can't think, can't breathe. I can't do anything except think about eating. And eat.

Feeling guilty for lying to my sister, guilty for possibly having been rude, and guilty for what I'm about to do, I'll walk up and down the aisles of CVS or the supermarket—usually CVS first, since the supermarket is three blocks farther, which means three blocks too far—in frustration. If the line at CVS seems too long, I'll leave and go to the supermarket, wishing desperately for an express binge line where I can at least buy a chocolate-chip muffin or a Twix bar to tide me over for the walk to the Safeway.

Let's say I start at CVS. Depending on how frantic I feel, I'll skip the charade that I'm here for anything but food (translation: I won't bother grabbing a magazine or some toilet paper first). I will not stop; I will not pass go; I will head directly to the shelves with Hostess cupcakes and cinnamon rolls. I'll wonder briefly if a chocolate bar would do it, but it would have to be in addition—at binge times I almost always want something sweet and cakey. I'll do the complex calculus that involves how many items of junk food I can buy without having it look like they're all for me and without looking like I'm going to eat them all at once. Unlike the supermarket, CVS doesn't really sell the sort of stuff packaged to make it look like you're having a last-minute party. Anyway, what twenty-three-year-old has a party where the hors d'oeuvres consist of Little Debbie cream-filled oatmeal cookies, Chunky bars, and a bag of mini blueberry muffins?

Usually two single-serving items are the most I dare buy at CVS, an amount that's never enough. So part of the choosing involves how long I can make what I've bought last: long enough to make it to the other CVS four blocks away? (Though there is always, always someone I know at that one.) To Safeway? To Marvelous Market? To Firehook Bakery? I scan for the shortest checkout line and evaluate the nimbleness of both the cashiers and the people waiting in the lines. Don't want to be behind the lady who takes a half hour to unload her basket and fifteen minutes fumbling with her wallet.

It's all a matter of time—I have to have what I want immediately, and the harder I try to wait it out, the worse it gets. I'll scan the shelves, debating how much more I'll be able to eat before even I can't eat another bite. I'll strategize: what order should I eat things in—what do I want the most? What do I need to eat first so I've gotten it down before I'm so full that even I finally have to stop eating?

A package of Hostess cupcakes, an iced apple-cinnamon roll, and three blocks later I'll arrive at the supermarket. In my case I'll try to pretend that I'm just doing normal grocery shopping, which, oh, just happens to include some junk food. Luckily, some of my "junk" includes things normal people eat in normal quantities, so along with my chocolate-chip-cookie-dough ice cream and mini apple pie, I can safely buy cheese and peanut butter and corn bread without anyone knowing they're binge ingredients. If I think about it—which often, so focused on the binge, I won't—I'll add some apples or tomatoes or mushrooms for the full-on I'm-normal effect. As I'm tearing through the aisles, I don't make eye contact with anyone. If I do, I wonder: *Can they tell that the contents of my little red shopping basket will barely last me an hour?*

At the grocery store I'll follow the same routine as at CVS, scanning for the quickest-looking cashier and the shortest line (usually *not* the express line). I'll head home, wishing I could snap my fingers and be there instantly, because there's a chance I'll bump into someone I know on the street—that I'll be caught eating. I'll take the back door to my apartment building so the guy at the front desk can't stop me to chat. And I'll lug myself up the stairs and collapse against my door, not sure which is more to blame for my exhaustion: the stomach overstuffed with food or all the planning, all the secrecy.

In real time the whole binge might take an hour or so. But in my mind the film is over in seconds, so I can replay it endlessly, torturing myself with it. It's only 5:00 P.M., but I can see the whole evening before me—the inevitability of it. Then, like a Choose Your Own Adventure book, there's the option of the unknown—at least, unknown for me. Yes, I've had a revolting amount of cake today, but what would happen if I stopped the binge right now?

I can't remember the last time I stopped in midbinge, but part of the reason I was so excited about this *Shape* project was I thought if I dieted properly—none of my crazy 500-calorie-a-day regimens—I might end the bingeing once and for all. I thought about losing the project before the first column's ever even made it into print.

So here's what really happened this evening: thinking about having to tell *Shape*—the arbiter of all things healthy—about my (extremely unhealthy) binge behavior made me more frantic than ever. So at 6:00 P.M. I gave up on work for the day and decided that for dinner I could have whatever I wanted—within reason.

Then I realized I didn't know what "within reason" is.

I considered all sorts of options: a couple of Chilean empanadas (but I do like the vegetarian ones, and also the apple ones). General Tso's chicken (shouldn't do that because I'll also want fried rice and dumplings). A burrito with lots of cheese (except every time I walk into the place I want chips and quesadillas, too). What I wanted was to be able to have a "normal" meal—where I felt satisfied but not stuffed—but I'm no longer sure what that feels like. Nor could I think of a single restaurant or take-out place I could go that would feel safe—where I wouldn't go in and feel my head about to split trying to decide what I wanted to eat the most.

On the way home I stopped at the grocery store and looked at all sorts of desserts: apple pie, cream puffs, carrot cake with cream-cheese frosting. I wanted them all, but more, I wanted desperately to stop thinking about them. It occurred to me that if I didn't buy them, and therefore didn't eat them, I might still spend the night thinking about them, but at least the night wouldn't be a total waste. There was still a chance I'd be able to read a magazine or talk to a friend without thinking: I'm so horribly full, I feel sick, I want to die.

So I didn't buy anything. I went home and had a salad and some chicken and half a cantaloupe, because it's a meal that doesn't require any thought at all.

Was the binge broken? I didn't dare hope so. For all I knew then, it was just temporarily stalled and would come back later in full force.

Getting ready for bed, I didn't congratulate myself for having broken the binge cycle, because for all I knew, it wasn't over. I had spent a day wanting all these things and almost tasting them. And although the immediate urge may be gone—I'd waited it out—the desire is like a tumor. You think you've successfully operated and removed it, only to find a few stray cells still there, hours or days away from growing into something ominous.

I gained two pounds.

And about a hundred pounds of dread. Weight gained. Will it ever come off again? Usually once I start gaining weight, that's the end of the diet.

I dread telling *Shape*. I'm tempted to lie, then I realize I don't have to. For the first few months I've had to file weekly journals that won't be printed, just to let Maureen, my editor at *Shape*, know how things are going. But now, because I'm doing so well—ha!—*Shape* trusts me, so I have to file only my monthly columns. And I've already lost enough weight this month (five pounds so far) that even if I've put on two, I've still got a net loss. I'm safe.

Safe in print, but not safe from myself. I haven't had a full-out binge yet, but I can feel one coming. Yesterday brought me to the edge. One of these days—someday soon—I'm going to fall.

That's what bingeing is—a free-fall. You know you're doing something you shouldn't do, something you swore you wouldn't do, something that's dangerous and destructive. You know you're going to feel like hell when it's done—you know it, but in the moment you just don't care. You close your eyes and jump.

Friday. Three days post-pig-out-that-luckily-didn't-become-an-all-out-binge. Spent the party tonight barely able to concentrate on anything anyone said to me, which always makes me feel lonely and disconnected. I was too busy fighting the urges I've been fighting all week, warily keeping one eye on the food like it's suddenly going to attack me. The urges weren't as bad as they were three days ago, when I ate the muffins and the cake, but with that first bite of the first muffin, my body suddenly remembered the taste of every sweet thing I'd been keeping myself away from, and wanted it all.

I kept away from the food and drank an entire two-liter bottle of Diet Coke, because I knew if I drank alcohol, it would be all over, food-wise. Sometime between my first and second drink, I'd stop worrying so much about my weight and feel like everything was going to be OK, even if I weighed a thousand pounds, and so I'd start eating. Thanks to the liquor, I wouldn't care—or care as much—who saw me. Everyone eats when they drink, right? You practically have to—no drinking on an empty stomach and all that. . . . And on what other occasion besides after drinking is it perfectly acceptable for a bunch of girls to head to the late-night pizza place, eating giant slices of pizza and not caring who's watching?

What I miss about drinking is the beer goggles you get on yourself. After a couple of drinks I can go to the bathroom and think I look OK, or at least not awful, instead of wishing I never had to go back out, wishing I could spirit myself from there back to my apartment and never leave home again.

Mary on the phone: "I think I found a marathon training program."

"What?"

Then I remembered Candace's party, where Mary had first brought up the idea of our running a marathon. She hadn't mentioned it since, so I didn't either.

Mary told me about Galloway—named for Jeff Galloway, the 1972 Olympic athlete who designed the program. It's supposed to be beginner-friendly.

"I don't know if I can run that much," I told her. What I was thinking was: *If I start bingeing, I'll be so full I'll barely be able to walk, much less run.*

"You only have to be able to run three miles to start, and you do that all the time," she said. After all, she was the one I often bragged to that I had just run six miles that morning: from my Dupont Circle apartment all the way up—and I mean up—Massachusetts and Wisconsin Avenues past the National Cathedral.

She paused. "Think about it."

And I did. Instead of immediately thinking of excuses for why I couldn't, I thought: *Hmmm. Why would Mary tell me I could do something I couldn't?* For just a moment I reveled in the thought of actually doing this. After all, if Mary thought I could do it, maybe I really could.

Then I came back to earth. I don't dream athletic dreams, I reminded myself. I'm the kid who mooned about writing a novel or winning an Oscar, never an Olympic medal.

I remember once seeing some Mylar-blanketed marathoners on the Metro and thinking they had done an amazing feat. I'd thought idly then that a marathon was a cool thing to do—for someone else. My athletic ambitions had to do with getting to the gym more often or getting my arms into a shape where I might dare to wear something sleeveless. They didn't have anything to do with running 26.2 miles in one day.

Trip to New Orleans to celebrate a friend's birthday. Again I did the extra-lunch-in-the-office-fridge routine, planning for myself to screw up. I consumed far too many beignets and praline samples, but I at least stuck to my exercise routine, running outside in the brutal, swampy heat. I had to laugh when, running by Lake Pontchartrain, a guy came up to me as I stopped for water and said: "You must be from Washington or New York or somewhere like that."

I looked down to see if I was wearing a *Washingtonian* T-shirt or some other dead giveaway. Nope. Just a faded one from the San Diego Zoo.

"Only some Type A type from New York or Washington would be out running during Jazz Fest," he told me.

Long pause while I tried desperately to think of something clever to say and failed miserably. So I just smiled, put my headphones back on, and ran off, laughing to myself at how wrong an impression one can get from meeting someone for five seconds. If I saw him again—and you seemed to see the same people again and again at Jazz Fest—I'd be "the crazy runner girl."

As if trying on the description, I tried to add a couple of sprints on the way home but had to stop and walk.

While I was away, Mary checked out the Galloway group.

"I haven't been running nearly as much as you, and I was fine," Mary said. "Abby was, too." Abby is the other friend Mary's managed to talk into this. I don't know why I didn't tell her then that the idea of my doing such a thing was ludicrous. Instead I told her I wouldn't be able to get out to Virginia to train. I don't have a car, and the Metro doesn't run that early.

"You can stay at my house on Fridays," she said. There went my last excuse. Why not? I figured. I'd join the group to ramp up my mileage—it would at least guarantee I got in a good workout every Saturday. When the mileage got to be too much, I'd stop. Besides, maybe knowing that I'd have to get up and run in the morning would keep me from bingeing—and if I did binge, maybe the running would help keep the weight off.

My twenty-fourth birthday—and my first day of marathon training. Our group had its share of diehards and its share of first-timers, some of whom looked no more athletic than I felt. We ran five miles.

After months of staring at flashing red numbers on a treadmill, running on the Mount Vernon trail with a group of people to distract me was easy. I was on such a high that when the Metro broke down in Rosslyn on the way home, I ran the three miles to my apartment. If you'd told me last year that I'd wake up at 6:00 A.M. and run eight miles on my birthday, I would have wondered what you were smoking and where I could get some.

Month 6 (June)

*T*his morning I practically skipped to work, still on a high from last night's boxing class, where I realized my body felt so much lighter when we were skipping around. (I still hate the instructor for bringing up my weight the second day of class, but I refuse to quit the class because I refuse to let him win.)

When we were warming up, bouncing from side to side, it seemed to take so little effort to move. It was like when you expect a door to be really heavy, so you throw yourself against it, but instead it's so light it flies open so fast you nearly fall over. I kept overestimating how much energy I needed to jump and ending up much farther across the room than I intended.

I loved it. It made me want to run for miles and do cartwheels. If I knew how to do cartwheels.

Of course the gee-isn't-life-swell feeling couldn't last.

Lunch with one of those "friends" Bridget Jones would call a "jellyfisher." The sort who say something that sounds perfectly innocent, maybe even complimentary, until you stop and consider it.

She's one of those friend types who seem much more difficult to jettison completely than to make polite conversation with ("Ooh!" Insert squeal here. "Haven't seen you in *soooo* long!") at various work events and to have lunch with about once every five months (after multiple reschedules), as we did today. She knows about the *Shape* project—she's one of those people who always seems to know more about my career than I do—and after we ordered, she looked at me critically.

She didn't say anything. Then, as if to herself: "Yeah, I can tell you've lost a little bit of weight."

I'm not sure if it's the way she said "little bit"—when I know it's more than thirty pounds—or the tone or what. But immediately I felt like fat girl squeezed into too-small size 14 black pants. Never mind that these are the same ones that this morning looked like they might be a bit too loose.

I didn't manage to leave over any portion of my plain grilled chicken and nearly dry noodles, the way I usually try to. I sat there and raged and ate and envied her for eating peanut noodles as she talked about the fact that she really should get her (size 8) self to the gym every once in a while.

Life is not fair.

I left lunch convinced I was hungry, though I had eaten more than usual. About 3:00 P.M., sitting in the Borders café—my office away from the office—I felt the urge to binge. I once read that when your diet motivation is flagging, you should try on clothes. So I headed down the street to the Gap. As soon as I reached the dressing room, it occurred to me that this was yet another one of those diet things that sounds good in theory but—depending on one's mind-set—could be complete crap in practice. What kind of motivation could I possibly get from looking at myself in clothes that all seem to be different sizes despite having the same number on the tag? (Size 14s in Gap classic jeans seem as small as a 10 in the rest of their clothes, but size 14s in reverse fit are just fine.) Am I supposed to get the shiny, happy "I want to stay this size" feeling or the self-loathing I seem to specialize in—the "God, I'm still so fat" variety?

I could fit into a couple of 12s, but a 14 still seemed to be my size. Which was frustrating because several years ago, when I weighed only six pounds less than I do now, I could get into 10s. Which does not make sense, as I'm working out more now than I did then—more muscle—so shouldn't I be smaller?

Post-Gap I was hungrier than ever. Yogurt, I realized, was not going to cut it. But I couldn't decide whether in that danger moment it was worse to eat my yogurt and feel cranky or to brave eating something else and risk a subsequent tidal wave of wants. I wanted a piece of this apple crumb cake I used to eat all the time in my prediet days, but I wasn't sure I was ready.

My new kick—courtesy of Nancy—is to start eating foods I desperately want. She says if I crave a food, that means it has power over me, and I need to eat it more often. Every day, if that's what it takes.

I started with peanut butter, which on the scale of things I crave is maybe a four or so, as opposed to the, say, seven or eight of apple crumb cake. I've eaten peanut butter nearly every day for the past two weeks. Two tablespoons—a proper serving—on rice cakes. These regular indulgences are supposed to keep me from dipping the spoon (or my fingers) in the peanut butter jar at 11:00 P.M., because I already know I'm going to have some for breakfast or lunch the next day.

It works—sort of.

If I'm fine and happy and not too stressed when I'm having my peanut butter, I eat it and feel satisfied and maybe a little smug that I've managed to incorporate such a thing into my diet. But if I'm feeling at all angsty, I don't feel any fuller or more satisfied from the peanut butter than I do from my usual (and by now nauseating) two Boca Burgers on two pieces of whole-grain bread with lettuce leaves—and I *do* want to stick my fingers in the jar. I also start considering what else I can eat.

But back to this afternoon. I lingered around the bakery like I was hoping to accidentally-on-purpose run into someone I have a crush on. Finally I bought the cake, took it to my office, and stared at it. Looked at the bit of grease from it that had seeped onto the napkin. Turned it around on the napkin on my desk. Thought I could practically taste it and wondered if that might be enough. Finally took one bite. Paused. Waited for the urge to eat the whole thing in three bites. It was there. Dare I take another bite? But could I even throw this out if I wanted to?

I tried another bite. Does it even taste *that* good? I considered. Maybe I should have gone for something else. Pause. Can't go down that road of options—that's the road of wanting everything.

Another bite. Chewed. Paused. Waited for fear. Another bite. And another. The last time I ate anything that slowly was when I had to make four bites last for at least twenty minutes or so, and not even because I was testing out the whole theory that you should eat slowly because your stomach takes twenty minutes to let you know it's full. That time I'd looked up at a restaurant and realized I'd gobbled down my food before anyone else at the table had gotten very far—and there's little more embarrassing to an overweight person than having the waiter ask, "Finished?" while everyone else is nowhere near there.

I felt full when I finished the cake—full enough to begin estimating the absolute most weight I could have gained from it. Could it have fifteen hundred calories? I told myself I was not overestimating, just being reasonable. After all, aren't I always reading that bagels from bagel chains have eight hundred—and they probably don't have nearly as much sugar and fat as the cake.

Though I thought about the cake and its possible effects on my diet off and on for the rest of the evening—and, in fact, am still thinking about it as I write—I ate my regularly scheduled dinner. No extras, no cutbacks. Progress, I suppose.

Today I finished the Race for the Cure, the nation's largest 5K. I'd like to be excited and call it my first race, except there were so many people that "trudge for the cure" is probably more accurate.

Mary and I aren't nearly fast enough to be out front, surging ahead of the masses, so we ended up quickly realizing that since there were too many people for us to run, we'd better let go of any ideas that this would be a workout and just walk along and chat. Except now that we've skipped marathon training to do the race, we're going to have to get up at the crack of dawn tomorrow to beat the unforgiving D.C. summer heat and do our eight— count 'em, eight—miles.

I'm sure someone has written something terribly pithy about how you're always a child in your parents' house, but pithiness is beyond me right now. I'm still dealing with the feelings of guilt that followed my three-day regression to childhood, complete with the raiding of the refrigerator. This weekend I spent at my parents' house was one where I felt like I ate as if the past five and a half months had never happened. I mindlessly grabbed chocolate from the box on the counter. I picked at leftovers on the table. I ate lunch because my mother announced it was time, not because I was hungry. I listened to my parents' constant snapping at each other—their undisguised disgust with each other—and ducked off to the kitchen for a snack. I tore through the cabinets looking for junk food when I was alone in the house.

Some of my eating, I'm sure, was due to my mother's incredible focus on it. Before I arrived, she'd asked me what I was eating these days so she could have it in the house. She had tried so hard to be considerate that I couldn't bear to tell her when I got there that she had bought the wrong yogurt—I'd wanted fat-free. And she'd bought five containers—how could I possibly eat that much in three days?

Guilt. Guilt. Guilt. I didn't want to hurt her—as always, my mother wants us to be the perfect happy family when we're all together, but we never have been, and I can't imagine we're going to start now. So I ate one of the yogurts, all the while feeling resentful that I had to eat it, wishing I could spend the calories in a full-fat yogurt on something I'd rather eat. Which was probably what led to poking through the refrigerator to see what there was that I *would* rather eat.

When it came time to choose restaurants for dinner, my mother was worried about me. "Will there be anything for you to eat there?" she'd ask about every restaurant my father suggested. I tried to tell her that there's a diet portion of everything and that I'd be fine. The trouble with my mother is that her diet ideas—like her ideas of what I should wear to a party ("Don't you think you should put on a skirt?")—are fossilized in the amber of her adolescence. Pasta, potatoes, and bread are verboten. Cottage cheese and tuna fish are diet manna.

All of the attention made me very uncomfortable. The more the spotlight shines on me, the more annoyed my sister becomes. My father usually sides with my sister, so I kept waiting to end up at some place that had nothing but fattening food and desserts my sister knows I adore. That would be just like her, I thought darkly. Think I'm paranoid? While I was on one of my diets of yore, Diana—who never passes up the chance for chocolate—ordered an apple dessert for the table to split. ("I knew it would make you happy," she said when I confronted her later.) Anything with "junky apples," as we both call them, my sister says so reminds her of me that occasionally in college she'd call me long distance from a restaurant pay phone just to tell me somebody was eating them.

In an attempt not to lose my temper, I reminded myself that it had barely been a year since my parents had moved from Miami back to New Jersey—the only living human beings, I like to tease them, to do so. So my sister couldn't know the restaurants in the area that well and couldn't make subversive choices. But I knew it wasn't the choice of restaurant that mattered—it was my (and my family's) behavior once we were there. I'm so used to getting upset or annoyed by things they say—whether it's about my choice of job or choice of entrée—that the slightest thing sets me off. *I have changed,* I want to yell. *I'm not the same person I was ten years ago.* Trouble is, the minute I'm around my family, I become that person, that child. I lose my temper. And of course, I eat.

Before Diana and I left for New Jersey, I had told myself that while I was at my parents' I'd try to incorporate some of Nancy's rules about eating what I crave. I knew, for example, that my parents would have cheese—something I never dare buy myself, since there's no one to help me eat it. But when I was faced with a refrigerator that kept yielding new and surprising delights, à la Mary Poppins's handbag, I couldn't handle it. There was too much choice, and

I felt like I had too little control over what I did and when. ("You don't really need forty-five minutes to go to the gym, do you? You better hurry up—we want to go to dinner.") I lay around at night berating myself for having eaten so much and freaking out that because in New Jersey we drove everywhere instead of walking, as I do in D.C., I technically should have eaten even less than I usually do instead of more.

The obsessiveness. I felt like I was being swallowed by it.

I knew I wasn't strong enough to resist the usual eat-our-way-home car trip with Diana, where we chow on Auntie Anne's pretzels (Diana) and Cinnabon cinnamon buns (me) and all sorts of other rest-stop grease. So I settled for deciding to stop eating once we hit New York Avenue on the way into D.C. No eating once we hit the city limits.

I thought that knowing there was a finite end to the eating might make me feel more frantic, but it didn't. Instead it sapped some of my desire to do it in the first place. I thought about how nice it would be not to go to bed really full this evening and not to wake up tomorrow sluggish but ravenous, both of which inevitably follow all the eating.

I concentrated on the feeling—where was the point that I could feel full but not sick? I decided I wanted only the frosting part of the Cinnabon, which you can actually order in a little cup for forty cents, so I must not be the only freak who likes that part best. Then Diana and I split cheese fries. At the third rest stop I looked at the convenience stores and the Burger King and the TCBY and didn't see a thing I felt like eating.

I felt empty, almost. I'm so used to the franticness and the panic when it comes to food, so used to those feelings blotting out everything else, that I literally didn't know what to do with myself. Then the joy took over. I kept looking at different foods and thinking: *Is it possible that I really don't want to eat that?* It was like discovering I had some sort of magical ability, and I had to keep testing to make sure it wasn't a fluke. I didn't eat for the rest of the car ride.

Today—four days after I got back from New Jersey, which is four days back on track—my friend Cindy had a dinner party. *I can do this*, I thought before I went, but really I wasn't so sure. I debated whether I should try to starve all day and leave as many calories as possible for dinner or follow the old diet canard that you're not supposed to arrive hungry—you should have a filling, healthy snack beforehand. The supposedly tried-and-true rarely works for me—I always eat my snack thinking there's probably going to be something at the party I'd rather eat. And of course—God forbid I should think positively—I'm convinced I'm going to screw up anyway, so shouldn't I skip the snack and save the calories as a buffer?

For once, though, I wasn't stressed out before I even got to the party. This was because things in my closet actually fit, and I wasn't throwing everything on the bed, looking desperately for the only pair of black pants that actually fit (and wondering if anyone would notice that I'd worn them about four times in the past week).

Though I'd already gone running, I decided to walk to Cindy's. It's a good half-hour walk uphill that I figured should be worth at least an extra something-bad-I'm-going-to-eat. It made me sad—sad for myself—that on the way I passed a good dozen places where in past years I had bought ingredients for a binge. Only six months ago I'd probably have been bingeing as I walked, the fear that I might not be able to eat everything I wanted at the dinner driving me to arrive at the party stuffed but still frantic for more.

On the walk it also occurred to me that I was nervous about the party. Yes, I'd been to loads of other parties in the past few months, but not a dinner party that wasn't at a restaurant (for as much as restaurants trouble me, at least you can attempt to order what you want without having to worry that you're offending the hostess by not eating the potatoes au gratin). I was nervous about this party not just because of what I might eat but because I was literally not sure what to do with myself—how to occupy the time. I've spent so much of parties past trying both to concentrate on the conversation *and* figure out how I could eat what I wanted without anyone's noticing—wondering if anyone would comment if I took a second or third piece of Brie *en croute*—that now, as at the rest stop when I didn't want to eat, I was at a loss.

For the first hour of the party, I focused intently on the conversation. Every time my mind began to wander to food, I'd pause and bring it back. When I finally braved the buffet, I started out slowly. Chicken and papaya and rice, the least diet-damaging dish I could find. I felt pleased with myself, almost smug. And whenever I get too confident that I know exactly what I'm doing, inevitably that's when I screw up. Lulled by a couple of glasses of wine and some comments about how good I looked, I figured I could have a bit of Brie and maybe some cheesecake. But soon all the comments about how good this cake or that paella was drove me back over to survey the buffet, where I had more Brie and a sliver of chocolate cake. Then more slivers. I should have just taken a piece and sat down and eaten it properly—savored it—but I couldn't. Where, I wondered, is the diet tipping point—the line where you think about food just enough to get it right but not so much that you're obsessed?

Soon I was feeling a bit too full—a feeling that these days is paired with panic and a sense of impending doom. When I went to the bathroom—I'd drunk nearly an entire two-liter bottle of Diet Coke in an effort to stop eating—I could see the imprint of the button and zipper of my jeans on my stomach. Fat. Fat. Fat. There was a scale under the sink, and though I was wearing jeans and boots—and it was the end of the day and I should have known better—I couldn't resist torturing myself.

It said I'd gained seven pounds. That I weighed 178 pounds instead of 171.

I got on the scale four times. The least I'd gained, this scale seemed to say, was six pounds. If I subtracted for jeans and shoes and lots of Diet Coke (wondered briefly if there was another full bottle of soda somewhere I could grab and weigh, just to be more precise), maybe I'd gained only two pounds? Two and a half?

This is why I don't have a scale in my own bathroom.

Yes, I'm a wee bit obsessive, but in the light of morning even I'm not so crazy as to think I could possibly have gained seven pounds in one evening. That would be the equivalent of nearly twenty-five thousand calories over and above what my body needs, or more than seven entire cheesecakes. Two pounds would be seven thousand extra calories, which is, I suppose, possible, but . . . seven thousand calories is still a little more than two cheesecakes, or eleven personal pan pizzas. I *know* I didn't eat that much. But still I can't stop thinking about it.

To put myself out of my misery, I e-mailed Peeke. Her response: a physiology lesson. When I'm eating by Peeke's rules, I'm not eating a lot after 5:00 P.M. and definitely no starches like breads, pasta, and rice. When I eat even just a little more than I normally do at night, I don't efficiently burn up those calories, so they sit there. Carbs are the worst: it's a biochemical requirement that you store four molecules of water for every one of carbohydrate. Therefore you put on disgusting amounts of water weight when you eat carbs. Which is what I did.

To pee out the weight—which is certainly preferable to having to work it off (what I'd have to do if I'd put on seven pounds of fat), Peeke said I had to eliminate starches totally for about forty-eight hours. Just protein, fruits, and vegetables.

The moral of this story: eat in the evening and you'll wear it the next morning. And for two days afterward.

For years I listened to my parents snipe at each other or just avoid each other and wondered when they'd get divorced. I wondered until the fights and the long silences and the retreats to opposite ends of the house became a part of everyday life, something I just worked around, like the one car window that couldn't be rolled down or the toaster that required a couple of strategic bangs to make it work. I stopped wondering when, and now that the day has finally come, it's caught me by surprise.

In typical understated Dad fashion—it really is a matter of life and death for the patients in his intensive care unit, and to him nothing else ever seems that dire—he mentioned the divorce as an aside when I called to ask him a quick question. I'd told him I was on deadline, and just as I was getting off the phone, he said, "Hang on a second."

Just like that. "Hang on a second"—as if he had something on the tip of his tongue to tell me and he'd forgotten it.

Then he said that he'd gotten a job in San Francisco and that Mom wasn't going with him.

I didn't have to ask what he meant. The tears started silently streaming. I'm twenty-four years old, I don't live with my parents, and they've already moved from my childhood home. I shouldn't be so upset about the divorce, but I am.

Dad talked on and on, in the overly soothing tone that I'm sure he used to use when he worked at the hospital in Miami, when he had to discuss a patient's imminent death with the family. I didn't hear most of it. I was concentrating hard on not making any sound as I cried. I didn't want him to hear me, because I didn't want him to try to make it better. That would make it worse.

Nobody was moving out of the house in New Jersey right away. But come January—six months from now—when Dad set off for San Francisco, Mom would go back to Florida. Almost thirty years of marriage—over, just like that.

I wanted to ask Dad what finally had pushed him over the edge—and I knew without even asking that it was he who had done it. Three things ran through my head. The first was a line near the beginning of Grace Paley's "Wants," a short story I had liked in college: "In many ways, he said, as I look back, I attribute the dissolution of our marriage to the fact that you never invited the Bertrams to dinner." The second was Mom asking—I think when I was in third or fourth grade—how many of the kids in my class had divorced parents and seeming so proud that having still-married parents put me in the minority. The third was from Mom's first brain surgery. Her best friend Bobbi from college had flown in from Israel and spent the night at the hospital with her. While Mom was in surgery, Diana and I asked Bobbi all sorts of questions about Mom and what she was like in college. We didn't ask the one thing we wanted to know the most: if she died in surgery, did Bobbi think she would have been happy with the life she had had?

I'll never forget one of the things Bobbi told us that day: that all Mom—capable Mom, who had once worked as a social worker and run a thousand different volunteer projects—had ever really wanted was to get married and have children. I felt both relieved and guilty. Relieved that Mom had gotten at least some of what she wanted (even if, when she got it, it wasn't what she thought it would be) and, if I was part of all she ever wanted, guilty that I had sometimes gotten so angry with her while she was sick. Diana and I occasionally tried to ease our guilt by wondering whether, since she hadn't seemed to be able to care about anything during all those years, she also hadn't been able to care about how we'd treated her. The thought never really made me feel any better.

This afternoon I cried while I finished a couple of items for my page in the opening section of the magazine. My page is supposed to be young and snappy and lighthearted, and I was feeling anything but.

I skipped a bar opening and went home, not sure what to do with myself. I didn't want to read or watch TV or talk to anyone or even eat. I suddenly realized what I wanted was to put on my headphones and just run and run and run until the sound of the music and the sound of my heartbeat drowned out all my thoughts.

Ran ten miles this morning! It sounded like a big deal until Juli, our running-group leader, asked for a show of hands from all of us who had just run our first ten-miler. Probably a dozen hands went up, and we high-fived and cheered.

I could barely hear what Juli said next: "When you're done, ten miles will seem like a joke."

Sixteen more miles on top of this?

Mary and Abby groaned. I made a show of doing the same. I still haven't told them I don't think I'm going to be around to train for much longer. I don't want to quit, but nor do I want to fail, and I'm pretty sure my body wasn't exactly born to run, much less born to run 26.2 miles.

Today would have been my parents' twenty-eighth wedding anniversary. I've never been so happy that I didn't get my act together and have my card in the mail early. In years past, I've ended up having to FedEx or send it by second-day priority, because I always had so much trouble finding the damn card in the first place. After all, there's hardly a Hallmark-approved (or even Shoebox-approved) card that says something like "Happy anniversary—hope you don't spend too much of the day thinking back to 1971 and wondering what you were thinking." Plus, there was always the chance that Dad would mostly ignore the anniversary, which would make Diana's and my anniversary cards or flowers seem even more mournful, like "It's a girl!" balloons that accidentally arrive at the hospital after the newborn baby has died.

It's been three days since I found out about the divorce, and I've cried off and on, mostly for Mom. I'm pretty sure Dad will be fine, but Mom is sick, no matter how much we might pretend she's OK. Her whole life these days has been him and us, and I don't know what she's going to do. She's saying this has been coming for a long time, and she's just sorry she didn't ask him for a divorce first, but that's Proud Mom talking, I'm sure of it.

I remember last year, when Mom and Dad moved to New Jersey. Since Dad had already started the job and was living in corporate housing, Diana flew down to help Mom drive her car up to the new house—Mom's driving was becoming scarier and scarier, though no one seemed to want to broach the topic of taking her license away. When Diana got back to D.C. after the drive, she told me Mom had complained about the move the entire three-day trip. Mom didn't want to go. She didn't want to leave Grandma—her mother—who had just turned eighty and whom she'd lived near her entire life.

Diana asked Mom the question I don't know if I would have: why, then, was Mom going?

"You go where your husband goes," Mom told her.

When Diana and I talked about the divorce yesterday, Diana told me something she'd left out of that story.

Diana had told Dad how bitter and upset Mom was on the drive up, and Dad said, "I told her she didn't have to come." He wasn't joking.

I haven't binged. I haven't even eaten extra. I feel drained, but I haven't used that as an excuse not to go to the gym. I've clung to my diet as the one thing that I can make go right when everything else is going wrong. I've clung to it like it's the only thing in the world that's going to save me.

Month 7 (July)

From the be-careful-what-you-wish-for files: the other night at a party, the most attractive guy I could ever hope would pay attention to me actually paid attention to me. It's "the other night" and not "last night" because it's taken me a few days to force myself to write about it. I haven't wanted to think about it, much less relive it.

I first met Larry briefly a couple of weeks ago at my friend Karen's apartment. Smart, cute, funny, and built—he must have the body fat of a Diet Coke, I remember thinking. No way could I be his type.

But he showed up with a couple of friends at Karen's party the other night, glanced around the room, and walked right up to me.

We started chatting about my job, his upcoming move to Chicago, and a couple of people we both knew. When the conversation passed the fifteen-minute mark, I stopped hearing what he was saying—stopped being aware of almost anything except that we were at a party and a cute guy was actually having a conversation with me. I was giddy.

I vaguely remembered something a law school classmate of his had said the first night I met him: "He doesn't go out with anyone who isn't at least an eight."

At the time I thought that made him sound like a jerk—so superficial and probably the sort of guy who was out-and-out rude to not-exactly-an-eight women like me. But, like knowing you shouldn't participate in catty office gossip but being unable to resist, there I was flirting with him.

I had to keep bringing my attention back to Larry's words. There were two conversations—the one I was having with him and the one going on in my head: *Why is he still here? When is he going to leave?* I was flattered and nervous—my voice a few shades too loud, my laugh overeager.

I loved my outfit that night—a pair of fitted light gray Tahari pants and a white tank top with a lavender cardigan to hide my still-icky arms. I thought the pants made me look thinner than I ever had. My skin was clear, my hair wasn't frizzy (despite the humidity), and earlier that day Mary and I had made a bunch of plans for the upcoming weeks. Life was good. I didn't feel like having my mood dampened by the blow-off from him I was sure was inevitable. So I left to go to the bathroom. When I came back, he was still there. I got myself a drink. I went to chat with another friend. When I stopped talking to her, there he was again. Larry and I talked some more, and I think I even made a joke about him leaving when I went to the bathroom—the sort of stupid thing I blurt out when I'm really nervous, when I feel, as I did then, like some guy is talking to me only on a dare and I want him to know that I, too, am in on the joke.

I don't remember what he said, but I know he reached out and squeezed my arm.

Larry briefly had dated a friend of a friend and had a few choice comments about her desperation to get married. His willingness to bad-mouth people he knew that I knew should have been a red flag, but it wasn't. His talk about what a catch he was going to be in Chicago should also have been a red flag. *Ick*, I remember thinking. But the novelty of someone—especially someone as attractive as he was—paying attention to me was too strong to walk away from. I looked around the room and caught a friend's eye. She winked. I focused on Larry again. Once, just once, I wanted to have something of my own to pick over and giggle about with my friends on Sunday morning.

Around midnight—after I'd been bantering with Larry for at least an hour—everyone decided to hit another party a few blocks away. Larry and I walked together through the darkened streets. I got the feeling that if I turned my head and looked at him he would kiss me. So I looked straight ahead, talking loud, fast, and nonstop.

"You're really tense," he kept saying, reaching over to massage my shoulders.

This made me more tense. I had the feeling of standing at the edge of a precipice, about to fall. I was sure there were rules and codes of behavior for this type of thing that everyone had learned back in junior high or high school—or at least college—but I had not. I had always dated men I was already friends with—and had drunkenly kissed a few others—but I'd never dealt with anyone like Larry, who seemed so out of my league, and who came on so strong. I wasn't sure what I wanted. Occasionally when I had too much to drink at parties I'd flirt a bit, but I always felt as safe as if I were flirting with a gay male friend. I was fat. Nothing was ever going to happen.

At the second party, Mary and I took one of those joint trips to the bathroom that men love to joke about. I wanted to ask her what to do. But I couldn't. I was giddy, and it was so much fun to giggle about what was going on. Besides, I wasn't quite ready to admit to anyone—especially myself—that I had only a vague idea of what I was getting into.

Larry invited me back to his apartment for a drink, but he lived in northern Virginia—a good twenty-minute cab ride from where I lived, just a few blocks away from the party. I was too scared to go home with him, anyway.

"No, I can't," I said.

So he walked me home. Standing outside the front door, under the watchful eye of the security guard at my building's front desk, he asked to come in.

"My apartment's a mess," I said. It wasn't a lie. My apartment looked the way it almost always does, like a hurricane had hit a bookstore: books, newspapers, magazines, and CDs everywhere. Whenever I went on dates, my friend Alexy would nag me to clean it so I couldn't use the mess as an excuse not to let a guy in (something I did once two years ago, but she still likes to tease me about it). But of course it had never occurred to me to clean it before going out to this party—who besides me would see it?

"I don't care," Larry said.

"I do," I answered.

"I really don't care," he said, following me in as I opened the door to the building. Once he was in the elevator with me, I couldn't—didn't know how to—make him leave. It didn't occur to me that I could just say, "I'm not comfortable having you here," or just "No." It was a similar dissociation to the bingeing—that resigned feeling that I can't stop, that someone else is in control and I just have to surrender.

"What a mess," he said—and not in a nice way—when he walked in. I didn't say anything. I don't know if I thought it consciously then, but I know now that I didn't think I deserved to be treated better.

I didn't have any liquor in my apartment, which I remember annoyed him. This was, I think, when he stopped seeming sarcastic—a trait I usually enjoy—and crossed the line to almost cruel.

We sat on my futon, kissing. He tried to pull me into his lap, which I wouldn't do—I was pretty sure I would crush him. He kept trying to take my shirt off, but I wouldn't cooperate. Instead, I tried to wriggle a bit out of his reach. He said something about not playing hard to get. Finally I muttered something about hating my arms, then wanted to kick myself for saying anything that lame. Besides, after what he'd said about my apartment, there was no way I wanted to hear what he might have to say about my body.

I wanted him to leave, but I was frozen—unable to do anything to stop this. He gave up on my top and started complaining about how the futon was too small and we really should switch to the bed, which, in my studio apartment, was just a few feet away. I didn't say anything. He began running a finger along the inside of the waistband of my gray pants. Instinctively, I sucked in my stomach. The pants were fitted, and I waited to hear something about the roll of fat above them.

He looked for the zipper, which he couldn't figure out was in the back. I didn't clue him in. I knew if that happened, I was pretty sure even I could tell what would happen next.

"We are *not* having sex," someone said—*I* said. I don't know where that came from. I thought he would leave then, but still he didn't.

"Oh, all right," he said, sounding disgusted. "You're going to have to get me off somehow, then."

I cringed. Without being invited, he climbed into my bed, and finally I did, too. I felt like I owed him this—that it was I who had done something wrong, and that somehow I had to set things right. When it was over, I lay awake all night, still fully clothed, feeling like I was trapped in a bad afterschool special, wishing I'd never let him in—and wishing my bed were bigger. He was well muscled, so it was like being in bed next to a heater.

Finally I got up and lay on the futon, wanting to scream, wanting to call Mary, wanting him to leave. *Where had it all gone so horribly wrong?* I kept thinking.

In the morning he made no move to go.

"You're a journalist—where's your Sunday *Times*?" he snapped.

"Downstairs at the front desk," I mumbled.

"Aren't you going to get it?" he asked.

I did.

"Don't you have any food?" He seemed to be enjoying this.

I didn't. I didn't want to suggest we go out and get some because (a) I didn't want to go anywhere with him, (b) I was scared he might say something nasty about my not needing any more food, and (c) I couldn't think of anything I'd want to eat in front of him.

He sat around for hours reading the paper, which for some reason made me feel even more violated than anything else he'd done or said. He barely said anything to me, except to tell me I'd never be Maureen Dowd.

Finally he left.

He gave me a kiss on the cheek. "Don't miss me too much," he said, then paused in the doorway and took a last look. "Oh—and clean up this place."

When he left, I took a shower, feeling like even if I stood under the hot water for a thousand years I'd still be able to feel his hands on me.

Then I called Mary.

She guessed instantly that our circle's standard teasing of friends who "got some" the night before was not the best idea here.

I told her the story in fits and spurts, pausing often, testing the waters to see if I could say any more without her being disgusted with me and hanging up and never speaking to me again. Mary knew quite a bit about my family and its problems, but other than that she mostly knew only my "normal" side—the healthy, exercising, funny/sarcastic, got-a-problem-and-here's-how-I'm-going-to-solve-it side. Sure, she saw some of the insecurity—I was constantly asking her if my jeans were too tight—but I wasn't sure I was ready to let her in on how totally *not* together I was on the inside.

"He's a jerk," she said. "He's not even that cute—his personality sort of covers up any cuteness."

I felt a little better, but not much. I had told her most of the story, but my excuse for what seemed, in the light of morning, completely idiotic and naive behavior on my part was the excuse that's almost always acceptable at our age: hey, I was drunk. The truth was I wasn't—in fact, at times the night before I'd wished desperately for a drink to soften the edges of the horrible, sharp self-consciousness.

She repeated several times that he was a jerk, occasionally substituting *asshole* and *psycho* and *loser* and my favorite Mary-ism, *dookie-head*.

"And be careful if you've been drinking," she admonished me. I felt crappy for lying—but I felt like I had to. Admitting that I really was that clueless about the Larry situation meant, I was sure, having to admit a whole pile of things about myself I didn't want to have to think about, much less tell anyone else. It was easier—safer—just to lie.

Near the end of the conversation she told me Larry wasn't going to be the only guy who ever flirted with me.

"Get used to it," she said.

I wanted desperately to ask her what I should say if something like the night before ever happened again—to ask for a script to write down, the way I do with interview subjects that scare me—but I couldn't.

"He's not the only guy you're ever going to meet," she said. "Remember that."

Didn't lose any weight this week. And I've eaten nothing but what I'm supposed to. People say that eating appropriately is supposed to be its own reward—don't I feel good that I'm taking care of myself?—but frankly, it's not enough. I feel like I'm hungry all the time, so the unbudging scale makes me want to pig out in frustration.

I'm trying to take it one day at a time. The marathon training is actually helping. My weigh-in day is Wednesday, and I know that if I binge because I'm disgusted with my plodding progress, I'll have to stop by Thursday afternoon, because it takes my body at least twenty-four hours to recover, and I don't want to feel like throwing up while trying to run on Saturday morning. (Actually, the runs are so early Saturday morning—5:00 A.M. because of the punishing heat and humidity—that I probably should consider them Friday night.) And if I can make it to Saturday . . . well, usually the run puts me in a good mood.

I've grown to love the ritual of Saturday morning runs, even if I don't always love the runs themselves. Sometimes I feel like I live for these mornings—for the order they bring, for how my life falls into place around them. Every week I have to get up and run three days and cross-train another two, or I know I'll feel terrible on the long run.

Thursday night happy hours have become a thing of the past—liquor is dehydrating, and (note to my bingeing self) Juli has drilled into us that what you eat and drink for two days before the run is as important as what you consume the night before. Mary, Abby, and I don't go out at all on Fridays.

On Saturdays after the run, no matter how horrible my week has been, I feel like all is right again. Often by the time I get back to my apartment, I'll have a phone message from Mary saying, "Can you believe we did that?"

Last Saturday my friend Cindy called at noon, expecting to tease me about my having just gotten up. I told her—almost smugly—that not only had I been up since 5:00 A.M., but I had run twelve miles, taken a shower, read the paper, *and* done my laundry.

"Where is Courtney?" she asked. "Who are you, and what have you done with her?"

"How's the weight?" Grandma on the phone. Apparently this week she's dispensed with subtlety, since her usual way of asking is, "What did you have for dinner last night?"

"Fine," I snapped. I knew I was going to have to give a little bit more information before the subject could be closed, but the trick is to offer just enough to get by yet not enough to provoke further discussion.

Grandma likes to hear good news—one of her standard opening lines is, "So what have you got to tell me that's good?" So I told her I'd bought size 12 jeans and planned never to shop in another plus-size department. Fourteens they sell at Lane Bryant (though I can't imagine why you'd buy them there unless you were trying to feel better about yourself by imagining the size 20 customers being jealous of your relative slenderness), but 12s . . . 12s you can't buy in any plus-size department. They're squarely in the "normal" range.

"That's what you said last time," she said. "Why is it any different this time?"

Mission to abort the subject failed.

I knew exactly where the conversation was going, because we've had it before. I knew I shouldn't take the bait, should just change the subject. But I couldn't.

"Do you have to remind me of that?" I asked. Whined, really.

"I'm reminding you so you won't do it again," she said matter-of-factly.

I wanted to tell her that her "reminder" wasn't helping, the same way her comments at dinner tables of yore about what I was eating never helped. But in the moment I couldn't. I just felt stung. Stunned.

I got off the phone and ate two cereal bars. I would have eaten ice cream if I'd had any in the house.

What I wanted to tell her—tell *somebody*—is that, truth be told, things aren't going so well with the diet these days.

Despite my saintlike behavior—this week alone I have passed up cake *four* times—all my virtue seems wasted. I haven't lost any weight this week—the second week in a row that's happened. (And no, it was *not* "that time of the month." Peeke and Shari and Nancy asked me that. Feel like I'm back in eighth-grade gym class, counting the weeks until I can use that excuse again.)

After a birthday party last night, some friends and I went on to another party at a gorgeous loft in Adams Morgan, a neighborhood just north of mine. I prowled around looking for a drink, and who should I find but Larry? In three years of overlapping circles of friends I'd never met him, but now there he was again, two weeks after Karen's party, at this random party, arm draped around some blonde woman's shoulder.

He walked right up to me and smiled. He looked evil.

He nodded toward his date across the room. "Don't you think Cara looks like Carolyn Bessette Kennedy?"

I paused, noticing how ugly his smirk made him look.

"No," I said, surprising even myself. "Carolyn Bessette Kennedy was *pretty*."

I strode off, feeling the silence solidify behind me.

"It's Sunday morning—do you miss me?" said a voice on the other end of the phone.

It was Larry. Where had he gotten my number? I had never given it to him—not last week and certainly not last night. For an instant I couldn't help being vaguely flattered that he'd taken the time to track it down. I'm crazy, I thought. If this is how I think, what happened last week was definitely my fault.

"Well, do you miss me?"

I couldn't think of anything to say.

"I've finished packing. Are you coming over to kiss me good-bye?" he asked.

I picked at my bedspread, flashing back to him lying on it, and how much I had wanted him to leave.

I didn't care about a clever—and cutting—closing line. "No, I'm going to tell you good-bye over the phone. Good-bye," I said and hung up.

Still, much as I hated myself for thinking it, a tiny bit of me couldn't help wondering if he'd call again. I remembered talking with a colleague about Bill Clinton and his way with the opposite sex: some women will take prurient interest over no interest at all. I wonder if I'm always going to be one of them.

Yesterday Abby, our friend Betina, and I ran the Rockville Rotary Twilight 8K—my first official race, if you don't count Race for the Cure, which I don't. I finished in 51:54, a 10:27-a-mile pace. And despite constant thoughts of "Will I come in last? What if I come in last?" I was 326th out of 460 women—so not even close to last. I actually felt like I could have run faster—Mary said Betina told her I was "positively speedy" at the end.

My reward for a week of good eating and finishing my first race? I *gained* a pound. I got on and off the scale six times to be sure. (It started out as best two out of three, and when one of those times it looked like I'd gained a pound and a half, I decided on an average of four out of five.)

Peeke said these things happen—that my body likes where it is now, and it's holding on to the extra weight. *Apparently it's as stubborn as I am*, I thought. This gain of a pound (I refuse to think pound and a half) means there has been no net change in my weight this month, since I lost one pound the first week and then stayed the same for two.

Frankly, after the weigh-in I didn't know how I was going to make it through the rest of the day, foodwise, and of course I didn't. I ate a jumbo chocolate muffin. Then in the afternoon I had two pieces of cake and swiped frosting from a third.

Have spent the past four days since the weigh-in eating anything and everything I want, thinking: *I'll get back on track tomorrow.*

I've also spent the past four days freaking out. I didn't want to call anyone for help, because I didn't want to think about the fact that I can't stop eating, much less write about it in my food journal. But this afternoon, with nightmares of return trips to Lane Bryant dancing in my head, I finally called Nancy. She reminded me that losing weight takes serious effort and asked what's been eating up the energy I've been so good about devoting to the cause. After hearing my catalog of stressors (looming deadlines, family issues), she said, "I give you permission to maintain for a couple of weeks."

"But I want to lose," I practically whined. Who wants to devote all this effort just to maintain? Still, maintaining beats gaining, I suppose, so I'd better give it a shot.

Month 8 (August)

*N*o net change in my weight last month, so today was just the thing to cheer me up (drench previous words in buckets of sarcasm): a *Shape* photo shoot. Woo-hoo! And this time they want to photograph me running. I begged Molly, the photographer, to do the shoot somewhere deep in suburbia, where we couldn't possibly run into anyone I know, but she said there had to be monuments in the background.

After a chat with the stylist about clothing—nothing too form-fitting, please!—she sent a box of clothes that contained loads of form-fitting things I would never wear. My usual aim for gym wear is for it to be as unremarkable as possible. But the stylist's first-choice outfit was a tight purple top and leggings and stoplight-red sneakers. I thought about lying and saying the purple catsuit, as I've nicknamed it, didn't fit right. But the other options in the box were at least as bad, and I certainly didn't want an "authentic" picture, which would be me in baggy gym shorts and a frat party T-shirt. So I put on the catsuit and wondered: could I smile, suck in my stomach, *and* run all at the same time?

Molly tried to be cheerful. "Look at your adorable red sneakers!" she said when I showed up for the shoot.

Doubt anybody was looking at them. Instead, I can only imagine they were wondering what the hell I was doing in the beastly heat of an August afternoon, running around in a workout outfit designed for winter (which is when the column will appear).

I spent two and a half hours skipping up and down steps that led to a path by the Potomac, running on the path itself, stretching, and pretending to tie my shoes. Pretending to tie my shoes was my idea—if the only thing

Molly could get excited about was the damn red shoes, well, let's at least make sure we see them in the picture.

That running for the camera is the last exercise I've done in five days. The first day after the shoot was a day off. But then I overslept the next day. Felt sick the third. Gym closed for a freak air-conditioning glitch the fourth. And I had an early morning interview the fifth and ended up staying at work until after the gym had closed.

But a funny thing has happened after five days of not exercising: I feel as disgusting as if I hadn't showered. I crave moving—make that sweating—the way I sometimes crave anything with frosting.

In diets past, too many days off caused a spiral into self-loathing: disgust over my slothfulness fueled forays to the local Mexican restaurant for the cheese-drenched comfort of nachos. Too full to move, I'd call it quits on the whole program.

This time I've stuck with it long enough to see benefits: I'm not out of breath when I sprint for the Metro. I don't get frustrated with fancy footwork in step aerobics class—I can focus on the moves because I'm in good enough shape not to have to struggle to breathe. A few days ago I e-mailed Shari to tell her that I'd run six miles Saturday, taken a two-hour bike ride with friends Sunday, and planned to try a ballet class. Her response was immediate: "You are an athlete! Do you realize that if you placed a personal ad, you'd have to put 'Must be fit'?"

Actually, I hadn't. Athlete?

I still haven't really told anyone—and especially not Peeke or Shari or *Shape*—that I'm running with a marathon-training group. I definitely don't say "training for a marathon," because I don't really think I am. Yes, I've planned my summer so as to avoid leaving town on the weekends—I'm sure if I miss a single Saturday I won't make it through the next one. But I still think of training as something temporary, a way to make sure I get in a good workout at least once a week. So I don't want there to be anyone to answer to—certainly not *Shape*—if and when I have to quit.

Ten-mile runs have become twelve, then fourteen, then sixteen. We pass the time on the run gossiping, singing, complaining about pains, and playing versions of drinking games, using the water in our water bottles. Abby, Mary, and our new running buddies, Stacy and Dagny, talk all the time about the day of the marathon and how they plan to celebrate when they cross the finish line. I never say anything, because I'm still not sure I'll be there.

Yes, I've done fine with the training—good enough, even, to think about quickening my pace. But every week I wonder if it's going to be my last with the group. I'm convinced there's going to be some number of miles at which my body will give out, proving what I've known all along: I was not meant to do this.

E-mail from Maureen, my editor at *Shape*: they've got the first copies of the magazine with my inaugural column. Gulp.

I've been so focused on the day-to-day of the diet that I've practically forgotten—at least as much as it's possible to "forget" something for which I've had photo shoots and deadlines—that anything about it will actually appear in print. Thus far there's been minimal editing on the columns, so after I turn them in, they don't reappear in my in-box with a bunch of questions from editors, forcing me to confront the idea that people are actually going to be reading what I write.

I was too afraid to go back and look in my files to see what I'd written for that first column. What I wrote privately for Peeke about my diet history and what I wrote publicly for *Shape* are a tangled loom in my head, and I'm not sure I want to look at how much of the former might have crept into the latter. All I remember for sure was deciding not to mention Mom's illness in print. Too private, too complicated.

Maureen said she thought I'd be pleased with the way the pages looked.

All I could think about was the "before" pictures I had to send *Shape* a few months ago, when they suddenly decided they should use a real "before" picture and not the me-minus-twenty-three-pounds one they had shot in March. I had to really beat the bushes to find them any shots of myself, since I was never one to pose willingly for pictures. Now I wish I could affix a Post-it to every copy of the issue, saying, "But I don't look like that anymore!"

That, I suppose, is the point.

Shape issues arrived at my office today, along with a note from Maureen saying she'd just seen the film from my running photo shoot (the catsuit shoot) and, "You look GREAT!!!! I mean it!!!!" (No extra exclamation points added.) Cannot say the same for the first column. It's a two-page spread, with two pictures: one of me sitting in a rowboat and one that's a fairly tight shot of my face. The size of my chin in the second picture is horrifying, but at least I got a good laugh out of it. If readers only knew that picture was from an out-of-control party and what I'm holding in my hands is a Jell-O shot. (Now, that would be an ad for healthy living.) There's also a picture of a hand writing in a diary.

Worse than the pictures, I think, is the text. My weight in print—something I've lied about on my driver's license, my gym membership application, and everywhere else but the column—is possibly more horrific than my face. I cannot believe I actually wrote about Grandma calling me "as big as a house" and my fear of walking up to men at parties. Cannot believe I wrote these amazingly personal things, and now they are in actual print. I guess the whole idea that the column wouldn't appear until a good eight or nine months after I started lulled me into a false sense of security—like, "Oh, that's not for ages. Somehow I'll deal with it when the time comes."

Then again, I have long believed no one actually reads most magazines—they just look at the pictures and headlines. I mean, why else am I always having to deal with the annoying comment, "I saw your article in such-and-such magazine"? I always want to answer, "Yeah? So did you read it?"

I showed the article to two friends at work. They didn't make any comments about what I looked like or how it compares to how I look now. They didn't say a word about the actual words. Instead, one asked if that was my hand holding the pen in the picture of a hand writing in the diary, and the other asked if that was my handwriting.

Yesterday Diana decided she wanted to try running and so came with me. It was definitely novel for *me* to be the fit one: I was running along just fine, and after ten minutes she was struggling. Every couple of minutes it was, "How long are we going to go? How long have we been going for?" Which I don't tend to think about—I just run my normal route and worry about the time only on "speed" days, those days once every couple of weeks when I'm feeling inspired and decide to add in some sprints. Diana said something about having eaten a lot that day and feeling full, so she quit after about fifteen minutes and headed home. I immediately broke into a sprint.

I'm going to run the marathon!

Or at least, I'm going to try, though I'm still not saying anything to *Shape* about it. I don't want the extra pressure, and I want it to be a corner of my life that's just mine—not for public consumption.

I decided to go ahead and try to run after not only surviving today's eighteen-miler but even feeling good at the end. Felt bizarrely like I could have gone farther and—is it possible?—faster.

My confidence in my ability to do this is still pretty shaky. (I'd say "my confidence in my athletic ability," except I still can't use the word *athletic* to apply to myself.) And ever since last month, when I had those few days of eating whatever I wanted after I'd gained a pound, I've felt almost perpetually on the brink of a binge. I haven't given in yet, but the fear that I'm going to lose control over food doesn't do much for my faith in myself.

But I have run eighteen miles, and now, somehow, it's a relief to admit: I'm going to do everything I can to cross that finish line, and if I can't, it won't be because I haven't tried. At the same time, it's scary. There have been things I wanted badly—admission to a seminar with a hotshot professor or a job—but other people had much of the control over those. With the marathon it's totally up to me.

An old male friend of mine used to say I had to be hit over the head to pick up on the idea that anyone was flirting with me. Today it was so blatant that even I got the message.

I was interviewing a young entrepreneur for a story, and he was over the top, saying that it wasn't fair of the magazine to send somebody this cute(!) to interview him. He was cute himself, if arrogant. He told me I should come to New York for his thirtieth birthday party. Later he asked if I'd go with him to a black-tie dinner he had to attend in a couple of weeks.

I kept changing the topic back to the interview, trying not to blush and wondering if this was a stunt he was pulling to ensure I'd write a flattering story about him.

Finally I said, "You do realize this is all on the record."

"You wouldn't do that to me," he said and winked.

"Only because I only have 250 words I wouldn't," I answered.

The rest of the interview proceeded as normally as I suppose it could have. He called later in the afternoon and left a voice mail. So I e-mailed him, saying I didn't feel comfortable talking to him until after the story goes to press next week. We'll see if he calls again after that.

Apparently I'm looking good enough that *Shape* has asked for a goal weight—the number at which they'll be able officially to declare this project a success. But Peeke is very resistant to the idea of a goal weight for me, somebody with a lifelong history of being overweight, because it's impossible to say where my body will be comfortable. It has never stayed at one weight for very long. Peeke would much prefer to focus on bringing down my body fat percentage, by both losing weight and upping muscle.

A good body fat percentage for me, Peeke says, is 20 percent. I don't know what I started at, though Peeke estimated 34 percent. Currently I'm at 169 pounds and 24 percent, which means I need to lose about 7 more pounds of pure fat to get to 20 percent. Except you don't lose only fat (you lose water and sometimes muscle), so it'll probably be a bit more on the scale—maybe 10 pounds or so.

If only when—or if—I finish losing weight I'll be done thinking about weighing and measuring and worrying. But I never will be.

Dad is coming to town for a conference—without Mom, of course. I can't say I'm looking forward to it. I don't like sitting there while Dad and Diana discuss the fine points of cars they like and—now that Diana has a Web job—go on and on about various computer- and Internet-related things. I often feel like the third wheel on outings with Dad and Diana, probably because they're so much closer with each other than I am with either of them. And ever since Diana told me she and Dad once had a conversation that involved something about how I'm too smart to have the job I have and write about the sometimes frivolous things I do . . . well, I just wonder what other things about me they've discussed.

Instead of waiting for the inevitable discussion/argument with Diana about what to do with Dad, I suggested to him directly that we go bike riding on Maryland's Eastern Shore. Dad biked across the United States as a kid (something that, I've often teased him, makes him sound a lot cooler than the Dad I know), so I knew he'd probably like the idea, and he did. And I knew that if Dad were into it, Diana wouldn't want to be the one to spoil it.

I didn't even really realize it until the words *bike ride* popped out of my mouth that I was actually suggesting we do something active—and suggesting it as though it was a totally normal thing.

I know Dad's on the phone with Diana now. I wonder which one of them brought up first how unlike me my suggestion was.

I joked to Mary that one of the reasons I'd suggested a bike ride was that it would be impossible for Dad, Diana, and me to talk much as we rode single file, wind whipping. In the car on the way to the shore, I couldn't wait for the silence. Dad talked a lot about the divorce, repeatedly referring to Mom as "Mommy," as if Diana and I were four years old.

I know he often wishes we were—these days he talks a lot about how sorry he is not to have been around much while we were small. But he seems to want it both ways—that we be little kids *and* adults. In the same "Mommy" conversation, he started talking about what he wanted in a "mate," as he called it. I was afraid that if I said anything about the appropriateness of the topic, Diana would glare at me and I'd snap back and we'd squabble. Then Dad would get annoyed and we'd all sit in stony silence—all before we'd even been together for forty-five minutes. But just as I was wondering if Diana wasn't a bit uncomfortable, too—Mom and Dad aren't even divorced yet, for heaven's sake—she said, "Dad, I don't really think we should talk about this. Or about Mom."

Which made conversation a bit stilted—all roads leading to the topic we weren't supposed to be discussing. On the bike ride itself, I couldn't help thinking guiltily that if Mom were here, there was no way we'd be here. Mom circles the parking lot for the spot closest to the door. She does not move any more than necessary.

My food problems began when we stopped for lunch. There was absolutely nothing on the menu that wasn't fried or mayonnaisey, and the fact that I haven't lost any weight despite having behaved on the food front *and* running miles and miles—well, it made me feel frantic. I had a crab cake sandwich—I think the bread was buttered, too—without the fries and was still hungry when I was done. The hunger—combined with knowing I was going to be with Dad and Diana all day and that if I were to say I needed a snack at 3:00, Dad would probably say we should get it later—made me anxious. I've never been able to explain—not to my family, not to anyone—that I can't wait. I'm sure part of it is that being told when I can eat or when we're going to eat reminds me of being a kid, of knowing that I was going to have to sneak food when Mom wasn't looking, because I probably couldn't eat all I wanted when she was.

I didn't want to say I was still hungry after lunch, because then Dad would suggest dessert and Diana would get annoyed when I said I didn't want any, and I'd get so frustrated with *that* that I'd probably eat.

Eat. It's still my knee-jerk reaction to everything.

We got back on our bikes, and I actually forgot about my hunger for a while. It was a clear summer day, I wasn't at work, I had lost thirty-five pounds over the past seven and a half months, and there were a zillion things in the upcoming months I was looking forward to. Life seemed pretty good.

But in the car on the way home, we stopped at a huge gourmet food store. Cookies and chocolate and cakes everywhere.

I didn't have to consider what I'd write in my food journals—aka how I'd explain this to Peeke—since lately the journals have become more and more sporadic. I've been doing so well—or so everyone thinks—that no one even asks for them anymore.

I pushed thoughts of what I might gain out of my head. I wanted everything.

I knew I could probably buy one thing in front of Dad and Diana, but what if what I bought wasn't a single serving and I wanted the whole box? And what if I had one bite of whatever it was and decided it wasn't really what I wanted? They would never understand that I had to throw it out and get something else. And what if that wasn't the right thing? And what if they bought something and I wanted more of it than was normal? I feared having to explain myself. If I were thinking rationally, I would have considered that I've lost thirty-five pounds and therefore should have been able to brush off any questions from them by saying I knew what I was doing. If I were thinking rationally, I would have considered that they might not question my eating at all, because they'd be eating themselves. But on the brink of a binge I don't think rationally. All I think is that I've got to get what I want, and I've got to get it without anyone I know seeing me.

I ended up claiming I was going to the bathroom and then going to a distant cash register—hidden from view by hundreds of jars of marinades—and buying a package of chocolate-covered raisins. Not really what I wanted, but my rationale was simple: (1) They were among the first things I saw. (2) The package was small enough to shove in my bag. (3) The raisins themselves were small enough that I could sit in the back seat of the car and eat them covertly—popping a few into my mouth while ducking my head and pretending to rummage for something in the depths of my bag. (4) Unlike with chocolate-covered nuts, my breath wouldn't really smell from raisins.

The fear of being caught plus the disgust that I was probably setting off a binge plus the fear that I was never going to lose more weight at this rate suddenly equaled wanting everything in the store. I knew the raisins weren't going to be enough for the car trip home—once I finished them, I'd have to have something else.

But I couldn't. I ate my chocolate-covered raisins, plus as many cookies as I dared from the box Dad and Diana had bought, and by the time we got back to D.C. I wanted dinner. Immediately. I knew that wasn't going to happen, so I made an excuse that I needed to buy contact lens solution and ducked out to CVS, where I bought a Twix bar and a Kit Kat. I would have bought more, but I knew I couldn't binge full out. I knew I couldn't handle sitting through dinner at a restaurant feeling as sick as I do when I binge. Plus today is Thursday, and I've got a race—a race, not just a training run—on Sunday.

Gained two pounds. Two pounds! And I didn't even have a major binge. The smaller I get, the less forgiving my body is of any extra bit of food. Call it the booby prize of weight loss.

Just so happened Peeke e-mailed today asking for an update, and I wasn't in the mood to put on my usual happy face. I didn't give all the details of my slipup—I said I'd eaten some junk food, including cookies and chocolate-covered raisins. I told her—flat out—that I was frustrated, that I didn't know how I was going to make it through another day on this diet because I was starting to feel like I was starving, and that I was thinking about food more than I ever have in my life. It's like a 1940s University of Minnesota starvation study I once read, where researchers restricted thirty-six men to half their usual food intake for six months. Thoughts of food consumed the men during that time: they read cookbooks, collected recipes, even hoarded kitchen utensils. I don't like to cook, but lately I find myself reading the food sections of the *Washington Post* and the *New York Times* and becoming unreasonably irritated that the *Times* doesn't include calorie counts for its recipes.

Peeke left a message for me in her great cathedral of a voice: "Don't you dare ever give up on yourself—you're doing great. Please, Courtney, nose to the grindstone and remember the regrouping you're doing is the hardest of all. You need to hold on now—it's the sixth mile of the 10K. And you never give up!"

If that woman doesn't have a contract for a motivational tape, she will soon.

I e-mailed Peeke to say I thought the problem was that I've stretched the diet too much—like an elastic waistband you stretch and stretch until it sort of flops. I do stick to the diet she set out in the beginning—except when I don't. I have a cookie and figure if I eat a little less for dinner it should even out. I have a few bites of pasta off someone else's plate when we're out to eat. For lunch I'll think, *How bad could it be to have a mozzarella and pesto sandwich for lunch just this once?* And because I'm not really keeping the food journals, and because these aren't binges, I conveniently forget about the extras.

So I've decided I need to go totally back to basics for a while. Back to everything Peeke told me on Day 1. Cereal and banana for breakfast. Boca Burgers or other protein on good bread with lots of veggies for lunch. Nothing fancy. Few or no choices. I did it at the beginning—I ought to be able to do it now.

Except it's just so tempting to have a bit of the chocolate on the lunch table or that cookie instead of my proper snack and say: tomorrow. I'll start tomorrow.

Feel like a huge weight has been lifted. I've been on this diet for more than seven months, and today was the first day I actually asked for help. I didn't make excuses or lie about why I didn't want to go for pizza with Mary. I just took a deep breath and said, "I've been having a rough time with the diet, and I'd like to go out, but I don't want to eat there."

It's such a small thing, but it's something I haven't been able to do before. I haven't wanted to call attention to myself and what I eat—I think because, as silly as it sounds, I've always feared the impact it's going to have on my social life. Eating is such a big part of life—dinners out, parties, brunches, "let's order Chinese and watch 'Sex and the City'"—that the last thing I want to do is be the person everyone groans about. Like, "Oh, God, we can't invite Courtney. We'll never be able to find a restaurant she can eat at." Or "Oh, God, is she going to sigh about the fat content of everything the way Katrina sighs about everything she can't eat because it has gluten?" Everyone has shorthand for friends: "my friend who plays in a band" or "my friend who works at the Justice Department." I'm usually "my friend who works at the *Washingtonian*" or "my friend the writer." I definitely don't want to be "my friend on the annoying diet."

Mary didn't blink—just asked where I'd feel comfortable going. I felt so free after that—and so safe. It's not like she's going to physically restrain me from bakeries, but at least for today there was no lying, no pretending everything was fine when my body feels like it's splintering from the tug-of-war between eating everything and resisting. My comment about not feeling like I could go for pizza touched off a long talk about food and weight (though not bingeing, which seems too messed up to tell anyone about). Food and weight are not anything Mary and I have ever really talked about, apart from Mary's girlie "I feel foul," which she says whenever she feels like she's eaten a lot. It's what she says instead of "I feel fat"—a phrase I have never used, even once, because to me it would be like saying I have brown eyes. It's a fact so immutable it doesn't require mentioning.

Sitting outside tonight at dinner, I felt like—I never thought these words would come out of my mouth—it was too hot to eat much of anything, even the fresh fruit I had ordered. The whole time we sat there—a good couple of hours—I could barely focus on the conversation. I kept thinking: *Am I really not hungry? Is that possible?* And I wasn't. Who knows? Maybe someday I *will* be one of those people who push away a chocolate dessert after three bites because it's too rich.

Finished my first big race: the Annapolis ten-miler. It's infamous for being a hilly killer—up and down these steep bridges—which I didn't learn until long after I'd signed up. And I finished—nowhere near last—in 1:45. Less-than-ten-minute miles! I did the last mile in 8:15, so I wasn't even close to beat from running the previous nine.

I was so nervous about this race you'd think I'd never finished that 8K or eighteen-mile training run. Mary said my nerves were part of my inability to give myself credit for anything. I couldn't seem to explain that there was something about a ten-mile race that just seemed almost overconfident on my part—a statement that I'm a runner and not just someone playing at it. Loads of people sign up for 8Ks and 10Ks, but ten-mile races attract a different— and serious—crowd.

The people at the expo—where you pick up your race packet and where every running-related company on the planet tries to sell you stuff—looked like real runners. What does a real runner look like? Well, thin. I wondered if people thought I was the (171-pound, size 12, giant of a) friend coming along to lend her friends support—if they thought I was the person who'd be holding Mary's and Abby's stuff and cheering them while they ran.

Call from the young entrepreneur. He left a message, not saying a word about the story other than that he had seen it, and so now that it was done, if I didn't want to talk to him, I'd have to give an excuse other than that I was writing about him. I wasn't especially interested, but now that he is, well. . . .

One thing that worries me is that he's not exactly discreet—during the interview, he skewered half a dozen people he had to have guessed I also know. Makes me feel like I wouldn't be a date—or whatever it is—so much as a scathing-anecdote-in-waiting.

I have run through stomachaches, knee pain, heat advisories, and rain. But today I hit a wall.

It was just a ten-mile run—and by now, I really can say "*just* a ten-mile run"—around the monuments, but it seemed like four marathons. My body felt like lead. I cried through the last three miles, tears burning my eyes as they mixed with sweat. I cried not just because moving my body felt like moving a rusted, badly put-together robot but because I was sure this was really it. No matter how much I want this, my body has realized what my mind has always known: I can't.

Mary reminded me that everybody has bad runs—hadn't Juli told us that? I want to believe her. I want to believe in myself. But today brought back every doubt. Yes, normal people have bad runs and then are fine the next week. But I am sure I am not "normal." Just eight months ago, I had barely run so much as a mile.

I don't want to go to the next training session—don't want what I'm sure I'll get: confirmation that I can't finish. But I don't want to quit, either. I'm so close. And I'm surprising even myself with how badly I want this. I make silent promises that have nothing to do with food or weight: *I will not gossip. I will try harder to get along with my sister. I will not claim not to have gotten an e-mail when in fact I've deliberately deleted it. Just please, please let me have this one thing.*

Even if Saturday's training session is OK, I can't help worrying: *What if my next "bad run" is the marathon?*

Month 9 (September)

*T*he bad news: no net change in my weight for the second month in a row.

The good news—unrelated to weight—is that I am not totally paranoid.

Knew the guy in line at the grocery store behind me was staring and couldn't figure out why. My zipper wasn't unzipped. I was wearing black, so there couldn't be any embarrassing stains on my pants. I wasn't on a binge, so there was nothing especially noteworthy about my groceries: Boca Burgers, Egg Beaters, mushrooms, bagged salad, grape tomatoes, low-fat shredded cheese, Special K, peaches. Got home to find a message from the guy on my machine. He had memorized my number when I gave it to the cashier (so she could log my order on my loyalty card). Wanted to call him back just to ask what about the method in which he had gotten my number was *not* creepy and stalkeresque, but decided to restrain myself. Wanted to call Mary and tell her, but as crazy and vaguely scary as the episode is, I am also oddly, shamefully flattered by it.

Am I ever going to have a day when I wake up and think, *Gee, I look fabulous today*? Forget the psychological benefits; it would definitely help me out with *Shape*. They've informed me I've not been taking nearly enough photos of myself to fill in the gaps between shoots. I'm supposed to be taking pictures every month, but without a set day to do it, I always put it off. It would be different if I woke up the odd morning and my skin was clear, my hair was falling at exactly the right angle, and I felt thin. But that never happens. So I put off facing the camera, hoping tomorrow will be better.

Shape still doesn't know about the marathon, but they know from the monthly "workout schedules" I submit with the columns that I've been running at least three times a week and doing some smaller races. So now that I've become such a "runner girl," as my *Shape* editor Maureen has taken to calling me, *Shape* wants authentic action shots of me at a race. Cynical me can't help wondering if it's because they don't believe I actually do these races. I can't really blame them, since I can hardly believe it myself.

The next race I have is the MS Half Marathon in a couple of weeks, which will be, at 13.1 miles, the longest race I've done yet. I know I've said this before every race, but I'm nervous about not finishing. It'll be bad enough to deal with myself if I fail, let alone a photographer who's supposed to be documenting my success.

E-mail from Maureen asking how I've managed to convince all these friends of mine to work out with me.

Her question made me consider how much losing weight has changed even the people I choose to hang out with. I never used to have any friends who were much into fitness, and most of my old friends still aren't. I think some of them are still adjusting to the new me, this alien creature who actually wants to go biking and try a ballet class. (Still haven't gotten up the nerve for that last one—I keep picturing myself looking like Babar the elephant in a pink tutu.) I even wonder if some of them are resentful, the way you feel when your best single friend starts seriously dating someone and there's some turbulence before your friendship reaches a new equilibrium.

It's not that I don't hang out with old friends anymore; it's that I don't see some of them as much because they're not game to do all the sorts of active things I suddenly want to try. Recently, one of them said—a hint of ice in her voice—that she hadn't seen me in forever because I was always out "running a marathon." I ended up staying up incredibly late—just like old times—to chat with her because I felt guilty, then had a hard time getting up for the gym, which made me feel resentful. Feel like I just can't win.

Speaking of old friends: one of the things I want to do this weekend—Labor Day weekend, when an old college friend is coming to visit—is try a body-sculpting class I've heard is fantastic. Despite my best efforts to like lifting weights, I still would rather run for hours than do a set of chest presses, so I figure a class might help.

I haven't seen Bonnie in two years, and I've spoken to her only sporadically since then. I could tell she was weirded out when I told her I had a ten-mile run Saturday morning I couldn't miss and that because of it I wouldn't be able to stay out very late on Friday night. Considering that our college friendship involved more dessert than I care to think about, and that the last time I mentioned running she told me she didn't even own a pair of sneakers, I shouldn't have been surprised that there was a long silence from her end. Finally she said, "Well, if that's what you have to do." So—despite her frequent comments that she wants to lose fifteen pounds—I'm not optimistic that she'll want to join me for the class, and I know I'll feel guilty about leaving her to go on my own.

I know what the standard diet advice about this would be: I'm supposed to teach my friend about my eating/exercise program and make sure she understands how important it is to me (because it is, isn't it?). But where's the line between being a good host/wanting her to have a nice time and then doing what I need for myself? I know what the diet experts would say about that, too: do you have to have food to have a nice time? Well, no. But when I haven't seen a friend in a couple of years, it seems more than a bit rude to say, "I've got to go run Saturday morning, which means I won't be much fun Friday night, and by the way, remember those two or three restaurants you've been wanting to try? Well, I don't want to go to them because it's hard for me to stay on a diet there." I want to compromise and say, "OK, let's go to whatever restaurant you want. But for me to do that without being totally, totally neurotic (as opposed to just sort of neurotic), I need to go work out."

As Shari says, if you decide to eat something inappropriate—like a "big old sit-down fancy schmancy," as she calls it—you must have a plan for how you will physically offset the calorie intake with running, biking, lifting, etc., that day. If that means that you have to run twice that day, so be it.

The amount of working out I need to do to offset the number of calories Bonnie and I might eat—one of the restaurants is Southern, with nary a vegetable that isn't fried—well, that's a lot of working out. So which is worse: disappearing for hours to work out so we can eat where she wants or not disappearing for hours but then being much more difficult when it comes to restaurant choices? I know, I know: how about moderation—a little working out and a little "bad" food? Two problems with that: one, I've been struggling to get (and stay) on track these days, what with not losing any weight and the constant struggle not to binge. So even just a couple of bites of something I don't normally (translation: shouldn't) eat can be dangerous. Two, the problem with going out to dinner with just one other person is that, especially when it's another woman, I don't know one who will order exactly what she wants even if you don't agree to split it with her or at least agree to have a few bites.

Side order of guilt with the salad, anyone?

This has been one of the longest weekends of my life. Bonnie decided not to come to D.C. until Saturday afternoon since I wasn't really going to be "available"—meaning "much fun"—Friday night or Saturday morning. Fine. Cool. Problem solved.

She got off the plane, gave me a hug (no word about how I looked), and promptly started complaining about the weather. She complained about the heat. She complained about the rain. She complained about what her hair looked like in the heat and rain. She complained that it was too hot to walk anywhere. She didn't want to go anywhere D.C.-ish, like to a museum. She wanted to shop but then complained that everything was too expensive and that it was depressing to see all these things she couldn't buy. She complained that the Metro stops were too far apart. (See previous complaint about it being too hot to walk anywhere.)

Things became so strained that I finally suggested a couple of movies, figuring the extra-strength air-conditioning plus the fact that you can't talk in the theater would shut her up. But she didn't feel like watching a movie. So we got a table at Xando and ran out of things to talk about halfway through our drinks.

I spent the weekend feeling trapped, alternately wondering on what, exactly, our friendship had been based and plotting how I could sneak off and binge. I couldn't escape her, couldn't seem to make things the way they used to be, so I ate to escape her. Yes, the urge to binge was in full force, in spite of—or maybe because of—the huge meals we were eating in all the restaurants I had been so worried about before she got here. I didn't even try to resist going, because the fact that we were both hungry seemed to be the only thing Bonnie and I had in common. The urge to binge was so strong I even resorted to ducking off to CVS while she was in the shower. I took the cinnamon rolls back to my apartment and ate them standing next to the kitchen garbage can, ready to hide the evidence the minute the bathroom door opened.

The gym would have been a good escape from the whole uncomfortable weekend, but by the end I couldn't even use it. I was that full.

Today I found out I've gained four pounds with all this eating, and still I haven't stopped. I can't.

I got on and off the scale, checking and double-checking. It was 173 all four times I checked.

I thought about all the starving I was going to have to do to end up with a net loss for the month. I thought about whether it was possible to run twenty miles—as I have to do for training—if I've been starving for the days immediately preceding it. Probably not. So I thought about just going back to the Peeke plan of the diet's early days—the days before I thought I could get away with having a drink here and a piece of chocolate there and still lose weight.

I thought about the possibility that I wouldn't be able to face the Boca Burgers at lunch today—the probability that I'd spend the whole day in a silent struggle between what I know I should eat and what I want. I couldn't bear it. Not today.

All together now: tomorrow. I'll start tomorrow.

Having my picture appear with the *Shape* column means that nobody wonders if the Courtney Rubin in the column is the Courtney Rubin she knows. The silver lining in this is that random people from my past are starting to pop up. My editor says she's gotten a handful of e-mails from people claiming to be high school friends of mine. Today I personally got an e-mail from Jennie, a former *Miami Herald* reporter who knew me when I was a sixteen-year-old kid working there but to whom I haven't spoken in years.

Jennie has heard from a colleague we both still keep in touch with that I'm running the marathon and wrote to ask how the training is going. Namely: am I dropping weight like crazy?

I wish. I wrote back that I was eating like a madwoman and that I'm probably the only living human being to worry about *gaining* weight on a marathon-training program.

I'm sure she got my response and thought I was exaggerating. The scary thing is that I'm not. I haven't been able to stop eating since Bonnie was here. The two and a half days she was here plus the three since then are the longest-running binge I've had since before I started this diet. The thought of running on Saturday—today is Thursday—isn't stopping me. Nor is the thought that if I keep eating like this, I'll end up with a net weight gain for the month and I'll have to tell *Shape*. This is how it is when I binge: tomorrow and next week and consequences cease to exist. There is just what I want now and how I'm going to get it.

Every day since Bonnie left, I've tried to stop. I've gotten up, eaten my breakfast—Special K, milk, banana—and gone to the gym. So far, so good. But it seems like only more food will cure the almost inexplicable, uncontrollable hunger I get the morning after a binge, as if the binge has literally stretched my stomach. I picture the things I've eaten in the past few hours—muffins, a calzone, a brownie, and cantaloupe (my pathetic attempt to eat at least one healthy thing)—all sitting whole in my stomach, in cartoon colors, pushing out my stomach into strange shapes, as if it were a balloon at the hands of a child's birthday party clown.

Jennie wrote to me that she didn't even like to drive twenty miles. Now I have run that distance, feeling the entire time that I'm going to throw up because I'm so full.

In diets past, I would have given up the exercise the moment I started bingeing. But the marathon training has become more than a way to burn calories. It's something to master besides my appetite. And I'll be damned if I'm going to let food keep me from crossing the finish line.

Today was a great day for running—cooler than it's been in ages—but I couldn't enjoy it. I didn't talk, and I didn't listen. Instead I concentrated literally on putting one foot in front of the other, thinking about lifting my knee as if it could be done only if I concentrated hard enough. I calculated the calories I was burning and the pathetically small amount of food—at least compared to what I've eaten over the past week—that the run would burn off.

Today is the one-week mark. I've eaten virtually nonstop for one whole week. Now in my mind the cartoon food (all in its whole, unchewed form) has filled my entire body, a gruesome collage of gluttony.

I'm terrified that nothing in the world—not the prospect of my jeans not fitting, not the prospect of dealing with *Shape* or anyone else—is ever going to stop me from eating. The weight gain last Wednesday didn't. The run hasn't. This awful, horrible weighed-down-by-my-own-body feeling hasn't.

And hating myself hasn't.

I can't explain what takes over when I binge: how I can know how destructive it is and yet, in the moment, just absolutely not care. When I binge, it's like being in midair, free of everything: the possibility of weight gain and the nagging fears that what I do is not normal, that it's sick. Except I can't hover in midair for long. Eventually I have to land. I have to deal.

Finally e-mailed Shari an official invitation to attend my pity party: I can't stop eating. Except for the baby carrots in the fridge—I'm not eating *them*.

I didn't detail the bingeing, just said I'd had a friend in town last week and hadn't been able to get back on track.

She told me to stop thinking so much and go for a run, to eat an entire bag of baby carrots, if necessary, when I want to eat, and to e-mail her a list of everything I ate from that moment on. Suddenly it all seemed so simple, so doable. As simple as that, I thought, OK, I'm going to do this. Someone is expecting me to. Someone wants me to.

Which begs one question: why is the fact that I want to not enough?

It's been twenty-four hours back on the diet, and already I can feel my resolve slipping. Going back to a diet after having been off it is much harder than starting fresh. There's no joy of the new, none of the sense of possibility. There's only endless thought about how long it might take to undo the damage I've caused, plus dread of constant hunger—and the failure that inevitably seems to follow that.

I've eaten two and a half bags of baby carrots in the past two days and nothing else except my exactly-according-to-plan meals, which I'm psyched to e-mail Shari. Frankly, the thought of eating so much as one more carrot is so unappealing that when I want to eat, I just don't. Why can I not get sick of, say, chocolate like that?

E-mail from *Shape*'s photo people saying that after the half marathon they think they'd next like to photograph me when I get to 160 pounds, and when do I think I'll be there? As if I could predict such a thing. That's when I realized I really haven't lost any weight all summer: I've just been losing and gaining the same two pounds, and now there's the six I've just gained.

When do I think I'll be at 160? "The Twelfth of Never," I want to e-mail back. I've never weighed 160 in my entire adult life, and at the rate I'm going, I'll be lucky just to get back down to 169 (which sounds better than 170). Thanks to my six-pound gain, I'm currently at 175. Which I know nine months ago I would have given anything to weigh, but now it seems scarily close to 180, which is scarily close to 190 . . . which is then only a few binges away from 200.

Diet advice, courtesy of *Cosmo*: every time you feel like having a hot fudge sundae, have sex instead.

Considering that the closest I've come to having sex recently is the screaming orgasm shot this guy sent me at a bar because he decided I looked like Monica Lewinsky, I have a vague sense that said tip is not going to work.

Lost two pounds. Two more pounds to go before I get back to 169. Considering my progress of late, I cannot imagine hanging on long enough to get there.

Ever since my friend Matt quoted me in an article he wrote for the *Fort Lauderdale Sun-Sentinel* when we were in high school, I've had zero trouble understanding why some of the people I call for my own stories don't want to be interviewed. I doubt Matt meant to, but he took my quote out of context, and I sounded like an idiot.

Which is how I sounded today. This radio station wanted to interview me about the *Shape* project, so I agreed, stupidly thinking there was only so much damage I could do in the two minutes max I was sure I'd be allotted on morning drive time.

I hardly got the chance to do any damage. The DJ did it all by herself. She had sounded so friendly on the phone the other day, but during the interview . . . well, she made me feel like some sort of circus freak, with her commenting on how unhealthy and heavy I was and repeating my starting weight on the air so many times I was starting to wonder if she was getting a cash bonus for each mention. She didn't seem to care that I'd lost any weight; she was obsessed with the idea of how anybody lets herself get to 206 pounds in the first place. She also made me feel deviant for ever craving blueberry muffins, by her insinuating that "normal" people—apparently, "normal" people like her—always confine their cravings to chocolate. Since I've never met her in person, I can only imagine she's one of those women who prances around in a string bikini, complaining loudly about how fat she is. (Anybody who thinks she's *that* fat doesn't walk around in a string bikini.)

I was hoping this morning was one of those cases when other people would think I sounded a whole lot better than I thought I did, but somehow I doubt it. No one has said anything except, "I heard you on the radio this morning," and then they give me what seems like a knowing little smile. I don't weigh 206 pounds anymore, but today I feel like the number is written in red across my forehead and every bit of fat on my body has been circled with Magic Marker, as was supposedly done to some sorority pledges in an infamous story told endlessly while I was in college.

I'm not 206 pounds, but I feel as fat as ever. I have trouble buying dessert without wondering if the person selling it to me is thinking, *So that's how she got so big*. It's practically a reflex to look for an XL at the Gap. And when I look at pictures of myself in an attempt to see proof that I look different, I still automatically try to pick myself out of a group by looking for the biggest figure.

I'm a size 12 and sometimes 10, but I look in the mirror and my brain morphs it into a funhouse mirror. On one level I know that, but still I can't stop myself. So *Shape* has a new expert they want me to consult: a body-image specialist. I never even knew such people existed.

It wasn't an auspicious beginning when she told me she wanted me to meditate. What's next? I wanted to ask. I know meditation isn't that out there anymore, but I still couldn't help wondering if next she'd have me dancing around naked, banging on African drums, and chanting affirmations like, "I am thin and beautiful."

But considering that in the past I've gone to crazy lengths (eating just four peaches a day and nothing else) to lose weight, I figured I should at least listen to this woman if there was a chance she could rid me of the ability to make myself so miserable.

She told me that because I've struggled with food and weight for so long, I don't see my body very clearly. No kidding. I told her about the (ridiculously Courtney-centric) thoughts that litter my brain, such as that people at a party are all noticing that my stomach sticks out in my jeans, and she didn't make me feel like a freak. She just said that, as with losing weight, stopping my toxic thoughts won't happen overnight.

Since I have a race coming up, I also told her about my paranoia that the spectators are secretly laughing at me.

"What is the evidence that these people are even looking at you?" she asked. "Most people are thinking about themselves. Maybe they're thinking, 'Gosh, how does anybody run that far?'"

I like this woman. I just wish I could believe her.

Something to obsess about besides food. A guy I met at a party last week—and didn't bother writing down that I had met because I'm a cynic and didn't want to jinx it—actually called. We ended up talking for an hour, and I had to grab another call before we fixed a date to get margaritas. (We both don't like beer.) Said I'd call him back but realized I didn't have his number and sent three emergency e-mails to Mary trying to figure out what to do before remembering she was out of the office.

I track down phone numbers almost every day as part of my job, but it seems a little stalkeresque to employ those skills here. If I don't call him, though, will he even give it a second thought? Will he think I'm blowing him off (which is what I would assume if the situation were reversed)? Or will he pick over the conversation in his mind, wonder if he shouldn't have said this or that, and suddenly realize he never gave me his number? Then again, I'm going to take a wild guess that because Mars versus Venus is a gazillion-dollar industry, men do not think this way.

Nothing is ever enough. I put on my jeans today for the first time in nearly two months—it's been so hot that wearing jeans has been unthinkable. With all the eating I've done recently, I should have been relieved that they still fit, but instead I almost cried in frustration that they weren't any looser.

I want a vacation from dealing with food. I'm either starving (or feel like I am) or bingeing, and either way the thoughts of food are constant. Not only do I want my jeans to be looser for obvious reasons (I want to be thinner) but I want my jeans looser because I feel like I deserve it. I want a reward just for having to deal.

Mile 12 of the 13.1-mile half marathon, and I wasn't thinking about Mark the photographer (no Molly today) or the fact that I'd almost finished. (Me, who once could barely run one mile!) Instead I was looking at the spectators, all of whom seemed to be staring at me. I was convinced they were thinking, *What is that fat girl doing running?* I was wishing I could hide, since I was sure they were laughing at my skimpy running outfit, a necessary evil, since it was ninety-eight degrees and anything else chafes.

Two guys—running buddies of mine—made me especially self-conscious. They kept poking each other then pointing to Mark (he was on a bike, riding ahead of me, then hopping off to take pictures) and saying loudly, "Who's that girl with the photographer? I think she's on that new NBC show." More than one spectator yelled: "Hey, can I get your autograph?"

Mary is off doing a triathlon(!) this weekend, so it was just Abby and me and the guys, and the guys thought this was the funniest thing ever. They clowned around for the camera until Mark finally asked them to stop; he said all of those photos would be unusable.

As I got sweatier, I got crankier. When Mark yelled, "Smile!" at mile 9, I would have yelled back, "I don't feel like it!" except it wasn't worth the breath.

Afterward, he took a picture of me eating a banana—please, please, please, don't let *Shape* run that one!—and chugging water, then of the guys and me having a water fight. Thank God I didn't wear a white T-shirt.

I finished in 2:15—just over ten-minute miles, which I was happy with, considering how hot and miserable it was.

Then I went to pick up my finishers' T-shirt.

The guy asked, "5K or half marathon?"

"Half marathon," I answered, and his eyes widened.

I was about to say something self-deprecating or defensive but suddenly realized he hadn't even asked me my size, just automatically handed me a medium T-shirt. Not an XL, not even an L—an M. That's when I saw a big red stop sign of the kind the body-image expert had told me to imagine whenever I thought negative thoughts. For half a second, I allowed myself to consider: maybe he's actually impressed. Thirteen miles *is* kind of far. Maybe, just maybe, he's thinking what I would have thought a year ago: "I wish I could do that."

Month 10 (October)

I haven't been able to write for days because I don't want to be alone with my thoughts. Yes, I've been bingeing again, with an abandon that scares even me.

I'm not particularly religious—God is reserved mostly for silent bargaining at hospitals and exams—but I am convinced something terrible is going to happen to me because I started this bingeing streak on Yom Kippur, the Day of Atonement. Not at the break-the-fast after Yom Kippur but *on* Yom Kippur. While I was supposed to be fasting.

Alexy and I had gone to the supermarket to buy some of the food we needed for the break-the-fast party she was hosting. When we parted at the corner, she went to her apartment to cook and I walked into the first café I saw. I bought two blueberry muffins and ate them on the four-minute walk home, panicking about what I would say if anyone I knew caught me. When I got home, my phone was ringing. It was Diana talking about how much she wished she could sleep away Yom Kippur because it's so hard to fast.

I tried to listen, but I felt so guilty I couldn't concentrate. Yom Kippur is a difficult holiday for anyone who's trying to learn moderation, as I am. There is no middle ground with fasting: you can't do it halfway.

I got off the phone and tore through my kitchen. Shredded low-fat cheese and huge handfuls of dry cereal. I was eating just to eat, and I knew it. But as usual, in the moment it didn't matter. Nothing mattered except eating.

After a week of bingeing—and in a binge-induced fit of desperation—I came clean to *Shape* today, about gaining weight.

I didn't use the word *binge*—too scary. Too much like a serious problem. I don't know if it was a conscious decision, but I also didn't use the phrase *pig out.* Instead I wrote to Maureen that due to a "variety of circumstances" I'd been seriously slacking this month, to the point where I'd gained about five pounds. Actually, it's six: the two I still have to lose from my binges when Bonnie was here, plus four I've just gained from this last fit. I told Maureen I was getting panicked about the fact that I was going to look horrible and stupid and idiotic in print and that then I just kept eating—that it was a nasty cycle that sort of fueled itself. I couldn't resist ending my tale of woe on a positive note, fully aware of the irony that I usually struggle for the shiny happy spin in the column: I pointed out that I have been saintly about exercise. Which I actually have. Maybe I should give myself a break and think about how much worse off I would be if I hadn't been doing all this running.

Shape column number three hit print today. (No word on how they want to handle the weight gain.)

I wrote the column so many months ago that now it's almost painful to look at. I see the picture of a girl who is nineteen pounds thinner than when she started, but I don't find it inspirational. All I see is a girl who had no idea what was coming. I was so full of optimism then, so sure that this was going to be the time I actually finished what I had started—that I'd get all of the weight off. For good.

Now I feel like only stop-action photography could capture my transformation from thinner back to fat again—that the bingeing is going to make it happen that fast.

What makes the weight gain even worse is all the people rooting for me. I've gotten mail about articles I've written for the *Washingtonian*, but nothing like what the *Shape* column has brought in: letters—six pages, some of them—and photos and cards and inspirational sayings and, of course, diet tips.

It's strange having people I don't know learn such personal details about me, but it's stranger having the people I do know learn them. It's occurred to me that when I was a child, the mere idea that my sister had been snooping in my journal would be enough to send me into a rage, but here I am dumping it out for the world to see. Yes, this is different, because I'm supposedly in control. But words are like eggs—they hatch things that grow beyond your control.

Like *very* responsive readers. My phone number is listed, and I've already had a bunch of calls from around the country, including one from a thirty-four-year-old woman who keeps calling at around 10:00 P.M., wanting me to talk her off the Ben & Jerry's ledge.

I want to help her, and I try to. I probably wouldn't call a magazine writer at home for advice, but I definitely can relate to the desperation that leads to such an act. I want so badly to be able to give this woman the one nugget of advice that she's looking for—the one bit that will make a difference, that will make the diet she's attempting different from all the others that preceded it. But I'm still looking for the nugget myself.

Magarita Man—the non-beer-drinking guy from the party the other week—called to say he's traveling for the next two weeks. Ugh. At the rate I'm eating I'm going to be at least a size bigger by the next time I see him.

Meanwhile, I'm feeling totally idiotic, because I just read an art review by a guy I spent two hours talking to at another party and who had asked for my number and said we should go out. In this one tiny 150-word review he mentioned a girlfriend—*so* hate that style of writing—so how is it that in two hours I got nary a mention of this chick? What is with this guy, anyway? Note to self: ask Stephen for the guy view on how much time should elapse before mentioning a girlfriend. Personally, I think the tipping point is somewhere around a half hour—too much earlier and the guy's being pretty conceited, thinking that wanting to date him might be the only reason you're chatting. But too much later is just not fair.

If—upon hearing I'm running a marathon—one more person says, "You must be able to eat whatever you want," I'll be so torn between screaming and crying that I just might spontaneously combust. I *cannot* eat whatever I want, because eating things other than what I'm "supposed" to eat—at least according to Peeke—induces fear and panic. I worry not just about burning off whatever extra I eat but about how full it's going to make me.

This morning I realized—in that blinding flash that comes when you can finally put a name to something that's been there all along—that while being really hungry inspires panic (When am I going to get to eat? What if I can't wait that long? And what if I can't get rid of this hungry feeling?), so does feeling full. Even if the fullness comes because I've eaten something as innocent as two bags of baby carrots—just the feeling sends me into a tailspin. I associate fullness with bingeing and with being fat. I think; therefore I am. I am full; therefore I am fat.

I am also cranky and frustrated. I'm tired of running and, on alternate days, using the elliptical trainer, but I'm afraid to try any new form of cross-training—like roller-blading—because I'm afraid I'll break or sprain something and miss the marathon after all this training. (Ditto for a pair of extra-high heels I wanted to buy myself as a treat.) Fear and anxiety about the marathon are making me want to eat and eat and eat, and the only thing stopping me is, of course, the marathon. I'll hate myself more than ever if, because I can't stop eating everything in sight for a few weeks, I ruin something I've been working on for nearly six months. For now I've given up praying that I'll stop bingeing for good. Now I just concentrate on getting through one hour without bingeing. Then the next. And then the next. Call it the ultra-marathon of the mind.

I have a new obsession: that I'm going to get injured in these last three weeks before the marathon, and it's not even going to be a glamorous injury, like from rock climbing or skiing. It's going to be a klutzy, lame injury—the sort that sounds like I made it up just to avoid running the damn race. This morning I banged my right ankle getting off the cross-trainer. And then I slipped getting out of the shower. If I could swathe myself in bubble wrap for the next three weeks, I just might consider it.

My other new obsession is slightly healthier. I'm going to move to London—not someday, not when I get around to looking into it, but on March 1, about six months from now. I've always wanted to live abroad, and lately I've had this acute sense of the passage of time, maybe because an ever-increasing percentage of mine seems to be taken up with diet and exercise and bingeing.

I have a friend from college living in London who has the amazing ability to make absolutely anything I want to do seem possible. I'm going to visit Elizabeth after the marathon, and when we talked today, leaving my friends, quitting my perfectly good job without another in sight, and moving across the Atlantic to an outrageously expensive place where it's gray half the year seemed like a totally rational idea. If not now, when?

The conversation with Elizabeth was a blur of plans and pep talks. For the half hour we spent on the phone collaborating on the invention of the new transatlantic Courtney, I felt so free of everything, from whether this guy from the other day will ever call me right on up to bingeing and paralyzing self-doubt, such as whether I'll ever make it as a writer. When I hung up the phone, all the fears came flooding back and I wondered whether running to London isn't just another attempt to escape myself—if moving is just the latest in a long line of things (losing weight and finding a great pair of black pants among them) that I think will make my life perfect—and whether Elizabeth is just the latest in a long line of gurus (like Peeke before her) who I've decided have all the answers.

A woman at the cash machine asked me if I was the girl who wrote for *Shape*, then told me I was "beautiful." No kidding. I wanted to ask her if she meant beautiful in the picture in this month's column or beautiful now, after I'm not even sure how many weeks of bingeing and then halfhearted dieting. I wanted to drag this girl to the nearest grocery store to grab a copy of the magazine so I could quiz her about whether I look thinner now than I do in the picture. I wanted to ask her what she'd think if she knew that the girl who initially was so faithful to the diet she lost nineteen pounds in the first two months—such an amazing weight loss that *Shape* mentioned it on the cover—now couldn't seem to manage two days in a row on the diet, let alone two months. I wanted to tell her I needed help and to grill her for any little tip, the way the Ben-&-Jerry's-eating *Shape* reader who calls me at home does.

But I didn't. And thankfully, she didn't ask me for advice herself, which these days makes me feel like a fraud.

I got my cash and went to meet Mary for a movie. The desire to binge is so strong that in the past few days I haven't even been able to think about getting through an hour without doing it, because that amount of time seems like an eternity. I have to divide the hour into manageable pieces, the way you do when you have a project that seems too monstrous to be one line on your to-do list. So I concentrated on walking from the ATM to the Metro—a short walk where I pass three convenience stores, two bakeries, and three coffee bars—without stopping in any of them. When I got safely to the Metro, where eating is not allowed, I was grateful still to be living in D.C. and not London, where there are candy bar machines inside every Tube stop.

Still no official word from *Shape* about how the weight gain will be handled in print—or whether it will be. Between worrying about this and worrying about the marathon, all I want to do is eat.

The night before the marathon. I'm a mess. Erica, my best friend from college, has come down from New York to cheer me on, and we rented a movie

I now can't remember a thing about. I worry that I've eaten too much at the prerace pasta dinner. I worry that I'll oversleep. I worry that it will rain. I worry that I won't be able to find my friends and I'll have to run alone. I worry that I'll lose the computer chip on my sneaker and my race time won't count.

I can't sleep. I worry that I'm not getting any sleep.

I did it! I ran the marathon yesterday. Twenty-six-point-two miles. I even have the medal to prove it.

About 7:45 A.M. yesterday morning—which feels like a lifetime ago—Mary, Abby, Stacy, Dagny, and I assembled by the Porta Potties. We worried that we'd miss the starting gun while waiting in line. We tried not to look at the red and yellow balloon arch that read "FINISH." Shortly before 8:30, we joined more than twenty thousand other runners pushing and shoving down a grassy hill slippery with dew.

Great, I thought. *I'll break my ankle just before the starting line.*

Waiting for the gun, I had the caged-in feeling I sometimes get on airplanes: this is it—once we're up in the air there's no way to get off, even if we're about to crash.

I could always just stop running. But I had vowed that after all the training I would crawl across the finish line if I had to.

All along, my family had seemed skeptical. They treated my training like a fad I would outgrow. I didn't think they believed I could finish, and even though I wondered myself, I resented that they did.

I'd been told the marathon was really two races: the first twenty miles and then the last six. Much of the first twenty are a blur, although I'm pretty sure I wouldn't have made it through them without the crowds.

Probably the best piece of advice I got was to write my name across the front of my shirt so people could yell it as I ran by. I had no idea how thrilling it could be to have someone you've never met high-five you and yell your name until you were out of sight.

I remember funny things the spectators did, like blasting Gloria Gaynor's "I Will Survive" as we ran around the dreaded Haines Point, an infamously long and boring section of the route. There was a guy at mile 16 who made us laugh by beating on a drum and yelling "Run! Run! You've got great buns!" (Another yelled, not so helpfully, "You only have a ten-miler left to go!") A handful of women called out, "Just think—you can eat whatever you want when you're done!" I didn't smile at that.

Passing through a water stop staffed by U.S. Marines, I had to laugh. *This has to be the only athletic event on the planet*, I thought, *where the volunteers are in better shape than the competitors.*

Much of the time I felt as though I were in a cheesy, this-is-your-life video: my friend Erica at mile 10 and points beyond, Alexy by the Reflecting Pool, Kelly somewhere in the middle. I got teary-eyed when an unexpected friend popped up, waving a sign or calling my name.

By the last six miles things had gotten so tense that Mary, Abby, and I were barely speaking. (We'd lost Stacy and Dagny along the way.)

The three of us had promised to finish together—something veterans had told us would be nearly impossible, because pace falls apart in the end—but Mary was having trouble with her knee.

Mary was about thirty feet behind Abby and me, with our friend Betina, who had come to run the last ten miles with us. I was torn about whether to slow my pace. Slowing down was painful by that point, and if I stopped running, I didn't know if I could start again.

"Go ahead," Mary said, but I knew she didn't mean it. I made a last effort to slow down, but physically I couldn't. At the prerace pasta dinner she'd been talking about us doing the Rock 'n' Roll Marathon in San Diego next year, but she looked so annoyed I wondered if we'd even be speaking then.

Our strategy for getting through long runs had been to obsess about small things: not "How will I get through this?" but "I wish So-and-So would shut up" or "These shorts are beginning to chafe."

To take my mind off the race, I decided to be annoyed that my parents hadn't shown up. They were driving down from New Jersey to bring my sister her car anyway, so couldn't they at least stop by? This is only the biggest thing I've ever done, I thought. If I get married, are they going to skip the wedding?

As we neared the end, all I could think was: "One foot in front of the other, one foot in front of the other." I counted steps. I looked down, because however close the finish line was, it wasn't close enough.

I'd heard horror stories about the last two-tenths of a mile uphill to the Iwo Jima Memorial, how the slight rise would feel like Mount Everest. I didn't notice.

I saw friends who'd already finished, and somehow I picked up speed. As Abby and I crossed the finish line, I saw my parents and my sister. They'd shown up after all.

"That was a great act of physical courage, ma'am," said the Marine who put the medal around my neck. Another wrapped me in a Mylar blanket, and a third unlaced the computer chip from my shoe.

Abby cried. Mary collapsed against us. Someone took pictures. I was numb. So much of my life for the past six months had been about getting here, and now it was over.

At home the phone rang nonstop. "Running a marathon must be like having a baby," I told everyone who called. "You need a while to forget about the pain before you can do it again."

Erica and I went to Pizzeria Paradiso to celebrate. (Mom and Dad had gone back to New Jersey maybe twenty minutes after I crossed the finish line—Dad had to work.) Erica tried to make me wear my marathon finishers' T-shirt, but I wouldn't. So she settled for stopping everyone we passed who was wearing one and saying that I had done the marathon, too. She also told any person who so much as looked our way.

This morning at work I traded e-mails with Dagny, who'd loved every moment of the race.

"I still can't believe I did it," I wrote. "It all feels like a dream—until I try to go downstairs with what feel like eighty-year-old knees.

"But I am HOOKED. See you next year?"

Have not gotten on the scale for two weeks, making excuses (ran outside, overslept) to Peeke—and to myself—for why I haven't gone to the gym on Wednesday mornings, weigh-in days. (If *Shape* is going to fire me—I still haven't heard from them, and I'm too afraid to bring up the subject myself—I don't need to suffer more by looking at the number on the scale.)

I don't need the scale to tell me I've gained weight. Nothing fits. I ran around today looking for a dress for Halloween—Mary, Abby, and I decided to do the eighties high school prom girl thing: frosted pink lip gloss, poufy teased hair, and even poufier dresses. After going to six thrift stores—all full of last-minute costume seekers holding up random items of clothing and saying things like, "Do you think I could be a pirate in this?"—I finally found a shiny turquoise monstrosity. It looks more sixties than eighties, but I don't care. The important thing is that it fits. It's a size 16. All I can hope is that it really is true that clothing sizes were smaller in the sixties.

Month 11 (November)

*T*he marathon is over, and so is a week of people—mostly women—saying, "Your body must still think it's on mile 24—I bet you can eat whatever you want."

So how did I celebrate that *and* the first day of November—or, as an overly cheery substitute teacher used to write on the blackboard, the first day of the rest of my life? I went to Dunkin' Donuts for breakfast with Mary—who, a week after the marathon, is still occasionally frosty to me about it—and Abby.

Two jelly doughnuts later, I headed to an appointment with Peeke, worrying that she would have some insidious way (a hair test? laser vision?) of telling where I had been for breakfast. I told her I had done the marathon, and she didn't seem surprised.

"I always knew you were an athlete," she said and hugged me.

Unfortunately, my haphazard eating—and that's putting it nicely—has been neutralizing all of my "well-intentioned athletics," as Peeke says. We didn't discuss the how and why, which made me wonder if the reason for the face time (something I've had with her about three times in ten months) was so she could see just how bad I looked.

She announced she was calling off the *Shape* project for a month or two, and instead of being relieved, I just wanted to ask her to tell me honestly if it was because I looked like I'd gained weight.

Instead I nodded as she talked about how I needed to regroup—how I needed to use this as a learning experience (no matter how much I exercise, I *can't* eat whatever I want) and how the diet was like mile 24 of the marathon (apparently I've now been upgraded from mile 5 of the 10K) and I just had to hang in there.

I do feel better after talking with her. Now if only I didn't have to go off to London next week. It occurs to me that I have yet to manage a week's vacation in my adult life without bingeing. But I've *got* to. My jeans are already on the verge of not fitting—I'm afraid to wash them for fear they'll shrink the tiniest bit. I can't afford more bingeing. I'm hoping that just knowing I've told Peeke I'll e-mail her every day while I'm away will keep me in check.

Turns out Peeke can't temporarily call off the *Shape* project, though to ease the pressure she got them to agree not to photograph me for a month. After all this dreading, what *Shape* said about my writing about gaining weight ended up being pretty similar to what they had said about writing about losing it: don't be too negative. And end on a positive note.

SOMEWHERE OVER THE ATLANTIC

Thankfully, despite boredom and frustration (and fear—this is a really bumpy flight; shouldn't I be able to have cheesecake, even if it's crappy airplane cheesecake, before I die?), I've managed to do OK on food. I wouldn't let the flight attendants serve me dinner or breakfast—just ate my own food so I wouldn't even have to consider what on the tray was appropriate. And I didn't do my usual airport pig-out, which I'm sure was partly because I bumped into an old friend.

Frankly, I'm terrified about this trip. I know Elizabeth likes to eat late, eat dessert, and drink wine—all of which could be a disaster. I know there's nothing I *have* to eat, but I loathe seeming so lame. And eating late is tough. I guess I'll carry the protein bars Peeke recommends (though they taste like dog food) in my bag and eat them in the bathroom if I have to.

Last night before I left, Diana came over. She does not fear flying, as I do, but she always insists on seeing me before I go on a trip, "just in case."

She showed up at my door with her new cat, and as Fred started sharpening his claws on my mattress, Diana and I had one of these very honest conversations we have maybe once every couple of years. One minute she was looking at the clothes I had scattered around (but didn't want to try on in front of her in case they didn't fit), and the next I was spilling out that I thought I might have an eating disorder.

Earlier today, as I was poking around on eBay, looking for a guitar (yet another in a long line of things I think will make my life perfect), I snapped.

The guitar made me think of my fear of playing in public, which made me think about all the things I will never do while I am overweight. So I looked around some diet websites, searching for something inspirational. For months I've come across mentions of binge eating disorder and immediately dismissed it as yet another excuse for being overweight, like "I'm big boned" or "I have a slow metabolism." But today I felt desperate enough to think (hope?) that if enough people do something like what I do for it to have an official name, maybe it also has an official solution. So I clicked on a description of binge eating disorder from the *Diagnostic and Statistical Manual of Mental Disorders* on the American Psychiatric Association's website:

1. Recurrent episodes of binge eating. An episode of binge eating is characterized by both of the following:
   - eating, in a discrete period of time (e.g., within any two-hour period), an amount of food that is definitely larger than most people would eat in a similar period of time under similar circumstances
   - a sense of lack of control over eating during the episode (e.g., a feeling that one cannot stop eating or control what or how much one is eating)

That is me, I thought grimly, reading faster and faster.

2. The binge eating episodes are associated with at least three of the following:
   - eating much more rapidly than normal
   - eating until feeling uncomfortably full
   - eating large amounts of food when not feeling physically hungry
   - eating alone because of being embarrassed by how much one is eating
   - feeling disgusted with oneself, depressed, or feeling very guilty after overeating
3. Marked distress regarding binge eating.
4. The binge eating occurs, on average, at least two days a week for six months.
5. The binge eating is not associated with the regular use of inappropriate compensatory behaviors (e.g., purging, fasting, excessive exercise) and does not occur exclusively during the course of anorexia nervosa or bulimia nervosa.

I read the whole thing three times, slowly, wondering if the "two days a week for six months" disqualified me, or maybe the "inappropriate compensatory behaviors"? After all, I've tried to starve. . . .

Then I noticed a warning above the description: "It is important to note that you *can* still suffer from BED even if one of the below signs is not present. In other words, if you think you have BED, it's dangerous to read the diagnostic criteria and think, 'I don't have one of the symptoms, so I must not have it.'"

I felt both heartened and horrified. Heartened because this description of my eating habits in an actual book means that I am probably not the only person who does these things. Horrified because the book is one of mental disorders, which suggests that stopping bingeing may not be as simple as exercising a little willpower—or having the pressure of the watchful eyes of thousands of magazine readers upon me.

Binge eating disorder, I learned, is sometimes called the "forgotten eating disorder," because it receives so little attention. Diana had never heard of it. When she heard the term *eating disorder*, the first thing she said was, "Are you bulimic?"

No, I told her, though there are times I have tried to throw up. I told her my understanding of binge eating disorder—that it is bulimia, only without the purging. She tried to be sympathetic, but her questions about it ended up making me feel like a zoo animal. ("Hey, look, honey—it eats *eucalyptus!*") She kept saying she couldn't understand the bingeing—how I could buy all that food in the first place, much less eat it (any bit of it) in public? What I couldn't make her understand is that I *am* ashamed of doing that, and the shame of it just fuels the cycle.

Then again, everything seems to fuel the cycle.

IN LONDON

I spent my first day in London jet-lagged, sitting in an Internet café just off Trafalgar Square, writing what I have privately nicknamed my "weight-gain diary." I couldn't write honestly about what, specifically, made me gain weight—I'm still trying to figure that out. So I ended up writing that after months of practicing healthful habits, it's terrifying how fragile I still am. In the beginning months of the diet, I'd trained my body so that after a few days of eating poorly I'd actually wake up craving cantaloupe and salad. But after the past few months of haphazard eating, the "healthy food, please!" mechanism just isn't kicking in again.

I wrote about the stress of the project itself: "I thought having *Shape* readers follow along with me would be the world's best motivation, but sometimes it spurred me to new heights of destructive eating patterns. I'd slip up for a few days and then be so stressed about ending up with a loss for the month and looking good in the photo that I'd eat more. Then I'd try to eat less than I should for a few days to make up for it, which only made me pig out in the end."

For the record, the plan for the photo this month is an empty pint of Ben & Jerry's with a spoon in it. I'm sure some friend will see the column and comment not about what I said but about whether that's my spoon and whether I got to eat the ice cream.

In the column I deliberately used *pig-out* and not *binge*. *Pig-out* requires no explanation—everyone understands it, though it means different amounts of food to different people. But *binge*—*binge* is a word that calls attention to itself. If I used the word *binge*, I knew I'd have to explain why and how it's different from a pig-out, and that was not something I was ready to admit to myself, much less in print. Yes, I told Diana I thought I might have a problem, but mostly I told her hoping she'd roll her eyes and tell me to stop being ridiculous and melodramatic. "You don't have an eating disorder," I could practically hear her saying. "You just eat too much." But she didn't.

For "current weight" I put 180—a gain of 11 pounds. It's an estimate. I haven't been able to make myself get on the scale.

Tonight Elizabeth and I went to a fair after Guy Fawkes Day fireworks on Clapham Common. We got some candy floss—that's British for "cotton candy"—and Elizabeth talked about how much she loves sausage and peppers and also fried chicken, something I never would have expected. Greasy fingers do not go with my image of Elizabeth in her fabulous vintage coats and pearls.

Elizabeth and I have known each other for four years, but we've never talked about food—until this trip. She's been full of questions about the *Shape* column, which she'd heard about from a friend of hers who saw it. I had never told her about it—Elizabeth has this image of me as always on the verge of writing the next great American novel. I didn't want to tell her that instead of writing about the green light at the end of Daisy's dock, I was writing about my inability to control my weight.

Last night we didn't eat dinner before going to the theater and were ravenous when we got home. I was having grapefruit, but Elizabeth was tearing through bread and Greek cucumber dressing. When at first I mistook the container of dressing for chive cream cheese, she looked horrified. "Do you think I'd be eating it like that?" she said.

I stopped short of saying, "Well, *I* have." It was the first time I've heard her sound aware of calories or fat—Elizabeth, who once told me that she just can't worry about food most of the time and that, anyway, she hasn't met a single guy who preferred Twiggy. Easy for her to say—she's a single-digit size with no major effort. Last I checked, she owned one pair of running shoes—and she bought them sometime in the late 1980s.

Thank God for Elizabeth—or whoever up there seems determined to keep me from bingeing. I can't duck off from her for more than a second, and I'm not even that frustrated by it. I think it's destiny that I *not* binge on this trip. I tried to sneak off after we got off the tube last night—said I needed to buy a Diet Coke—but Elizabeth insisted on coming with me. (I did manage to sneak an extra Cadbury's chocolate in addition to the one I ate publicly.) The one other lapse was when we were at the cinema: I ducked off to go to the bathroom and bought a chocolate muffin. I didn't even really want it—would've much preferred a cream scone I saw earlier today. But it's a habit: the sneaking, the stockpiling just so I won't have to say I'm hungry (much less actually be hungry) later. Must go running tomorrow before consuming huge amounts of chili and bread-and-butter pudding at the Sunday lunch we're planning.

Ran for sixty-five minutes today—got a bit lost—and (victory!) didn't eat the popcorn at the movies just because it was there. I was stuffed from lunch, anyway—the chili.

Debating extending my vacation and going to Barcelona for a few days. I got an e-mail from a friend who lives there, and he was urging me to come on over. I so hate for food to be the determinant of what I do, but I guess I should wait and see if I start bingeing. I know that once I start bingeing on a vacation it's a free-fall, and I won't be able to stop. Every morning I'll wake up promising myself I'll stop, but I'll end up clinging to the idea that I'll stop the minute I get home—clinging to the idea of home the way a lapsed November dieter clings to the idea of January 1 and New Year's resolutions.

Some people come to Europe and find inspiration for novels, short stories, and films. A week in London, and I've written in my journal not about the people I've met or the shows I've seen or the quirky things I've noticed or the long talks Elizabeth and I have had. I've written about food: What I'm eating. What I'm not eating. What I want to be eating.

Have eaten nonstop for two days. Loads and loads of chocolate. Not sure what kicked it off—possibly the constant worrying that I *would* binge, the constant refusing of food, and the constant mental noting of what I have and haven't eaten already balanced against what I might eat later.

I have a pair of black pants with me that I now can't button. Feel like I need tent-size tops to hide the doughnut of fat around my middle created by too-tight jeans. And now I'm in Barcelona. I'm trying not to wish I'd just gone back to D.C. yesterday, as planned, but it's not working. I can't stop binge-ing. I keep thinking that if I'd gone home yesterday, today I'd be getting back on track. But it's not about location—it's about me.

I'm trying to convince myself that everything happens for a reason, even if I have no idea what the reason is while it's happening. Maybe I'm going to meet the love of my life on the 3:00 A.M. bus to Barcelona's airport?

Ha.

Finally back home, and panicking because I have just a week and a half to stem this disastrous tide of overeating before heading to New Jersey for Thanksgiving. Feeling fat—though as Shari repeatedly tells me, fat is not a feeling. At least I was the diet saint today, though I could manage only twenty-five minutes at the gym.

Today was, as I've privately been referring to it all week, the Last Thanksgiving Predivorce. I was dreading it—and joking that I'd have to take notes for my novel—and now that it's over, I'm not sure what to think.

Diana and I missed a big chunk of it. She got a flat tire last night, and since we drove around until 1:00 A.M. or so looking for a place to buy a tire (I could have told her we wouldn't find any), we got a late start this morn-ing. And predictably, there was traffic, so we didn't end up getting to New Jersey until nearly 5:00 P.M. Mom's guilt trip—for showing up late and not helping—stopped at all ports of call. Secretly, I was glad to have missed all the yelling that goes with Mom as perpetually frazzled hostess: yelling for helping, yelling for not helping, yelling for being in the way. . . . I think Mom's getting frazzled when she has people over must have started happening in the past few years, since I can't imagine she could have gotten quite this crazy in the days—twenty-five years ago—when she used to like to throw huge parties. It doesn't fit with what we used to hear about Mom as entertainer, organized and efficient. And I'm instantly uncomfortable with frazzled Mom—it reminds me too much of The Beginning of the End, my melodramatic way of thinking about our bat mitzvah, which is when we started to notice something was wrong with her.

There was more food than I remember there ever being, probably because Mom made spanakopita in an attempt to use up the phyllo dough in the freezer before she and Dad go their separate ways in a month and a half. "Need to use it up" was also the reason given for the acorn squash and the forlorn pile of cocktail napkins imprinted with "Jerri & Eben." Then there was all the usual stuff, including mashed potatoes, which poor Mom left until late, hoping Diana (who's the reason we've always had two kinds of potatoes—she hated sweet potatoes as a kid) would arrive in time to peel the five-pound bag.

The conversation at dinner was the usual patchwork quilt, punctuated with long silences. Aunt Missy admired the new dining room table—which Grandma had bought this year as an early wedding anniversary present, just days before the divorce was announced. Uncle Ronny spent the time he wasn't eating reading the paper in the corner. Uncle Murray—in bolo tie—was doing his usual mischievous deliberate mixing up of names (calling me Diana) and equally deliberate mishearing of everything anyone says. He's been doing this sort of thing since Dad was a kid, and even Dad can't begin to guess what he might say.

Despite—or maybe because of—the impending divorce, Mom and Dad didn't really seem to be sniping any more than usual. Maybe because this is the way it's been for more than twenty-five years and they don't know any other way. All the guests were Dad's family (Grandma stayed in Florida, though she did call to recite what she'd eaten), and I wondered if we'd ever all be together like this again. Probably not.

During dinner, people kept disappearing in twos. Diana and Dad ducked off at one point for what I later found out was a discussion of one of Dad's latest electronic toys. When I found them, Diana went back to the table and

Dad and I ended up talking about the divorce and why he hadn't left the marriage earlier (because of us, he says). Then it was Mom and Aunt Missy going upstairs to measure Diana's and my old bedroom furniture. In case someone in the family wanted it.

When Dad and my little cousin David got up to go look at something on the computer, I decided it was my turn to leave. I wanted to play the piano—the one Grandma bought for Diana and me fifteen years ago. It's been sold with the house, and this is probably the last time I'll ever see it. I opened the piano bench, which for years has contained a history of my life in sheet music: the "Für Elise" I marked up for my first recital; the Springsteen "Thunder Road" I bought to give myself something to concentrate on besides a failed relationship. But the bench was empty—cleaned out and ready for its new owners. I wish I were.

After everyone left, Diana, Dad, Mom, and I stood around the kitchen. I felt sad looking at some of the dishes that were barely touched: the mashed potatoes, the special Jell-O heart Mom makes instead of cranberry sauce. I wanted to eat them myself, to make a big fuss over them, because I knew she would be pleased. The harder Mom tries to make things the way they always are (or always were), the more we all change or don't want them the old way anyway. I'm not the only one watching calories, and I know almost everyone at the table wished Mom had made a little less food than usual—but instead this year she'd made more.

The standing around the kitchen kibitzing, as my mother calls it, is the only part of our family Thanksgiving I think I'll miss. Teasing Dad about eating all the walnuts off the pumpkin pie. Teasing Diana about eating all the marshmallows off the sweet potatoes. Various dishes jogging our memories of other times they've been served and what happened at those events. For that ten minutes we feel like a family. Is food the only way we know how to connect? Is it all we really have in common?

Month 12 (December)

*I*n the never-ending search for the one thing that will magically restore my ability to stick to a diet, here's another possibility: time of day I work out. Today was the first day since I got back from London three weeks ago that I managed to get up before work and go to the gym. I've been going at night, which I think has been contributing to my haphazard eating. It's probably psychological, but there's something about going first thing in the morning that makes "I'm going to be good today" less of a vow and more of a reality.

This morning all the guys at the gym front desk and in the weight room asked me where I've been for the past few weeks. It was amazing to realize I've been at the gym at least five days a week for nearly a year—and that people have actually noticed.

Thanks partially to the 6:00 A.M. gym visit—which means that smug feeling of sitting at my desk knowing I've already accomplished something—today was one of those days where everything feels, if not right with my world, at least on its way to being OK.

I hate writing about other writers, particularly ones who are so much better than I can ever hope to be. I would much prefer to write such profiles in a question-and-answer format, so that none of my words clutter theirs.

I spent the morning trying to write the beginning of what is supposed to be a short profile of Natalie Angier, a *New York Times* science writer and author of *Woman: An Intimate Geography*. Except I'm stuck, and what are the chances our nice family magazine is going to let me open with: "A moment of silence, please, for the sadly shrinking clitoris. Despite *Cosmo*'s best efforts, it's actually wasting away from lack of use"?

I've never had any job besides writing, so it would be hard to defend my private (and semi-self-serving) contention that mine is among the professions least conducive to losing weight—chocolate taster and food critic not included. When I write, I wish yet again that my vices were cigarettes, liquor, or nail biting, because every time I struggle over a sentence I try to think of something that might make the writing easier and inevitably decide I'd be able to concentrate better if I weren't hungry.

More ammo for my idea that a social life is not conducive to dieting: got my fifth party invitation for the same Friday—the annual Christmas pileup. And I have something to do every night this week. And we're on deadline. And I'm leaving Saturday morning for a weekend in New York, including the party of a friend I haven't seen in ages. She e-mailed me about having seen the new *Shape* column (and picture), and I'm nervous because I think I looked better then. A lame excuse to avoid a party, I know, so I'm going anyway. Assuming I can find anything to wear, which—given that I refuse to buy size 14s again, which is what I seem to need—is probably not an assumption I should make.

This has been a week full of eating out and going out, but I've made it to the gym every day, and the part of my brain that looks at things like French fries and says, "not Courtney food" has finally switched back on. I forgot how good being in control feels.

I also forgot how crummy it feels to get on the scale knowing you've been good all week and not see the results you want. I've lost not one pound of the ten I gained—though I haven't been able to bear getting on the scale since before London, and I'm sure I gained weight there—so perhaps this week I lost whatever I gained while traveling? Either way, I'm at 180. Thousands of minutes of exercise and seven months of watching and weighing and wondering—and now I weigh about what I did at the end of Month 4.

Got up at 5:00—that's 5:00 A.M.—to make it to the gym before an 8:00 breakfast meeting. I needed the feeling of having worked out—I feel the binges coming on again.

Yesterday was a miserable day, the sort that makes me question everything about my life and the choices I've made. I wrote crap; was totally broken out (feeling shitty and zitty, as I told Mary); had no idea what to say to Mom when I talked to her in Florida, where she's looking for an apartment; and wanted to hang up on Grandma when she asked about my weight. I thought she'd be happy I had a bunch of parties to go to, but all she wanted to know was whether I had any "escorts" for them. So much for my idea that the silver lining of the divorce would be that she'd be less eager for me to get married.

After I felt fat and unmarriageable, next came poor and pathetic. Why, Grandma wanted to know, couldn't I get a holiday bonus like Diana did? Because I work for an ink-on-paper media company, not an Internet company.

I had too much cake at a birthday party and tried to make up for it later by not eating dinner, which by now I should know better than to do but still try every once in a while. Kind of the way my sister tries sweet potatoes every Thanksgiving—just to check and confirm that she does, indeed, still hate them.

So I narrowly managed not to binge today. I had to break the day up into little chunks of time to get through. I cannot imagine how I'm going to have the time and energy to plot a move to London in three months when it seems like 90 percent of my brain is consumed with a minute-by-minute struggle not to eat.

After a fiction reading I went to tonight, I had to fight the urge to stop into so many places on the walk home. I concentrated on remembering that horrible, full, tired, out-of-control feeling I get when I binge and how much more difficult that would make all the things I have to do this week. It worked. And I got home to discover that my purple (well, eggplant-colored) suit fits again. In dark moments I think I'd better wear it tomorrow, in case it doesn't fit again for a very long time.

E-mail from Diana saying that she saw a picture of me on the party page of a magazine and, "You look great!" That picture was taken three weeks ago. The skirt I'm wearing in it doesn't fit, even with control-top pantyhose. I know because I wanted to wear it today.

So today I wore the eggplant suit, attempting to stop myself from looking like an actual big round eggplant by wearing four-inch heels. I promptly fell on the rain-slicked pavement while running to a happy hour, and the woman who helped me up sort of peered at me and said, "Are you Courtney Rubin from *Shape*?" I stood there, hose ripped, knee (and ego) slightly bruised, while she told me how much better I look in real life than in the pictures. Hmmmph. Not sure how to interpret that.

Total parties I was invited to last night: five. Parties I made it to: three. Parties I really enjoyed: zero. It had nothing to do with the parties and everything to do with me. I spent most of the night looking at the tiny tops the women were wearing and remembering how just about this time last year I was swearing that next year I'd be one of them. I'm still down more than twenty-five pounds from where I started, but I know from past diets that the 180s for me are slippery territory. Gains of a pound can suddenly make an entire size not fit—and it's ridiculously easy to gain a pound after a couple of drinks. I badly want those drinks so I can float away from my body, forget about it at least for the evening.

I had a couple of drinks and then—inconspicuously, I thought—some chocolate fondue. But my friend Michele called this morning to say a friend of hers had called and said, "I didn't know you were having celebrities at your party."

Michele, of course, answered: "What are you talking about? What celebrities?"

"I saw that girl Courtney who writes that weight-loss column for *Shape*," came the response. "And she was eating chocolate fondue."

That body image expert was wrong. Everybody *is* looking at me.

"Oh, my God! How did she get so fat again?"

I'm sure that's what everyone's thinking.

I don't want to get on the scale. I don't want to be seen eating anything "bad." Putting on pounds is never good, but it's even worse when in the not too distant past you were just getting used to shrinking, not expanding. It's depressing that all the compliments and encouragement from friends have been replaced by dead silence, when now I need a boost more than ever.

In yet another terrifically timed e-mail from *Shape*—not their fault, but still—the photo folks want to know when next week they can shoot me. When I'm feeling melodramatic, as I do now, I wish they could literally shoot me. Put an end to all of this.

Am torn between trying to push off the photo shoot for as long as possible and angling to have it done immediately, before I can gain so much as one more pound.

My body seems to be conspiring against me.

After three days with a miserable cold, when the fact that I couldn't go to the gym made me frantic, I did something funny to my back yesterday while using the triceps rope. It doesn't really hurt when I'm sitting down, but there's a sharp pain when I switch positions. It takes me several minutes to stand up, and this morning it took me about fifteen minutes to change clothes—I could hardly pick up my feet. If this is the sort of thing Grandma gets when she mentions back pain, how does she not complain about it more often?

A doctor friend suspects a compressed cervical disk, but I'm hoping it's just a garden-variety pulled something. I thought of Emily, my roommate from college, and her exhortation that I exercise even when I don't think I can.

I tried to do a few leg lifts, but the pain made me catch my breath.

Back a bit better, but I'm still moving gingerly, and I'm afraid the gym might undo whatever healing seems to have occurred.

Got an e-mail from a *Shape* reader who says she needs moral support—that she's very overweight and thinks she could never look the way I do. She wants to know if I've ever thought of giving up on the whole weight-loss thing entirely.

I was about to fire off an e-mail telling her I knew exactly how she felt, but then I realized I have never thought of giving up. I have been frustrated and negative and hopeless, but I have never once said: I'm going to stop trying. I don't know how, but some tiny shred in me clings to the belief that maybe someday I will do this right. Someday I will learn. And somehow I continue to believe this despite all evidence to the contrary.

Actual evidence to the contrary: tonight I tried on some of my "fat" clothes and noticed some of them fit disturbingly well.

At the grocery store tonight, I chose my snack food not just on calories per serving but on how much damage it would do if I finished the whole box.

E-mail from a guy from Michele's party, who skipped all pleasantries and got directly to the point. My e-mail address is easy to track down—I work for a magazine and not one of ten million government agencies with their bizarre acronyms—so he e-mailed me for contact details for a friend I was with that night. Not, "Nice to meet you" or anything like that. Just, "How do I reach your friend?" Now I really feel like the elephant in the room: huge but invisible.

This incident does not make me kindly disposed to going to a couple of "Jewish Christmas" singles activities my friend Betsy is insisting she needs company for. One is called the Matzo Ball, and the other is called the Gefilte Fish Gala. I'm not in the mood to find the titles cute. Instead they're more evidence that food is everywhere and against me.

Though for one reason or another I have not gone running since Thanksgiving, I signed up for the Cherry Blossom Ten-Miler in April.

The phrase *cherry blossom* reminds me of something I wrote in my very first *Shape* column: "I hate knowing that my weight keeps me from doing things I want to do, including going biking around the monuments in cherry blossom season." Another spring is coming, and it looks like once again this year I'm going to be wishing it weren't—that sweater weather would stay indefinitely so I can hide.

The *Shape* project is technically supposed to be over in a couple of weeks, though I'll still be filing the columns through March, and they'll be in print until the September issue. No one has said anything about how we're going to end it, seeing as I'm hardly a *Shape* success story. Maybe they're hoping what I'm hoping—that I'll magically pull it together in the next few weeks and lose nineteen pounds in two months, the way I did the first two months of the diet.

Tonight I dug out the journal I kept from the Summer of a Thousand Peaches—that summer I ate four peaches a day and nothing else and ran for an hour a day. If I thought I could do that again, I just might try it. That's how desperate I feel.

I flipped through the pages, looking for a clue to how I managed it. But there was very little written. Suddenly I remembered: I couldn't keep a journal that summer. Writing about a relationship that was falling apart hurt too much. Nor did I want to submerge myself in the doubt (about my job, about my life, about whether D.C. would ever feel like home) that was already chest-deep. So I didn't write and I didn't eat, letting hunger blot out all the other feelings.

Christmas Eve. I did indeed end up at the Matzo Ball. I'm going to be dining out on stories from it for at least a week or two. (If one more guy made a joke about how he was the nice Jewish doctor my grandmother was hoping for, I was going to start handing out her phone number directly.) Nearly two thousand people there, and let's just say that if nearly every Jewish guy who's single in the D.C. area was in that room, I'm in very big trouble. Mostly I skulked around, playing wingwoman for Betsy. It's a role that I loathe but that seems to have been assigned cosmically to overweight women everywhere. The best you can do is to be the funny sidekick, and tonight I wasn't feeling up to it.

I wanted to go home, but Betsy made it clear that if I was a good friend, I wouldn't desert her. So I stayed. When finally we left—she with four phone numbers—I got out of the cab a couple of blocks away from my house and went to CVS, looking for anything I thought might fill the empty hole.

I knew better than to think I'd find anything. But I bought some ice cream anyway.

The day after Christmas, one year anniversary of the diet. This time last year, I thought I'd be thin by now. I imagined my awe-inspiring "after" picture, where I'd wear something sleeveless and impossibly trendy, preferably from a shop I walk by nearly every day but only once have had the nerve to enter.

I thought my life would be perfect.

I certainly never thought that a year after I began the *Shape* project, I'd still be fighting a lot more than the last 10 pounds—I'm at 184, up 15 pounds from the summer—and that even with professional support I'd still be struggling.

Where will I be at this time next year? I hope not here.

Month 13 (January, Again)

*N*ew Year's Day 2000. In New York City. Despite all the dire millennial predictions, everything is still standing. Including me, even though I was so sick two days ago I didn't think I'd be able to get out of bed, much less get up to New York and go to a party.

The flu—or whatever it was—came over me suddenly, virulently, five days ago. One minute I was packing for a New Year's Eve trip to Lake Tahoe, and the next I thought I was going to collapse if I didn't sit down. I lay down for a minute and then couldn't get up again. When Diana came by with apple juice and water, I had to crawl to open the door.

I lay in bed staring at the ceiling. I couldn't even read because my eyes kept tearing and glassing over with fever. From my window I could hear the sounds of D.C. slowly emptying out, everyone heading to millennial New Year's Eve celebrations. The phone was silent. All my friends were leaving town, and they thought I had left, too.

But I couldn't. Diana had changed my airplane ticket to thirty-six hours later, in case whatever I had was a twenty-four-hour bug, then she left herself. On December 30 I was still running a fever of 103.2. I called Dad, who wasn't especially freaked—I always run high fevers.

I felt sorrier and sorrier for myself, alone on New Year's Eve. The only thing that cheered me up was thinking about how much weight I was probably losing, because I couldn't eat and was only drinking water. Why ruin a perfect fast with apple juice?

On New Year's Eve Day, when I was feeling slightly better and bemoaning that there wasn't enough time to get out to Tahoe before New Year's, my friend Keith called from New York to leave me a Happy New Year message.

"What are you doing home?" he asked when I picked up. He insisted I couldn't spend New Year's alone in bed and that if I didn't think I could get up to New York by myself, he'd come down on the train and get me.

Love my friends. Also loved that after five days of not eating, I could fit into my little black dress. Wondered if I could make it through to 2000 without eating a thing.

New year, old me. Ate my way through New Year's Day, where I recovered from New Year's Eve by watching endless amounts of E! and eating endless amounts of Chinese food with my friend Erica, whose apartment I stayed at in New York. Then ate my way through the train trip back to D.C.

Now am getting fatter by the minute. And freaking out because out of nowhere I got a call to come up to New York for a job interview at a magazine that has always intrigued me. Of immediate concern is what to wear—something black, obviously, but not sure anything in my closet fits. (The first thing that popped into my head when I heard the word *interview* was: how much weight can I lose in two weeks?) Then there's a much bigger issue: if I get this job, I'm not sure what I'll do. I don't want to move to New York just now—don't think I could handle living somewhere that makes me feel circus-freak large, much less having to go out and talk to people, as my job would require. Anyway, if I could get it together to move to New York, shouldn't I just move to London, which is where I really want to go?

I'm not sure I'm ready to move anywhere. I don't want to start my life over somewhere looking like this. I want a fresh start—to leave myself behind. But I always get there first.

Mom found a two-bedroom apartment in Hollywood, only a couple of miles from our old house. Same zip code, totally different life.

Dad is en route to San Francisco.

They're about as far as they can get from each other and still be in the same country. I picture them, little lit-up dots on the *Sleepless in Seattle* map.

Except *Sleepless in Seattle* has a happy ending.

You stress and stress and stress about getting all the facts right in an article. You consider who might object to what details so that maybe just once you'll be prepared when someone calls to complain. But the one thing people pick on always turns out to be something I haven't thought about twice.

E-mail exchange with Natalie Angier, the *New York Times* writer I pro-filed. She apparently never reads stories about herself but broke her policy to read mine. She said her husband liked it, and he's picky.

I had described her as seeming fragile, and her e-mail about that made me laugh. "Fragile??? What about me seems fragile??? You've got to go weight lifting with me sometime. I bench press 140 and can do, oh, fifty to sixty push-ups at a stretch; how about you? All in good cheer, but honestly, frag-ile I ain't."

I wrote back that I could manage a mere forty push-ups but that I had just run a marathon—how did that figure in the scoring?

She promptly replied that she, too, got a laugh out of this exchange. And—something I've been thinking about since she said it—that we'd all be a lot better off if women saved their competing with each other for these sorts of things.

Got a raise, came up with a couple of story ideas I'm actually excited about working on, got a call from an editor at another magazine asking if I'd write for her, went to a (very difficult) spinning class, heard a friend's band play, had a long conversation with an old friend I haven't spoken with in ages. Today was one of those days when I felt happy enough with my life to con-sider—for at least a minute—why I'm doing something (dieting) that seems to make me so unhappy.

I thought back to that e-mail I got from a *Shape* reader about whether I had ever thought about giving up. There are two ways to give up. The first is to lose hope completely. I don't want to do that. The second is to accept myself at this weight or whatever weight I might become. I know there's an entire fat-acceptance movement that does this, but as yet I can't, and I'm not sure I want to. I don't think I look good this way. I won't say thin is better—as in thin people are superior to overweight ones—but I definitely think thin (but not necessarily model size) looks better. Frankly, I don't *want* to wear miniskirts or bustiers or halter tops at this weight. Just because it's in my size doesn't mean I should wear it.

What I want is to stop looking at my life through the prism of food and weight. I want to get an invitation to a party and not immediately worry about whether anything will fit and whether I should eat beforehand. I want to be able to look for a new job without wondering if there's truth to those studies about how overweight people are paid less and looked at as less competent.

At this point I would gladly trade the ever elusive possibility that some-day I'll be thin for a certainty that I could stay the same size (even if it's a 16) for the rest of my life.

Shape has decided to extend the project for another year. Despite the pressure and the constant worrying, it didn't really occur to me to say no. Knowing I have a whole other year—the luxury of time—makes me hope that maybe now I'll do things better. Maybe now I'll succeed. Besides, I'm too far into this now. Giving up would feel as though I'm totally giving up—that because I couldn't lose weight in this one year, I'm never going to. And I'm not ready to say that yet.

What this translates to on the magazine page is that what was supposed to be my victory lap is now just another mile on the trip. I'm getting two pages in the September magazine (my one-year anniversary issue) to dedicate to what I've learned this year. My summation of the past twelve months has an optimism and cheer I don't quite feel, about how I'll get this right some-day. The ending in particular: "I haven't quite conquered the food and weight issue, but . . . I never went more than five days without exercising, and usu-ally never more than two. No matter what I ate, I never stopped running, and I know that's a major achievement. Maybe life isn't perfect, but it's pretty darn good."

Spent all day with Mary and Abby at the outlet mall. I should have known it would be depressing. Outlet malls always are. Because the best stuff you can find is usually stuff for a season at least four months away, I always end up spending the whole day contemplating my weight (or contemplating it even more than usual, if that's possible). Do I want to invest $100 on this spring jacket—and on the fact that I'll be this size in four or five months? Should I buy it smaller as an incentive? The way things are going, the smartest bet would probably be to buy it bigger, but who wants to do that?

Of course I couldn't find a single New York–appropriate black pantsuit—or any other interview-appropriate attire—that fit. Toward the end I got des-perate enough—or is it realistic enough?—to give up on finding anything in a size 14 that would fit, and I tried on 16s, a size I definitely did not want to buy. I finally found a pair of black pants and a jacket. I don't love them, but I don't know that I'd love anything at this size. The interview is tomorrow, so I guess I have no choice.

I'm having flashbacks to an interview for a prestigious scholarship I had in the winter of my senior year of high school. I was wearing a navy blue suit

I'd bought for debate tournaments and feeling crummier than usual about myself—the suit had an elasticized waistband, which made me feel fat and sloppy. By then the adjectives *fat* and *sloppy* had become an indivisible pair in my mind, so I always felt like a cross between Pig Pen and one of those huge women I'd see in the supermarket—the kind who wore tent dresses and sneakers because their feet were too fat for normal shoes. I'd been trying to diet for the week beforehand, and I was wishing, as I did with all important events in my life, that I could put off the interview until I'd lost some weight.

The interview—with the president of a community college—started innocently. First question: what books was I reading? Easy. I relaxed and chatted away.

The next thing I remember is his asking me about being fat—and that was the word he used. *Fat.* First it was a poke, a nudge at the side of an anthill to see if anything was really alive in there. I don't remember his exact question, only that it so stunned me that I answered it, the way I would years later when a guy asked me ten minutes into our first date when the last time I'd had sex was.

Then the president began kicking sand everywhere. He quizzed me about the way being fat affected my daily life, whether I thought it would hinder me in the future, whether I thought being fat would keep me from ever having a date in college. Fat. Fat. A drumbeat of fat.

I didn't cry. I discussed these things clinically, as if speaking about another person. My mother, my father, my sister, my grandmother—all had called me fat before, and I'd cried or exploded all of those times. True, those responses weren't options in an interview for a scholarship I desperately wanted, but mostly I think I did neither because of the way he'd asked me the questions. He didn't blurt out the word *fat* in a moment of anger or disgust the way my family did (then often tiptoed around for days after, trying to pretend they hadn't). He phrased his questions the way I'd later learn to phrase questions for reluctant sources—assume what you know is a statement of fact and work from there. He talked about my weight as though it were a perfectly normal thing for a fifty-something man in a position of power to say to an awkward, nervous sixteen-year-old.

As we talked, the image I had of myself in my head kept getting fatter and fatter, blowing up like Violet, who chews the not-yet-perfected gum in *Willy Wonka & the Chocolate Factory.* In my mind I was a tiny pin of a head on a huge round body, arms and legs sticking out feebly. The image made it awfully difficult to concentrate on his questions. All I remember thinking was: *I'm fat; I deserve this.*

I left the interview feeling raw and exhausted, hating myself more than ever. I stumbled out into the sunlight, got in the car, and headed off to numb the pain in the only way I knew how. I drove to Kentucky Fried Chicken and ordered half a dozen biscuits.

I didn't get the scholarship.

Back from exactly nine hours in New York. I have no idea how the interview went, though now I'm not sure I want the job—or *a* job, really, since they still don't seem clear themselves on what they're offering.

One of the editors was talking about having me freelance from D.C. Another spent a half hour complaining about her job.

After I waited two hours to meet the top editor, when I finally got in to see him he didn't say anything for a full five minutes. Then he looked down at the letter I'd sent with my writing samples and said, "You look like you have a really friendly signature."

"My sister tells me it's really easy to forge," I answered.

He laughed.

Just got off the phone with Mom. Sometimes I feel so stung by how abruptly she ends a conversation. It's like she can't wait for me to finish my last sentence so she can say, "OK, Sweetie," in this tone—and it's always the same tone. Resigned. Tired. I always wonder: am I boring? Is it the long-distance bills? Is talking to me just another thing to do—like once she's heard my voice on the other end of the line, it doesn't matter if the conversation lasts three minutes or thirty, because it's now an immutable fact that her daughter has called?

Much as I want to prolong the conversation, I know I can't. I'm starting to wonder how much of what I say she can actually process. Tonight, no more than thirty seconds after I'd told her about all the snow, she asked me how the weather was. And lately she's taken to commenting that I shouldn't be talking to her while I'm at work.

"Mom, it's Sunday," I always say. Sometimes gently and sometimes not. She'll give a little laugh—a no-big-deal laugh—and change the subject to something she thinks will make me happy. She'll say she's read my latest story and that Grandma is excited to see it. Lately I've stopped asking her what she thought of specific portions of the story, because I'm starting to realize she doesn't remember what she's read. She never admits this, of course.

"Such a long article, Court," she'll say, usually more than once, with an audible touch of awe. "So many pages. How long did you spend on it?"

Whenever she does this, I think how much I wish that I couldn't tell that my mother is hiding something from me. I think of my last glimpse of her before I was wheeled to the operating room to have my tonsils out as a kid. The slender fingers ("the only part of me that's thin," she would always joke) tucking a stray hair into my surgical cap, the whiff of Shalimar perfume as she bent down to kiss me. The final squeeze of the arm telling me that as long as she was around, she would take care of everything. Nothing bad would happen to me.

I didn't know then—none of us knew then—that she was already sick.

Month 14 (February)

I haven't gotten on the scale in four weeks, and now I can't face it.

The first Wednesday—weigh-in day—I overslept and didn't get to the gym in the morning, and even a casual dieter knows you can't weigh yourself at night. The second week it was that time of the month—another "legitimate" excuse. At the three-week point I thought, *Well, I ate a lot, and pretty late last night, so . . .*

This morning was four weeks. I lay in bed this morning dreading it—the whole routine of weighing myself. The inevitable feeling of being starving—even though I've eaten my usual breakfast—just because I know I'm getting on a scale when I get to the gym and therefore don't want to eat even one extra bite. The attempt not to drink anything at all beforehand so as not to push up the scale so much as a quarter of an ounce more. The skulking around the locker room, waiting for the moment when the fewest women seem to be near the scale. The debate about how high to push the indicator. Start at a number I can't bear so I can flick it down a bit? But what if I start at a number I already think is horrendous and then have to flick it up?

Then there's checking to make sure the weight really is at zero—that everything is aligned properly. Then getting on and off the scale to double-check the number the indicator lands at. Should it be best two out of three? Three out of five? What is the exact point at which the silver balance beam starts to waver but doesn't quite hit that top bit, thus indicating that I've got to move the indicator up at least a quarter of a pound?

Finally, there's that sinking feeling—even if the number isn't quite as bad as I feared—that it will only go up. I've never once managed to stem the scale's upward climb when it starts in the middle of a diet—why will now be different?

I lie in bed, debating, plotting, *weighing*. Choices. Deal now and spend the day with the inevitable depression I know will result? Well, I do have a lot to do today, and it would be nice not to have the fat thing weighing on me even more than usual. Would one more week off the scale hurt? If I'm saintly for a week, maybe that will make a big difference. . . .

I don't really *need* to weigh myself, I rationalize. Isn't Peeke always saying that I should worry more about the clothes-o-meter than actual numbers? Numbers don't lie, but nor do they tell the whole truth.

I know I've gained weight. Do I need the scale to thumb it in my face? At the same time, I know that not weighing myself means another week of drifting. Of pretending to myself that it really is OK to have a chocolate-chip cookie instead of yogurt for a snack. Of pretending that my jeans shrank in the dryer or that I'm bloated or—biggest lie of all—that today I'm going to put a stop to all this eating.

The questions about what to do—from the scale to *Shape* to this frightening bingeing—get bigger and bigger until finally, in a split second, I push them out of my head and decide to go running outside. The perfect solution. Won't have to face the scale but will still have exercised. No one can say I'm being self-destructive there.

But I am. I know I am. I'm not dealing.

Today I had to deal. I had a *Shape* photo shoot this morning. I wanted to wear a tent and a paper bag, but I wasn't even being allowed to hide myself in all black. Bright colors, said *Shape*. Fitted clothes.

"We want to see your body," the photo editor chirped on the phone yesterday.

Trust me, you don't.

Peeke, who knows I'm struggling, had suggested a close-up of me lifting weights. My face and my arm doing a biceps curl—"vim, vigor, and vitality," she wrote, and "that beautiful face of yours." I laughed every time I thought about that. My face and an arm levitating with a dumbbell is what I pictured. I could just hear the questions from people I knew if there were a picture like that: *Is that* your *arm? Is that the weight you usually lift?*

But alas, no shots of me lifting weights. They decided on a "lifestyle" shot—ideas for possible pix: me reading a book in a café, me walking down a street, me ordering a smoothie—and Molly, the photographer, thought Adams Morgan would be a good, colorful place to shoot. Thankfully, nobody I know works there. I wore a French-blue shirt—the first time I've worn something besides black or gray in several weeks—and control-top hose beneath my black pants.

Today makes two weeks that Diana and I haven't been speaking. We've gone this long before without actually talking to each other—the semester I spent in England, for one, and weeks we've been busy, for another—but never because we were angry, which we are now. It's a fight about money I owe from the New Year's Eve trip I didn't end up taking. The trip involved a cabin in Lake Tahoe to be split among a bunch of people. Because the size of the group was in flux until the last minute and because I was a last-minute addition who would have just made everyone's bill cheaper—and, OK, because I already had to eat a $600 plane ticket—I contended that perhaps I didn't owe my entire share. Diana didn't agree. We couldn't even discuss the subject rationally. It seemed to be a touchstone for every other problem we'd ever had with each other. I was the selfish bitch who was concerned only with myself, and Diana was the martyr.

I'm starting to dread speaking with her. I'm sure she's going to be furious when I finally talk to her again, because she calls at least two or three times a day and hangs up on my machine. (How do I know this? Thank you, caller ID.) But she hasn't left a message, so I haven't felt obligated to call back.

Mary and I call it friend-dating: getting coffee or a drink with a woman you've met to see if you might want to hang out again. I haven't done much of it in the past year or so—Mary and I have joked that the bar has been set very high for new friends, because we love the friends we have and there already isn't enough time for them. But lately I've been friend-dating Victoria, a Capitol Hill staffer I met in November. We were at three of the same events in a week—and having a good time making fun of all three—and decided we should get a drink. And then actually followed up.

Part of my decision to expand my circle was a postmarathon freeze episode with Mary. Nothing was ever really said, but I knew Mary had been getting annoyed with me in the last few weeks of training because I'd gotten so competitive at the expense of fun—and friends. I wanted to run faster, and I didn't stop to think about whether Mary's bad knee could weather it or about how my friends felt.

I couldn't admit it then, but I was clinging to the marathon as the one thing in my life that I was still doing perfectly. I was bingeing again, I had screwed up the diet, I felt as if I hadn't written a story worth reading in months, but damn it, I hadn't missed a marathon training session yet! So I wanted it to be perfect. I wanted it to make up for everything else that was going poorly. I didn't just want to finish—if I did finish, I wanted a decent time, too.

Mary was a little frosty after the marathon, but I didn't say anything. I figured everything would be OK by the time I got back from London. It's against my nature to deal. Eating is how I deal—or how I have dealt. I avoid. That's part of why I eat in the first place. Because I *can't* deal.

As I'd expected, after I got back from London things were fine. Not as good as they had been over the summer, but OK enough that I could avoid saying anything about my behavior. I didn't want to hear what Mary might say if I brought it up. She might not know exactly why I had been behaving as I was—obsessively, hypercompetitively—but she knew enough about me that she'd probably ask enough of the right questions. Pointed ones. After all, she's a lawyer. Her questions, I was sure, eventually would lead to talk about bingeing and why I did it and how I needed help.

I wasn't ready to think about the answers.

So—in a sort of unspoken way—Mary and I haven't been avoiding each other, but we haven't spent nearly as much time together as we usually do. So Victoria and I have gone out at least twice every week—to drinks before some event we're both attending, to movies, to dinner at restaurants we've been wanting to try. We always order dessert. Victoria doesn't worry about her weight. She doesn't seem to have to.

In a way, the whole Mary thing is defiance and self-destructiveness on my part. She hasn't said anything about my weight or otherwise indicated that she's noticed I'm not following my diet as closely as I once was, but I'm sure she's noticed—and not just sure she's noticed in that paranoid, everyone's-looking-at-me kind of way. I'm sure she's noticed because she notices things like that, and though she would never say anything, that makes me feel caught. Guilty as charged—guilty of eating too much.

Victoria doesn't know about the diet or *Shape* or my mother or anything. I don't think she would care. She's not callous, but I know all she wants is a good time: Let's have a few drinks and a laugh and not let anything heavy ruin it. I'm happy to go along. I want to be the way she is: I don't want to think about anything heavy, either.

Elizabeth on the phone. Neither of us mentioned the fact that I had planned to move to London on March 1, which is only a few weeks away, and clearly

I haven't made much of an effort to do so. I got off the phone feeling empty. Yet another thing I've publicly announced plans to do and failed at.

Saw Diana at a launch party for a politics website—the first time our lines of work have brought us to the same event. She looked right through me.

Everything is a mess: my apartment, my office, my life. I feel if I could make progress on just one tiny thing, I'd be inspired to keep going. I decided to get my bills in order, to make little piles all over my rug, and then realized I had no file folders and the stationery store was closed because of a snow day. Frustration. It makes me want to shred all the bills and throw them around my apartment—a paper snowstorm. Not like my apartment could possibly look any worse.

As part of my I-am-not-moving-to-London-so-must-make-some-other-change-that-seems-like-progress mode, I decided I would work on my fiction for a half hour every day.

All I could think about was Mom and Dad's last night in the house in New Jersey before they went their separate ways. It seemed like a good scenario to set a story in motion: two people with a long history and just one more evening to get through. How do you spend those last eight hours? What do you *talk* about? Who gets the wedding album—or wants it? If there's an odd number of spoons, who gets the extra?

I didn't end up writing anything.

Saturday night at Rock-It Grill, this dive of a karaoke bar in Alexandria, Virginia—the sort of place where people know the words to the most obscure country songs. It was Abby's birthday, and we planned to order revolting shots (flaming Dr. Pepper, anyone?) and make complete fools of ourselves in relative anonymity—we've never seen anyone we know there.

During breaks from the singing—yowling is probably more accurate—Rock-It plays dance music. I was relieved not to be the one friend not dancing with a guy (and therefore having to spend the evening pretending to get drinks/go to the bathroom/look for someone) but not drunk enough not to feel self-conscious dancing. The (drunk) guy who had pulled me out on the floor went on and on about how he hadn't had a girlfriend in a while, and did I have a boyfriend? (Yes, idiot. That's why I'm dancing with you.) He had that, "I'm going to kiss you if you look directly at me" expression, so instead I looked over his shoulder at Mary and made faces.

After we finished singing "You're the One That I Want" from *Grease*, a girl—a *Shape* reader—came up to me. Often readers who come up and talk to me don't say anything besides that they like the column, but this girl wanted to discuss—what else?—diet tips. On a Saturday night past midnight in a karaoke bar.

I didn't want to be rude, but I couldn't think of anything I wanted to do less, with the possible exception of kiss the drunk guy. She wanted to know whether I thought potatoes were OK and what I thought of Weight Watchers versus Lean Cuisine and whether, since we obviously live somewhere near each other, I wanted to work out sometime. She was so sweet and full of compliments, but I wanted to yell at her: *Look at me—look at how much weight I've gained! Do I look like I have all the answers?*

Diane—a *Washingtonian* editor I'm close to—called me into her office to chat yesterday: enough of the stalling, she said. When am I going to write the eating disorders story? Which issue of the magazine? She wanted me to be specific.

I've been putting it off for a few months, doing preliminary research and claiming that a thousand other little projects are keeping me from focusing on it. The story originally was my idea—I'm so obsessed with food and exercise that they're almost all I can think of to write about. I didn't say anything about myself in the pitch—just mentioned a few tales of friends from my days in the sorority house in college.

Diane had suggested I actually use some of what I saw in college in the story, and I've been halfheartedly writing it up whenever I have a free moment. I know it's missing something.

Today—with a just-set deadline of mid-March, about three weeks away—I had to confront what was missing. Me.

I sat in the office until 10:00 P.M., frozen. Then I began writing furiously, pouring out stories: sneaking food. Lying. Starving. Steeling myself to climb into a bath so hot I burned myself in a desperate attempt to steam off some weight. (I'd read the idea somewhere.) Sitting around in sweatpants, eating all weekend, and being afraid that nothing would fit on Monday. Reading the Sweet Valley High series and wondering if I was the only reader who envied that the Wakefield twins were "a perfect size 6" (a phrase every book in the series included)—even though they seemed to eat pizza after school every day at their high school hangout.

I wrote until 4:30 A.M. I didn't stop to eat or surf the Web or change the CD I was playing. I couldn't stop to think, because I knew if I did, I'd stop writing.

I went home and slept a deep, dreamless sleep. I woke up at noon, exhausted, and stumbled into the office.

"Let's hear about the wild party last night," an editor teased me. Writing about nightlife has its benefits: no one ever raises an eyebrow when I show up at work late.

If he only knew. I thought of the file sitting on my computer. Even if I edit the hell out of it before turning it in, how will I ever be able to face my coworkers again?

"I've never read *Vanity Fair*. Should I?" said the guy sitting next to me at the coffee bar, tapping my magazine. It was yet another one of those gray days of February—holidays long gone, spring seeming impossibly far away—when it feels like nothing exciting will ever happen again.

He was cute, studying a GMAT prep book, and listening to Bruce Springsteen, who I love. We chatted for about twenty minutes. David was a nice Jewish government lawyer setting up a nonprofit. *Who says nobody ever meets anybody normal in bars?* I thought smugly. I also thought, *I've gotten no sleep this week because I've been on deadline, I don't think I even washed my face this morning (much less put on cover-up), and I've been sitting here raking my fingers through my hair as I read. I look like hell.*

My friend Alexy showed up—we had planned to meet—providing a convenient "Let's continue this at another time" opening. He took it—and my number.

After more than two months of e-mails to try to set a date, Abby, Mary, and I finally had dinner with Stacy and Dagny, our marathon running buddies. We all barely recognized one another with makeup on and in normal clothes—we were used to seeing one another only at the crack of dawn, in running outfits and wearing water-bottle belts and wary, how-bad-is-this-going-to-be expressions. Dagny was talking about signing up again and working on her finishing time. I remembered my private vow in October to do the same, but I can't imagine it now. Even when I do run, I never get the "I'm flying" feeling—not even for a second—that I'd occasionally get during workouts. Instead, my body feels like I'm wearing a wet sweatsuit—literally weighed down by what I've gained.

If there are indeed people who meet normal people in bars, I'm not one of them.

Drinks with David, the Jewish lawyer I met at Xando. Yes, that omission of the word *nice* before *Jewish* this time was deliberate.

The first thing he said when I arrived at the bar was that he can't drink alcohol and that drinking is expensive anyway.

So I ordered a Diet Coke. He ordered quesadillas and a Perrier and lurched into an excruciatingly detailed account of a long-term illness he's had.

"If I hadn't had to miss so much school, I could have gone Ivy League and then to an Ivy League law school," he said. Instead he was stuck at a D.C. law school with people he considered "intellectually inferior."

Oh.

He couldn't tell me enough about himself. He said he planned to redeem himself by going to an Ivy League business school and then to Harvard Divinity School—the last because so many U.S. presidents had gone there. He wanted to run for public office, and everything he'd done—from high school up to and including the nonprofit—had been for appearances.

I needed a drink.

"Where would you run for office?" I asked, taking a huge swallow of Diet Coke.

"Well, I don't really have any roots, so what I want to do is get married and run for office wherever she's from."

Mayday! Mayday!

Suddenly he began rhapsodizing about how stunning the women in South Carolina are.

I was tempted to tell him I had the solution to his problems: move to Charleston and find your wife there. Instead, I said I had to get going.

The check came, and he mentioned—again—how much debt he was in. He made no move to get the check, so I handed over a $5 bill—for one Diet Coke. He didn't offer change.

"Thanks!" he said brightly as I stumbled over my chair in my haste to leave. "We should do this again."

Just what D.C. needs—another steakhouse. But I went to the opening of this one because the cast of "The West Wing" was making an appearance, and I knew my pop-culture-vulture friend Alexy would love it.

Bumped into a college acquaintance, and we talked about another person we both know—a funny guy named Mike with whom I used to commiserate over our history theses senior year.

"Odd duck," Frank said affectionately of Mike—not words you'd expect to precede what came next: "He's had some bad luck. He had to drop out of law school because he's got brain cancer." A one-inch-by-one-inch inoperable lesion.

I thought briefly about Mike and getting in touch with him but didn't think I knew him well enough to say anything. Thoughts about the mini steak sandwiches and the crab cakes being passed fell away, and I thought about the relativity of unfairness. Unfair is not having a weight problem, as I do. Unfair is having brain cancer at age twenty-four.

I know this, and still I rage that food and weight are problems I have to deal with. It seems such a ridiculous thing when I put it down on paper: that I sit there in a restaurant thinking about the bread basket like it's *Attack of the Killer Rolls*. Or that when someone asks me if I'm hungry, I panic and think, *Well, is it OK to be hungry now?*

A guy I went to high school with saw me in *Shape*—he's a personal trainer now—and tracked me down. Talking to him was like attempting to put in an old retainer: it fit once, but it's almost painful now. He yanked me back at least ten years, to my awkward, unsure tenth-grade self. However dissatisfied I sometimes am with my life now, I'm a lot happier with it than I was in high school, and for at least a few minutes I felt grateful.

Signed up for the marathon again. Maybe that will give me the kick I need.

Can't help thinking that size-wise I'm the same—maybe even worse—than I was at this time a year ago. Tonight I could barely fit into the size 14 jeans and red sweater I remember buying so proudly to go to a party friends had early last March—the party where everyone told me how good I looked.

I'm too depressed to go and try to pin down the exact date of the party. I don't want to think about how much energy and effort I've expended this year only to end up, weight-wise, in the same place.

Last night I called Diana after nearly a month of not speaking over the New Year's Eve money. I ran into her at 2:30 A.M. as we were both walking into the building. After chatting for a couple of minutes, she asked about the money. I tried calmly to explain my side, but she said she didn't want to talk to me until I gave her the money. She followed me upstairs and tried to force her way into my apartment, keeping me from closing the door. When she got back to her apartment, she left a message on my machine. It ended: "You're a big fat liar, emphasis on the *fat*."

I listened to that bit twice just to believe it.

I wasn't enraged—just really, really hurt and sort of exhausted. So today, before I left for the gym, I wrote her a check and left it under her door with a note: "It's going to take me a very long time to forget that message on my machine, and I don't want to speak to you until I do." I thought about explaining how it wasn't her bullying that had worked this time—that I just didn't want there to be *any* reason for us to have to speak. But I didn't want to get into it.

Bought a ridiculously expensive new guitar, which I had absolutely no business doing. You know you're getting into seriously pathetic justification when you're thinking, *Well, if I'm playing my new guitar, I won't be able to put anything in my mouth.*

Breakthrough! I had been craving chocolate literally for two days and decided I'd better just give in and get some before it sent me off to do something even worse. Normally, trying to decide what I really want—considering the options—can set me off on a binge, but today it was like: don't want anything cakey, just want chocolate. So I got a Dove bar, had one square, and put the rest in my desk drawer. Where it sat all day, not really tempting me at all. Occasionally I'd open the drawer to check that it was still there and to marvel at the feeling that there it was and I didn't care.

Now, of course, I just need to figure out how I did that.

Gave in to the guilt that I'm a crummy sister and the nagging feeling that I was the one who had done something wrong: I called Diana. It's almost scary how easy it was to let a few weeks slide by without speaking.

I hadn't really actively not been calling her, if that makes sense. The first two weeks sped by—I was busy. I occasionally thought about calling her this week, mostly because I'd been worried about how she'd behave when we did start speaking—how angry she might be and how much she'd yell at me for being so wrapped up in myself.

Part of the reason I decided to call her was that I spoke to Mom last night and decided Diana and I shouldn't add another rift to the family pile.

After talking with Mom about the whole idea of family holidays that would include Mom and Dad—which the two of them keep talking about— I desperately wanted to talk to Diana. I wanted to know if the idea drives her as crazy as it drives me. One of the divorce's fringe benefits—at least from my standpoint—is that we'll get to give up the charade, even if it's just a couple of days a year, that we're a happy family.

"You're in the middle of a divorce!" I want to scream. "We don't have to pretend anymore!"

I know if we ask them why they're doing these joint holidays, they'll say it's for us, so we don't have to choose. I don't think that's it—I think both of them aren't sure how to navigate the upcoming year and are looking for at least one or two familiar days, even if the familiar is uncomfortable. Or perhaps they want to remind themselves that the route they've chosen is the right one?

Diana wasn't home. I left a message.

Month 15 (March)

I haven't looked at myself in weeks. Even when I'm in the bathroom at work—where there are mirrors everywhere—I keep my eyes trained to either the sink or the floor. I know if I catch sight of my reflection, I'm not going to want to go out and face the world again. Even though in my mind I'm huge—cue the exploding Violet from *Willy Wonka* paired with circus-freak music—I was still shocked when I saw myself in the pictures from Abby's birthday last month.

"As big as a house," I can hear my grandmother saying.

How did I let this happen? Does anyone on the planet gain weight as quickly as I do? Three months ago I could still squeeze into size 12 jeans, but now I can barely squeeze into size 16 suits. I wish I could just bury myself in a hole somewhere and not come out until I'm at least a size 14 again. I'm sure *Shape* will fire me after the next photo shoot. They know I'm not losing weight, but even I'm not sure how much I've gained. I've guesstimated that I'm somewhere north of 180, but in these birthday pictures I swear I look like I'm back at 206, where I started.

I remember the subject of the marathon coming up at Abby's birthday—how she laughed and told a couple of guys at the party that it was one significant thing she'd done before she turned thirty—and how quickly I tried to end the conversation when Abby said Mary and I had done it, too. I felt self-conscious enough running when I was a size 12. But now people *really* must be thinking, *How the hell did that fat girl finish?* Because now I really am fat again.

I have to learn to stop bingeing—and to stop hating myself for it. Today I ordered three books from Amazon on compulsive overeating.

Finally talked with Diana. She didn't apologize for what she said last month—we didn't really discuss it—but we agreed that there's enough going on in this family that perhaps we ought to at least make an effort to stick together.

During the conversation she kept mentioning that she wanted ice cream. I considered telling her that I wished she wouldn't tell me things like that, but I worried it would ruin the let's-get-along spirit. When she launched into a list of everything she had eaten that day, I finally said, "Can we not talk about food?"

She looked annoyed. "Why not?"

I thought for a few seconds about how to phrase this in a way that wouldn't bring up too many more questions and wouldn't sound too accusing. Finally I gave up. I've never once been able to script a conversation with Diana.

"Because I've gained weight and I'm having a really hard time getting back on track and this makes it even harder," I said carefully.

"Well, I'm hungry," she said. "So how much weight have you gained?"

Ugh. The start of questions I never feel like answering, because all they do is make me think about how miserably I've failed.

"I'm not sure," I said.

"Ten pounds?"

"I haven't gotten on the scale," I said.

"Fifteen pounds?"

She wasn't going to drop it.

"I haven't gotten on the scale." Pause. "Enough that things don't fit."

The mood shifted then, subtly. We've both always talked about how much we dislike change, and hearing I've gained weight was proof to her that things were returning to the familiar. I could see her relax slightly.

"What doesn't fit?" she asked.

I got reckless then. Given where her line of questioning seemed to be headed, I figured we were going to end up yelling at each other in another minute no matter what, so I might as well say what I really wanted to.

"Why does everything about my losing weight seem to make you so angry?" I asked.

"Because," she said.

"Because why?" I felt like I was five years old, asking my mother why I couldn't stay up for another half hour.

"You've said it yourself before," she said. "You're the smart one, and I'm the thin one. You can change yourself, but I can't change myself. If people are going to label us that way, why would I want you to be the same size as me? What do I have left then?"

It wasn't the answer I was expecting her to give. I didn't know what to say. I didn't feel sorry for her, exactly, but I felt sad, thinking about the two of us locked in this struggle—the Thin One versus the Smart One—that seemed to have no resolution we could make peace with.

We sat there in silence for a few minutes. I think her answer stunned us both, and we knew there was nothing either of us could say to make it better.

"I don't know what to say," I said. "I probably should go now." I got up to give her a hug.

"So that's it? Now you're done?" Diana asked. "Thanks for fitting me into your schedule." I could see the ice clinging to her words.

Any goodwill I felt was quickly evaporating.

"Well, I don't know what else there is to say."

"We can talk about something else," she said.

I didn't want to point out that our usual topics of conversation were food, how much we wanted to eat, how fat we were feeling, and the family— and we'd already covered or dismissed most of those.

We ended up talking about the Summer of a Thousand Peaches, and she said she'd figured out I wasn't eating and was lying about it and that she had snapped at me all that summer because she'd wished I'd tell the truth and stop sneaking around.

When I got back to my apartment, I thought about all the relationships in my life food had ruined, poisoned, or just dirtied. It had caused me to lie to nearly everyone in my life in one way or another, even if it was just "I'm not hungry" or "I already ate." It had made me keep people at a distance, so they couldn't glimpse my secret life. I pictured myself, sumo wrestler sized, surrounded by a pile of food that was like a moat, with everyone I knew on the other side, unable to get across.

The purple-catsuit picture—along with a column about discovering my inner athlete, when I was in a sports-experimenting frenzy—has hit print. Editors keep calling me up and asking me to write about exercise—always a variation on new research or new ways to work out—and I feel like a fraud.

These editors probably don't care what I look like—much less that I don't look like the *Shape* pictures anymore—but if there were a not-ridiculous way to bring up in the phone conversation that I've gained weight, I would.

The annoying thing about having gone on a date with a guy I met at Xando (David, the not-nice Jewish lawyer) is that now I don't feel like I can go there anymore to read my newspaper. I saw him and so couldn't deal with the idea of a torturous conversation with him that when he came up to me I pretended not to recognize him.

"Oh, you must mean my sister," I said. "We're twins." Little does he know that Diana is one inch taller and I can't bear to think about how many pounds thinner.

Got the compulsive-overeating books today. Two of them I immediately put aside as not much use. Dull, preachy, clinical, and like trying to swallow a particularly loathsome energy bar—reading them reminded me of sitting in Weight Watchers meetings as a kid, wondering why I had to be doing this when all of my friends were out doing something fun. But I got through a bunch of the third, *Breaking Free from Compulsive Eating*, by Geneen Roth.

She is the first person to make me feel not alone—not the only person who has ever struggled with this and not a bizarre case study waiting to be written up in some medical journal. Which is ironic, considering that "You make me feel like I'm not alone" is definitely among the top three things *Shape* readers write to me.

Roth writes about deciding what she's hungry for and eating chocolate-chip cookies at every meal for two weeks. Which is, I suppose, sort of what I had tried to do with the peanut butter and the apple crumb cake so many months ago. Except it didn't work because I still considered those foods "bad." I felt guilty when I ate them and didn't dare eat them as much as I wanted.

I'm afraid to try eating whatever I want, because the potential for weight gain terrifies me. Forget that I'm gaining weight by the minute anyway—I'm still *trying* to lose weight, even if you can't tell from the scale. I don't think I can call up *Shape* and say flat out that I need a few months to gain who knows how much weight so that maybe, possibly, someday I can have my head in a place where I can lose some. I feel trapped.

The problem with Roth's book is that I can already see that for it to work you have to surrender to it completely. You can't do it halfway—put limits on it, saying, "Well, I'll eat whatever I want as long as I don't go over sixteen hundred calories a day." You have to genuinely start believing that you can indeed eat whatever you want in whatever amount, if that's what you're hungry for.

It seems like you should need a lobotomy to believe this, not a $12.95 book.

I've been brooding on *Breaking Free*. Despite the fact that you can't really do it halfway, I'm still determined to try. If I could just hold myself to three reasonable meals a day *and* exercise—well, who knows what could happen?

But it's so hard to figure out what I want to eat. It's like breathing when you scuba dive—the more you think about it, the harder it is. Today I spent two hours in the grocery store trying calmly to consider things I might like or want. It was scary, because the only times I've considered so many things in a grocery store is when I've been bingeing, and I had to keep reminding myself that I *wasn't* bingeing. Not yet anyway.

I ended up leaving without buying anything. What looks good to eat at 9:00 P.M. on a Tuesday is rarely what looks good to me at noon or 7:00 P.M. or some other hour on another day. Eating what you want is really about living in the moment—not planning out of fear what you're going to eat and when. Eating what you want is also about trusting yourself to know what you want, and diets are about exactly the opposite. You can't trust yourself, so you have to look to someone else—or to some finite calorie count—to tell yourself what you can have.

After being too nervous to hit the "send" button all day, I finally e-mailed to Diane an edited version of my struggle with food for the eating disorders story. I didn't explain that it was no longer really about my friends. I just sent it, maybe hoping the desire to binge would leave me the moment the story left my computer.

Diane called two hours later with her edits. She didn't say much about the writing or the content or the fact that I had spilled this with no warning. I wondered if her reaction to the bits I had sent her was like Ms. Clark and my high school essays about Mom: so raw with emotion that they had to be handled gingerly.

All she really said that touched on its personal nature was: "Are you going to use a pseudonym?"

That's when I thought, Oh, God. What I do really *is* sick. I shouldn't want anyone to know it's me.

I've never been able to explain to my sister why I don't like renting movies. I've finally realized why. I'd rather go to the theater because it may be the one place I've never binged—a safe haven. At the theater, I never buy anything except a giant Diet Coke. I want to lose myself in the movie, which I can't do if I'm sitting there debating every last mouthful of popcorn or chocolate— and thinking about what else I might like to eat. But at home—or at someone else's—there's always a nearby kitchen to consider.

Pride and Prejudice marathon at Alexy's: a bunch of girls and all six tapes. And brunch food: bagels, pastry, and—an English touch—scones. À la Geneen Roth, I tried to focus on eating what I really wanted, but of course that was something that wasn't available—pancakes. Grrr. "I will conquer this," Mr. Darcy was saying on-screen. Me, too.

"I am determined that nothing but the deepest love could ever induce me to matrimony," Elizabeth Bennet says, and I considered—as I always do when I watch a period film—whether I would have liked to live in her time. Not as I am now—being overweight, sarcastic, and a terrible housekeeper probably would have been even more of a liability then than it is now. I need to have been born when being overweight was considered a sign of health and wealth—instead of the opposite.

Ran the St. Paddy's Day 10K—my first race since the marathon. It was also my first 10K: last summer I skipped directly from an 8K to a 10-miler.

I met up with my friend Christie and her boyfriend, and I remembered that the last time I saw her boyfriend—a year and a half ago—he had just finished running the Army Ten-Miler. It's strange to think I wasn't regularly running so much as a mile then.

It felt good to be back in the weird world of runners: families waving silly inspirational signs, The Juggler (a guy who juggles as he runs), power gels (though you don't need them for a 10K), and all. I felt out of shape. I kept switching speed and length of stride and the position of my water-bottle belt, hoping suddenly everything would fall into place and I'd feel a surge of adrenaline. It never happened.

As I ran, I wondered how many weeks of proper eating and regular workouts it would take to get my pace under ten-minute miles. Running is easy to obsess about—the mileage, the speed—but it's probably a healthier obsession than any I've had yet.

The trouble with acknowledging your feelings instead of just eating to "stuff" them is that you're still stuck with the feelings once you've acknowledged them. Or is that what running, meditating, and yoga are supposed to be for?

Tonight, at a scary dinner party filled with New York media types, I felt like an idiot—partially for talking so much, which I always do when I'm nervous, and partially because I wasn't happy with my all-black ensemble. I can't say it flattered me—it mostly just covered me up, which is all I seem to demand of clothes these days. I grab practically the first thing that I can actually zip or button. I don't scrutinize the fit, because that would require scrutinizing myself.

The evening got off to an inauspicious start when I walked into the room and everyone—including the only person I knew at the party—appeared to be in the sort of deep conversation you don't just go join. At dinner, the woman sitting next to me—a scary (and scary-skinny) New York editor—apparently had heard from somebody that I'd worked for the *Miami Herald* as a teenager. She asked me rather pointedly how I'd done that, as if she didn't believe it, and proceeded to preface her response to any other comment I made about stories I was working on now—she asked me about them—by saying I was young and naive. The only bonus was that she made me so nervous I could barely drink or eat—I wondered if she would correct which fork I used. Or maybe she was waiting for me to ask for a straw to sip my wine?

It starts as a tiny crack of uncertainty that becomes my own personal abyss. I let evenings like tonight call my whole life into question—what I'm doing with myself, what I *should* be doing with myself. Do I really belong in this field? Compliments about my work still catch me off guard, because what I write seems to me to be virtually indistinguishable from the rivers of words everywhere.

I wonder for the millionth time if I should have gone to law or business school, where I could end up with a career that would be so much easier to quantify: *I won this case. I signed that deal. I made X amount of dollars for the company this year.* Concrete signs that indicate whether I'm heading in the right direction.

I know some journalists spend their entire careers at the tier of magazines that includes some I now occasionally write for, never breaking into the very top tier. I can't stand the thought that at age twenty-four, this could be as far as I get. I could spend my whole life "almost but not quite"—a whole life of feeling, so keenly, what my limits are.

Skipped the party of an old friend partly because I had to work but mostly because I feel so fat. I haven't seen this friend since before I started the column, but he has seen the column—as well as, of course, the pictures, and the ones making it into print now are me at my thinnest, from the summer. I don't want to be asked about the column or wonder if people are wondering if the pictures are retouched because I don't look like that in person.

I trekked to a supermarket twenty-five minutes away to buy a piece of cake with the crummy, cheap buttercream frosting I've always loved because I decided that was what I was craving. It tasted overly sweet and just horrible. I ate four bites—the last two spent double- and triple-checking that there was actually a "forbidden" food I don't even like anymore.

I feel spent from the eating disorders piece. And now I've got to decide whether to use a pseudonym, which I go back and forth on. I'm not sure I want people to know these things about me, but at the same time not using my name seems like a validation of the idea that eating disorders are too shameful to admit to.

The story is part personal, part reported—all about the cult of thinness that surrounds us and how young most women are when they first begin succumbing to it.

It's estimated that 90 percent of Americans regularly consume low-calorie, sugar-free, or reduced-fat foods. Disordered eating—cutting out big groups of food, restricting yourself to nothing with more than five grams of fat, or social pig-outs—is rampant. Depending on which statistics you read, as many as 85 percent of college women indulge in it.

"I haven't met a woman yet who hasn't had some type of problem with food," one therapist told me. "It goes from throwing up ten times a day to just thinking a lot about what you could or should or shouldn't eat. I mean, who hasn't said, 'I can't eat that'?"

The statistics, stories, and experts made me feel both less alone and more depressed than ever.

In an *Esquire* magazine poll of a thousand women, more than half said they'd rather get run over by a truck than get fat. In another poll, a group of college students said they'd be more inclined to marry an embezzler, cocaine user, ex-mental patient, shoplifter, nymphomaniac, communist, atheist, or marijuana user than a fat person.

And my own story: Bruce the Spruce telling me to eat my vegetables so I'd be thin; the private eating in college so I could hold back in public—never mind that everyone could tell from the way I looked that I had to be eating more than was on my lunch tray; and the Summer of a Thousand Peaches.

The irony of the article is that I've been told if all goes well, I'll get a promotion to senior writer when it's done. Over the past few years my mind has been so consumed with food that I started to fear it was affecting my job. Now it is affecting my job, but not in the way I'd expected.

I turned in the piece at about 9:00 P.M. last night, possibly among the earliest I've ever turned in a long piece. The top editor is taking it home over the weekend to read, which means a whole weekend for me to freak out about it.

Mary called to say a friend of hers I met last week asked about me. Apparently he thought I was really funny. That's me—a regular court jester.

Got an e-mail from the editor about the story with the subject line "Relieved?" It didn't say much, other than that I needed to go somewhere fun after this piece and that I should take the offer I've gotten to go on a press trip to Australia in May. Woo-hoo!

I feel like I'm stuck in some sort of Middle Earth, unfit for any world, for any way of coping. I'm beginning to recognize the feelings that lead to overeating and bingeing, but lots of the time I binge anyway. No part of the binge is comforting anymore, but I still do it because it's what I know.

After a month and a half of going out every week, I'm not hanging out with Victoria anymore. The turning point came when we saw each other four times in one week. It was too much. Too many hours of frantic, forced fun and too much time with someone who, I've realized, doesn't particularly care if it's me sitting next to her at the bar or arriving with her at the party. It could be anyone—it's just a role she needs filled, and it makes me feel empty.

There's been nothing to say to her except that I've been really busy with a story. She seems to have already moved on.

Must be a better friend to the friends I have. And must be more open about what's going on—like my behavior with Mary around the time of the marathon. But I feel like there's a tipping point for how much you can pile on any one friend: How can I tell her about my mother and my parents' divorce—which I have done—and then pile the bingeing on top of it?

My close friends never say whether they've read the *Shape* columns, and I never ask. But occasionally someone will bring the subject up at an odd moment. I was telling Mary about another friend who has started being overly solicitous about what kind of restaurant we can go to together and whether I'd be OK with it. Which of course makes me not OK with it, because then I feel like if I order what I want and what I want is not a salad or grilled fish, this friend then thinks, *Why have I bothered?*

Mary didn't say anything for a couple of minutes. Then she said the columns made her much more conscious about what she says about food and her own weight around me. She also said that she'd suggested to Abby that she do the same. I hate the thought that being around me is so much *work*.

Have spent the past couple of days e-mailing this woman named Kellie from D.C. who figured out that "Courtney Rubin from *Shape*" and "Courtney Rubin from *Washingtonian*" are the same person. Her first e-mail caught me off guard, and I responded.

She had written—as nearly everyone does—that she couldn't believe she was writing a letter to someone in a magazine and about how bizarre it was to be so proud of someone she's never met and how much I had motivated her, even though she was struggling. I wrote back that contrary to what she was currently reading in the magazine right now (the marathon column with a picture of me at my thinnest), I too was struggling.

She wrote back: "Even if you never lose another pound, I love to hear about someone else's struggles and how they are just like mine. Keep writing."

Inspired by Kellie, I sent Peeke an e-mail asking for help. She told me to get a calendar and some star stickers and give myself red stars for days I do destructive things, silver stars for days I struggle but don't act on the temptation, and golds for days where I really stick to the diet. The immediate aim is to get rid of the reds. Silvers, I suppose, are the realities of daily living. Golds I can hope for but not count on. I'm not entirely clear on what this is supposed to do, other than, I suppose, make me face how many days a month I'm self-destructive.

A silver star day. My head is so filled with voices—Peeke's, Nancy's, and Geneen Roth's telling me it's OK to eat—that it's hard to sort out what I feel from what I think I should feel.

I had two jelly doughnuts for lunch today. Two doughnuts—nothing more. This is progress.

Date tonight with this guy Dan I met more than six weeks ago—long enough ago for me to have given up on his ever calling.

We went to dinner downtown and talked mostly about our jobs. I never talk about the *Shape* column, and I didn't this time either. It's not the sort of thing I want to end up talking about with some guy I've seen just twice in my life.

When the waitress came to tell us about dessert, she stopped in midrecitation and stared at me.

"You're Courtney Rubin from *Shape*," she said. "You can't order dessert."

I felt trapped then. I never would have ordered dessert anyway, but I didn't like it that after her comment I felt like I couldn't. I wanted to point out that I'd left more than half of my mashed potatoes and hadn't eaten any bread.

I also felt trapped because I knew Dan would ask about *Shape*, and the moment she left he did.

"I didn't know I was out with someone famous," he said.

I tried to explain the column in the vaguest terms possible, wondering if he was thinking, as I would if I were him: *Shouldn't someone writing about weight loss be thin?*

Month 16 (April)

*A*nother day, another reason my life would be easier/better if I were thinner. At a Passover seder I sat next to a cute guy, a cartoonist. The whole time I was talking, a little piece of my brain was thinking: *If I weren't overweight, maybe I could be one of those people who meet a potential boyfriend somewhere random.* When I went to the bathroom, I was afraid to look but figured I'd better face it. I examined my reflection and actually pronounced it not *too* repulsive.

Then I sat back down at the table, and Diana whispered: "We've got to do something about your hair. It's all frizzy."

Crazy athletic weekend. Saturday I ran the Cherry Blossom Ten-Miler. It was pouring, and with the windchill the temperature was sixteen degrees. I was supposed to be doing something healthy and good for myself, but I nearly made myself sick. Everyone I knew had dropped out of the race because of the weather, but I wouldn't let myself.

On Sunday I went hiking with Mary and Stacy. I'm glad I didn't know ahead of time that it involved lots of rock scrambling and a bit of rock climbing, because I probably would have wimped out. We were far along the trail before we started getting to bits that scared me, and at that point I just had to do them.

"I've heard even six-year-olds can do it," Mary said, trying to be encouraging. OK, I thought, but there are six-year-olds who do backflips off ten-meter diving boards and ride Space Mountain at Disney World—both things that scare me.

A couple of hours into the hike, we came to a sheer wall of rock. The higher I climbed, the harder the footholds got to find, and the farther apart they were. Worse, there were bunches of people at the foot of the wall, all waiting for me to finish climbing so they could have their turn.

My knee-jerk response was to climb back down and wait by the car. But climbing down rocks is even harder and scarier than climbing up, and Mary and Stacy were having none of it. They waited close to twenty minutes in one place for me to move a few feet. I didn't hear anyone on the trail laughing at me, either. In most cases they offered to help. It seemed the world was conspiring to keep me from quitting.

I was exhausted when I finished, but it was a good kind of tired. I won't say I loved every minute of it, but I definitely loved having done it.

The past few weeks have been the kind where half my wardrobe is at the dry cleaner because I'm never around in time to pick it up. The kind where it takes me three weeks to find a free hour to get coffee with a friend. It's the most unlikely of times, but all of a sudden food and exercise are falling back into place. There are lots of possible reasons, but I think it's this: after a couple of months of feeling again how it feels to be eating anything and everything and too much of it all the time—in a word: *yucky*—I've had enough. The high I got from the hike didn't hurt, either.

It sounds so simple and so weight-loss-success-story kind of cheerful: I woke up one morning and decided to do it. But as Nancy has told me repeatedly, everyone knows how to lose weight—it's just a matter of wanting it badly enough to make it work.

I'm tired of racking my brain for what I might possibly want to eat and then heading out to get it, all the while thinking: *I must eat it now because I am absolutely, positively getting back on track tomorrow.* These days the only thing I crave is control. But I know I've got to be careful. Last year I ate the same things over and over: things that were safe. But here's the rub: you eat the same thing every day, and suddenly you can't take it anymore. You can't figure out what you want to eat first. You've fallen into the diet trap—where foods feel forbidden because you're afraid of them or what might happen if you started eating them. At least that's what happened to me.

Forget about the gold and silver and whatever other color stars there were. That lasted a week until I tired of it, like a fad diet. Now I'm working on straddling the middle ground—halfway between eating exactly what I'm "supposed" to and eating anything and everything. My plan is to balance my fear of what I might eat if given the choice with my desire to plan to eat healthy by bringing lunch three times a week and eating whatever I want (within reason) the other two days. The weight won't come off as quickly, I'm sure, but maybe, just maybe, this time it will be for good.

My eating disorders story is getting a mention on the magazine cover, and one of the cover-line options was something like, "Fear of Fat: One Woman's Struggle with an Eating Disorder." I vetoed that one fast. I'm OK with talking about my bingeing in an article when I can pretend, as I'm doing, that the article really is mostly about other people. But seeing "one woman's struggle" is somehow just too revealing.

I can't believe I'm really publishing this. Tonight I sent the parts involving Diana to her. Not so much for her approval, but as a heads-up. She wrote back something I wasn't expecting: that she remembered a lot of the moments I was referring to with Mom and Grandma. She used to feel so awful during them—so unsure of what to do—she wanted to cry herself.

I keep envisioning myself someday writing an essay or short story titled "After the Flood." But all I can do now is look around at the rubble and try not to cry.

I got home Thursday night at 12:30 A.M.—I'd just put the eating disorders piece to bed, and I still had some freelance assignments to plow through. But I'd decided I deserved to go out and so had a couple of drinks. All I wanted to do then was sleep for hours, but when I walked into the building, one of the guys at the front desk said, "I don't think you want to go up there, Miss Rubin."

The guys often tease me about my piles of mail and the hours I get home, so I thought they were joking. I smiled wanly and headed for the elevator when one of them took my arm.

"Miss Rubin, you don't want to go up there," he said. "There's been a flood."

I didn't believe him. I'm still not sure what happened—they said something about a pipe being left open. All I know is it took the building extra long to discover the problem because there was no one living beneath me, so the water had to get all the way down to apartment 203 (through two floors) before anyone called the front desk.

There's so much stuff ruined I don't even know where to start. Of course, tons of this is my own fault, because my apartment was an absolute sty—I'd been telling everyone for weeks that I was going to take off a couple of days just to clean my apartment and get my life in order. So of course, loads of things were on the floor that had no business being there: magazines, CDs, clothes.

I keep trying to look on the bright side, saying that at least I'll really have to clean everything now. But I'll also have to replace so much stuff, which I don't have time for.

I felt so violated, seeing my stuff strewn around the hallway in soggy piles and knowing that the maintenance guys had seen my apartment in an embarrassing state. But I only started to cry—of all times—when I couldn't reach Diana. I was so tired, I had to go to the bathroom, and I just didn't want to have to deal with anyone. Diana and I are so used to seeing each other at our worst that I wanted to be with her not so much because I thought she'd make me feel better but because I wouldn't have to be on my best behavior around her. There's nothing I could say or do that could change her opinion of me.

Finally Diana came home, and I collapsed on her futon but couldn't sleep. Something was bothering me. So I begged Diana to dig out her copy of the lease. I had to know: can you be evicted for being a slob?

Insanity, I once read, is doing the same thing over and over again and expecting different results. If that's true, I'm certifiable.

As always, it's my instinct to call Mom when something goes wrong, so I called her this morning about the flood. I wanted her to tell me exactly what to do, and she didn't, or couldn't. She talked about what she was watching on the news—not because she doesn't care, but because her illness means her attention span is severely limited.

So I left Mary a half-hysterical voice mail, and she promptly called back, saying she was ditching her happy hour plans this evening to come over, help me assess the damage, and then take me to stay at her place. She must have spread the word about the flood to our friends, because the offers of places to stay and rides anywhere I needed started coming in.

In daylight, everything in the apartment was even worse than I'd remembered. College newspapers and high school yearbooks ruined. Pictures I'd meant to put in albums stuck together in clumps. Journals smeared to the point of unreadability, because I love to write with felt-tip pens. Mary and I threw out bags of stuff. I tried not to cry.

Sitting on Mary's couch alone on a Saturday night. It feels good. I've read maybe a hundred pages of my book-club book, practiced my guitar, done two loads of laundry, hand-washed a shirt and a rug, and made a stab at finding all the phone numbers to call various companies whose bills are now too soggy for me to see how much I owe them.

If this would have been a nightmare for anybody, it was doubly so for a weight watcher. Dealing with the aftermath of the flood—getting things cleaned up, fighting with the phone company, trying to replace dozens of things—is like a full-time job on top of the overtime I'm already working. I'm lucky to have a friend willing to let me crash in her apartment for several weeks, but Mary's place is far from mine, not to mention far from the gym I'd deliberately chosen because it was convenient to *my* place. I'm on someone else's schedule, without my own space, time, or even refrigerator. I hate having anybody—even Mary, *especially* Mary—see what I eat all the time. Knowing that I can't, say, have pizza for dinner two nights in a row—because that's not really normal—makes me want to binge. (What *doesn't* seem to make me want to binge?)

It's all I can do not to lie on my couch—OK, Mary's couch—and eat myself through it. I can't figure out how I'm going to exercise, and all the planning required to eat properly for a week just seems like one more thing I don't have the time or energy to do.

Every time I go back to my apartment to investigate, I find that something else has gone wrong. Now my stuff has been ruined four times. First with the initial flooding and then when things I had salvaged were thrown on top of ruined ones when maintenance men came to deal with the carpet. After that, I told our building manager I wanted to be told when there were people working in my apartment. But when I checked up on my apartment Thursday, I found work had been done in the bathroom, and more of my stuff was thrown on the floor, broken, soggy, and otherwise ruined. Later that evening, when I wasn't there, a sink backed up and made everything in my kitchen muddy and unusable. There's still mud on the floor.

On top of this, our building manager had told me they'd pay for dry-cleaning all the clothes and other things that were salvageable. But today there was a note in my mailbox saying she had to follow what the building owners said. They are insisting it's not their fault and that my lease absolves them of any responsibility.

I threw my cell phone across the room and cried.

I've been crying off and on for days. Even someone asking me how I am—in just the right sympathetic tone of voice—sets me off. And everything—

even getting myself to work, which from Mary's is a commute—seems to require more energy than I have.

I've eaten haphazardly, and I don't think running around town trying to do a million errands exactly counts as exercise. So once again I've turned to food as one thing I can—maybe, possibly, if I try hard enough, please God—control.

Nancy reminded me that every day I have a choice: to lose, to maintain, or to gain. We have a limited energy pie, and losing weight takes a slice—unfortunately, not the calorie-burning sort—that, when life is crazy, might be needed for other things, like dealing with landlords. "Times of chaos are not lose-weight days or weeks," she told me. They're maintain-if-at-all-possible weeks.

I also have to adjust my definition of *successful* when it comes to weight. The classic definition is, of course, the scale going down, but for now I may have to define *successful* as coping with the flood without gaining weight—forget about losing. After several months of ups and downs, I'm so frustrated that just when I was finally ready to rock again, my life seems to be conspiring against me. But really, what can I do? Given the option to gain or maintain—well, the choice is a no-brainer.

My weight-gain diary is in this month's *Shape*—the column I wrote nearly six months ago, at the beginning of November.

The column makes me ache for myself back then, writing with an everything's-going-to-be-OK-in-the-end cheer I'm sure I didn't feel. Then there's the ending: "The key, Peeke says, is to regroup. Dust yourself off, figure out what went wrong, forgive yourself, and get on with it. If only it were that easy."

Six months on, and I still haven't. Haven't forgiven myself. Haven't gotten on with it.

But the response to the column has been unlike anything I ever expected. This is the first issue that has my e-mail address in it, and the account overflowed. Lots of all caps and exclamation marks. "You are the most REAL part of the magazine!" and "I just wanted to tell you that you are amazing, and such an inspiration" and "We're all rooting for you, you can do it!!!!!!!" (no extra exclamation points added) and "Thanks for sticking your neck out and taking this project. You rally my spirit and help strengthen my resolve." And one of my favorites: "The first time I looked at my friend's *Shape* magazine I thought this is another magazine with stupid ideas on how to motivate you, but then I saw your article and subscribed to *Shape* right then and there. Every month I can't wait to read your diary. We're all behind you 100 percent."

Sherri, one of the senior editors at the *Washingtonian*, came into my office today carrying a bunch of pink roses and a card. In the card was what she had nicknamed "Getting Courtney's Head Above the Water Fund"—a mall gift certificate that much of the office had chipped in for.

I was speechless. It was one of the nicest things anyone has ever done for me.

Love everybody. Love my office.

Am swearing off complaining about anyone at the *Washingtonian*.

At least until next month.

The eating disorders story is out. Cover line: "Fear of Fat." Headline: "Losing It." I hope nobody but me knows just how apt that seems to be for my state of mind these days.

I jump every time my office phone rings, but it's never about the story. Instead, those calls seem to come when people don't think I'll be around—or maybe when no one is around to hear these women call. The time stamps on my voice mail are at 11:12 P.M., 2:37 A.M., 3:07 A.M. Women (and it's nearly all women) reaching out in the darkness—or possibly, I imagine, by the light of the refrigerator.

The e-mails have been very encouraging, though sad. One 260-pound woman wrote about how just after she read it she was walking across the street and some guy yelled, "Why don't you go on Weight Watchers?" There are flattering e-mails from two novelists I've profiled, plus a sweet one from a guy I know about the struggle he had helping an old girlfriend who was bulimic.

Despite the nice e-mails, I wish I could go into every book and grocery store in the Washington area and buy up every last copy to keep anyone from reading it. I especially wish there were some way to prevent my friends from doing so.

When I got back to Mary's today, she seemed to want to talk about something. Finally she said, "I read your story in the magazine." The eating disorders piece.

The magazine story is mostly about college and right after I graduated—before Mary knew me. But she wanted to know how much of the behavior I wrote about is still a problem. The piece ends on an upbeat note—that it has been long enough since I've binged that I'm starting to forget what it feels like (true at the moment I wrote the words, but not now). Still, she was worried about me, especially because the last lines of the story suggest that I'm still struggling: "My story doesn't have an ending because it never ends. You never completely stop thinking about food. You just work on doing it less. Instead of thinking about it all the time—100 percent of the pie—you aim for 75, then 50. You hope for 25. And whatever you do, you just keep going."

That was it—my opening to talk about all of this with her, to explain some of the behavior—the obsessiveness—that I'm sure sometimes has repelled her. I answered her question—told her that I didn't do some of the more extreme things in the story anymore, that I didn't starve. (I didn't add that sometimes I still think about starving and wish that I had the willpower.) But I didn't tell her anything more than that. Between the flood and the divorce and my mother and my constant worries about a thousand other things, I already feel so needy; so depressing. So heavy with grief.

Month 17 (May)

*G*randma hasn't said anything about the eating disorders story. (I'm not expecting Mom to say anything other than the story is long, which, in fact, it is.) I want to force the issue, the way I often do when I know I've gained weight and just want to hear it from Grandma already. But I can't bring myself to say anything.

Dad's e-mail: was Bruce the Spruce really that insensitive?

I avoided a *Shape* photo shoot because of the flood—it was supposed to be two days after. So now I've been told to take lots of pictures of myself this month because we're very behind. There's a plan for an extended photo shoot next month, where they'll take pictures for four months in one day. I can't decide which is worse: to have more photo shoots (and more chances to look bad/stupid/fat) or just the one. I hate the fact that with one, even if I make major progress, it's not going to show in the pictures.

I want to call *Shape* and say what they're doing is cheating, but it's not like I've been telling the whole truth, either.

My new, productive, going-to-make-my-life-perfect thing is that I've joined a fiction-writing group, hoping it will force me to finish some of the short story fragments I have lying around. Except after reading the stories for tonight's meeting, I'm no longer sure this was such a good idea. Everyone is so good it's daunting.

"Just from the way you talk I can't wait to read one of your stories," one of the group members told me as we were leaving.

Great—no pressure there.

Tonight was supposed to be my first night in my new apartment. But my mattress doesn't fit my bed frame, so I can't sleep on it. I had to trek back to Mary's, and tomorrow I'll have to deal with Mattress Discounters again. As if I need any more things to do.

When I went upstairs today to collect my phone from my old apartment it was gone. Stolen. A small thing, but another thing to replace. The money pit, this flood is.

It's also been a diet buster. I've gained six pounds. It's hard to take solace in the fact that if this had occurred a couple of years ago, it might have been ten or fifteen.

For the past few days I've been trying to wear myself out. I can't bear being alone with myself at night, lying awake hating myself for gaining weight, for bingeing, for being so desperate to get food that I lie to people I love. I feel like my relationship with food has taken precedence over all others—it's an abusive love I can't seem to extricate myself from.

I make mental lists of all the things food has ruined, damaged, or stolen. Time. Concentration. Happiness.

I feel like I've tried everything I can think of to lose weight—every last tip I've ever read. My resolve to lose weight is fading—worn away by every morning hoping today is going to be the day I get back on track and then, sometimes an hour into the day or sometimes twelve hours, failing.

Tonight I talked to Shari about the bingeing. I didn't try to prettify it as pigging out or attempt to put a positive spin on it—"at least I'm exercising"— as I have before. I told her I'd started to think I was getting over it—hence the upbeat ending to the eating disorders piece, which she read—but I'm not. It's back, and I don't know what to do.

I haven't discussed the bingeing with anyone associated with *Shape*. I talked with Shari about it partly because I should have done so ages ago, but also selfishly, so I could feel like I was making a fresh start—this collaboration on inventing the new Courtney. It's my perfectionist thing again: I'd rather start over and have the chance—unlikely as it seems—for all to go perfectly than constantly have to stare at my mistakes, the non-gold-starred days on the calendar. Also, I was starting to feel dishonest every time I had a conversation with her about *Shape*—like I was hiding something, which I was. Dishonesty, like every other crummy emotion, leads directly to eating.

So now I have a new plan of attack: food journals. Again.

I'm supposed to write down absolutely everything I eat (especially if it's a binge) and how I feel—not so I can be chastised for not sticking to a diet, Shari says, but so we can see the cause and effect and I can learn to short-circuit the system. It will be a slow process, and Shari says I'm not supposed to be worrying about losing weight while I do this. But how can I stop worrying about that? Even if I try, the obsession gnaws at the edges. My brain automatically thinks things like: *I ate this instead of that—that's a calorie savings.* Or: *We've spent all day walking around—that has to cancel some of what I ate at lunch.* And I know that in order for what Shari's proposing to work, I've *got* to binge for us to have something to work with.

I don't want to have to write down that list of foods, to confront it, to contemplate it. But I'll try anything now, and keeping food journals and analyzing them sounds so simple, so doable.

I feel hopeful again.

Four weeks and three days after the flood—or the Great Flood of '00, as Erica has taken to calling it—I've finally gotten my (sometimes still soggy) stuff out of all of my friends' apartments and moved into my new one, just two floors below my old one.

It's clean and new and unsullied by memories of starving or bingeing. I don't look at the futon and remember how I can never find a comfortable spot on it when I'm binge-level full, because the futon was ruined in the flood. I don't walk into the closet and see the mark on the wall from when I threw a shoe in frustration because nothing was fitting.

I want a new, clean life to go with my new, clean apartment.

The Sunday night blues. Mary has a date, Abby and Andrea are off shopping, Alexy is annoyed that I don't want to hold my birthday dinner tomorrow late enough (8:30—but it's a Monday night) for her to do her volunteer work first. And I've been getting answering machines for everyone else I call.

Diana got back from visiting Dad in San Francisco tonight and informed me that they had been talking about me. Don't get mad, she said, but (a guaranteed way to annoy me before she's even said whatever it is) I was too smart to spend my life writing about the silly, fluffy things that I do. I asked if there was anything else they had discussed about me that she'd care to share. She said my fear of driving.

"Anything else?" I asked.

She didn't say anything. I have a funny feeling they also discussed how much weight I've gained.

May 15, 2000: my twenty-fifth birthday. At the gym this morning I kept thinking about how different this birthday is from last year's. Well, how much heavier I am, though doing the math to come up with an exact figure is too depressing.

It didn't seem like an auspicious start to the day. But I got in to work and the phone was ringing. My friend Josh in Chicago, who is not generally a phone person. He was about the last person I'd expect to remember my birthday, and he hadn't.

"Hey, All-Star," he said. Turns out this media gossip website we're obsessed with linked to a *Washington Business Journal* article mentioning my promotion to senior writer. Except the article says I'm twenty-four, which, as of today, I pointed out to Josh, I am no longer.

So Josh e-mailed the website, and a line appeared beneath the article, identifying Josh as "a Rubin pal"—we got a laugh out of that one—who wanted to correct the record on my age, since it was my birthday.

I got "happy birthday" e-mails all day from journalists I barely know or don't know at all, including one from a reporter I met once before he moved to New York. "Congrats," he wrote. "It's fun being young and successful." I laughed at that one.

Because I'm going to Australia on Friday, the real birthday party is when I get back. Tonight's gathering was a low-key girls' night at a Brazilian restaurant in Adams Morgan. One caipirinha, no dessert.

I'm getting nervous about the Australia trip. It's exactly the sort where I can't confess my worries to any of my friends, because I would sound whiny: I have to go to Australia and go to a bunch of press dinners that will involve a lot of expensive food and wine. Waah.

What I can't say is that I become panicky at long meals where I can't escape food or where people are pushing it at me and I'm required to give an explanation for why I'm not having any. I debated saying I couldn't go on the trip, but as always, I loathe having food be the determiner of what I do.

This is supposed to be the fun trip I get to take after all of my work on the eating disorders piece, and it's starting to seem anything but. I'm too anxious to be amused by the irony that I've just published six thousand awfully honest words about my troubles with food yet can't say ten honest words to my boss about it, even though he has clearly read my story and so something like this might not come as a total surprise.

Trips for me are also still all-or-nothing food propositions. I can't get my mind around the fact that I can, theoretically, stop overeating or bingeing at any point. Once I start, I can't stop until I get home. Witness last November's trip to London.

Food makes it hard for me to enjoy vacations. Or really, *I* make it hard for myself to enjoy vacations. I go on them with unrealistic hopes. I think amazing things are going to have to happen to make all the struggle I'll have with food be worth it—that whatever I do or see has to be unbelievable or else it will be lost in the food.

Meanwhile, I'm having a tough time with the food journals. Usually the idea that anybody is going to look at them means I either eat saint-style or tidy them up a bit, the way my mother used to clean the house before the cleaner did. Even though I'm not technically dieting, I don't want to answer to Shari why I've eaten, say, a Dove bar or a muffin. I don't want her to know. It's like I'm going to get a grade on my food journals. As always, I want to be a good student. Have to keep up appearances.

It occurred to me the other day that my gotta-get-an-A instinct is probably part of the bingeing problem, so finally I admitted it.

Shari says I'm right—my instinct to edit *is* key to figuring out how to stop the bingeing. Why do I worry about pleasing other people when I'm hurting myself? The simple answer is that I crave outside validation, that it gives me something I'm not able to give myself. But the more complicated question— and answer, which Shari says won't come quickly—is why I can't.

SOMEWHERE OVER THE PACIFIC

On a flight from Los Angeles to Sydney, a flight I should have been on at this time yesterday. Am angry, angry, angry that even though I showed up for my flight two hours early, I still missed it because of the lines.

I've been prone to rage this month over the smallest things—late Metro trains, lines that move maddeningly slowly, my inability to find a receipt to return a ten-dollar hammer to the hardware store. Worse, with the rage has come the new and unattractive propensity to burst into tears, as I did yesterday when I found I wouldn't be flying out until today. I can't remember the last time I cried—was it the day I heard about the divorce?—before I started doing it practically every other day since the flood. I'm hoping the tears are just from general stress/bad luck/exhaustion. I'm also hoping maybe—like sweat being the sign of a fever that's breaking—the tears are a sign that I'm letting feelings out some way other than bingeing, even if crying isn't exactly my ideal response.

IN AUSTRALIA

Palm Cove, this Australian resort town, feels like it could be in South Florida. Pink and turquoise buildings. Surf shops. Tacky souvenirs.

But the sky here is so clear—and so star-studded—it actually seems fake. I wish I knew half of what I was seeing, though I did finally find someone who could point out the Southern Cross. Both days we've been here, I've gotten up early and run on the beach at sunrise. It was so beautiful I didn't even think about how many extra calories I was probably burning by running in the sand, which is harder than running on pavement. Well, I didn't think about it for long, anyway.

People keep bringing up things they saw the first day of the trip. I'm trying not to get too irritated and to take comfort in the things I won't miss. And I'm hoping to find out that there's some great cosmic reason I didn't make it onto my original flights. But neither of those planes crashed.

Went snorkeling and scuba diving in the Great Barrier Reef today, even though almost no one else did. I felt self-conscious, especially because one of the men on the trip—the sort of overly friendly grandpa type who started referring to me as "Court" five seconds after he met me—kept loudly teasing me that I was doing it because the guy in charge was cute.

If I were really into this guy, I was tempted to say, do you think I'd want him to see me in a bathing suit?

This is like something out of a dream, and not just because the sharp edges of life have been dulled by too much champagne.

I'm on the Orient Express—actually, it's the Great South Pacific Express—and it looks like something out of the 1920s. Deep polished mahogany with gold fixtures. Velvet. All sorts of things emblazoned with the train logo that I'm sure more than one guest has filched.

Wrote to Grandma because all this gracious living reminds me of nothing so much as the black-and-white picture she has in her bedroom of her and

Grandpa standing on the steps of a cruise ship sometime in the 1950s—she in a sleeveless dress and he in a dinner jacket. They look like movie stars.

I'd love to come back on a train like this and be slim. Be able to wear sleeveless dresses with strappy sandals and no control-top hose—and not have to worry about bulging out everywhere and whether my feet resemble Miss Piggy's.

Daydreaming about coming back here keeps me from thinking about the picture I got two days ago of me with a koala. My arm is so huge—it looks bigger than some people's thighs—that I can never show the picture to anyone. I know it's possible it's just an unflattering photo, but I'm really *that* unsure of what I look like, and there's no one I can ask.

Being on the train is frustrating, because there's no way to exercise. I can't even take a walk—the corridors are so narrow you have to stop every two minutes to let someone else by. There's practically nothing to do but eat, and that's what I'm doing.

I've managed to miss tea today, a fact I know I'm going to spend half of dinner trying to slide gracefully into the conversation in case I feel the need to explain why I may be eating more than everyone else.

It's official: I have the travel bug again. I've been collecting tips for places to go in Australia and New Zealand, thinking: *How can I get off a couple of months to go traveling, and who could I convince to do it with me?* People in England do this sort of thing all the time—work for a couple of years, quit their jobs (or just take their six weeks' vacation), and hit India or Australia or the Far East—but it seems so rare for Americans. The biggest obstacle for me, though, seems not to be time, money, or company, all of which could probably be solved. It's weight. How can I take the trip of a lifetime and not be able to bear to look at the pictures?

Am I replacing an addiction to food with an addiction to things, or am I just becoming obsessed with *things* because I can't have what I really want—to be thin? Lately there are so many things I want to own, and I keep coming up with new ones. Earrings from Tiffany's. CDs. Books. Cute shoes. Chanel lipstick. The newest spa product from Bliss. Forty-five-dollar Diptyque candles. A Birkin bag. A $24,000 Cathy Waterman necklace (which, depressingly, I will probably never be able to afford).

A tidal wave of wanting.

But I still want to eat.

Month 18 (June)

*B*etween Australia and the flood, I haven't gone on a proper grocery-shopping expedition in nearly two months.

I never officially decided to stop going weekly—somehow it just happened. Staying at Mary's disrupted the routine. Then a Sunday away, another Sunday busy, another Sunday lazy, and there you go. With the end of weekly grocery shopping also went my mental fast forward of the upcoming week, looking for potential food land mines. And then the slow unraveling of the rest of the routine: the weekly bag of healthy snacks for the office, which means I contemplate eating things at 4:00 P.M. that I know I shouldn't. When I eat the cookies or chips, I debate skipping dinner, or some part of it. At 10:00 or 11:00 P.M., I realize I'm starving and there's nothing healthy in my apartment to grab. So I buy something else I shouldn't, then wake up full and tired the next morning and don't go to the gym.

Losing weight is like wearing a watch that needs daily winding—if you don't start from the proper place, you're always going to get it wrong. I opened my refrigerator tonight and wondered if it was actually possible to make dinner (forget about tomorrow's lunch) out of nail polish, Healthy Choice string cheese, diet salad dressing, and a bottle of soy sauce of indeterminate age.

No more excuses. I'm getting up at 5:00 A.M. tomorrow so I can hit the gym and the Safeway before work.

Shape wants me to work on a feature story called "Does Your Environment Make You Fat?" I love this story, and I know exactly why: I love the idea of more excuses. *See? It's not my fault I'm overweight.* Then again, a sign over my body that says, "It's not my fault I'm overweight" will never ever replace a sexy black dress as the perfect party outfit.

My *Shape* e-mail account keeps overflowing. I can't bear to read the mail. Depending on my mood, it makes me feel like an impostor (so many of the writers think I've got an answer for them), depressed (because the readers haven't yet seen how much weight I've gained), or guilty (for not answering it all personally).

Shape again. Their patience with my gain-a-few, lose-one, gain-some-more routine is starting to wear thin. Got an e-mail from my editor asking whether I've been successful at losing any more weight. Maureen says she doesn't want me to feel like she's pressuring me, but maybe it's time to shake up the routine. "What have Peeke and Shari been saying?" she wants to know.

I told her I've just seen Shari, which is true, and that we're working on things. That I'm keeping food journals again. That we're trying to identify the emotional triggers that make me want to pig out (again I avoid using the word *binge*). That I plan to start lifting weights again. That I start marathon training again soon.

Just knowing that *Shape* was getting impatient—or seeming to—made me panic all day: Oh, no. I'm hungry. I'm *never* going to lose weight. I kept thinking I was hungry because I knew I couldn't eat any more—because I have got to start losing weight again. And to think that this was exactly the sort of pressure I thought would motivate me to lose weight when I decided to get myself into this *Shape* thing last year.

Since in the past I have obviously not been able to leap back on track—at least for more than a couple of days—I've decided to break my return to ideal diet behavior into baby steps. I went to the grocery store this week. Next week I'll work on getting my workouts back up to fifty minutes (I'd slipped to forty-five and now it's more like forty). Maybe then I'll be able to deal with lifting weights again, yet another thing I've let slide. At this rate nothing will happen fast. But I'm trying to remind myself that it's a start.

This month—per discussion with Shari—I'm supposed to work on setting boundaries, because if I can't do it with the rest of my life, I'm apparently never going to be able to do it with food. I'm supposed to decide how many freelance assignments I'll take per month and—because I'm the original girl who can't say no when there's an editor on the phone—I'm to post this number on my desk (along with a script for what I'll say when someone calls and

I'm up to my monthly limit). I'm supposed to decide ahead of time what time I'm going to bed and not answer the phone after that. The goal is to master my life and let food follow.

I'm scared that nobody—editor or friend—will ever call again. For me, being overweight has always meant that I have to take what I can get—as if with each extra pound I have I lose a little more of the right to demand more, or to demand better, whether from friends or anyone else. I'm not sure where and how this idea took root, only that it's been there for as long as I can remember.

Shape online chat. Sample questions: What's my favorite flavor of Ben & Jerry's? What did I eat for dinner tonight? What's my favorite snack? What music do I like to listen to when I run? What do I do when I'm hungry right after lunch?

I answered all the questions, but all I wanted to type was: "You don't want to copy me." You do not want to replicate my results or, more accurately, lack thereof.

Grandma is too busy worrying about someone else's weight to ask me about mine.

Mom is losing weight. At first Grandma sounded pleased: "Your mother never eats," she told me one Sunday, sounding awed. "You should see your mother," she told me another.

I can't quite pinpoint when, but lately the "You should see your mother" has been sounding panicked. Not "You should *see* your mother," but "*You* should see your mother." The tone is accusing, too: what kind of daughter am I for not getting down to Florida more often?

I know I should go visit, but I'm afraid. Mostly I'm afraid to see what her life is like now: the dining room table—the last anniversary present—crammed into Mom's apartment instead of the big house it was intended for. Occasionally Mom mentions—always offhandedly—that the phone rarely rings, and that pains me so much I immediately have to cauterize the wound, which I do by making suggestions I know aren't helpful: has she looked up that old friend? What about the organization she used to volunteer for? Grandma wants her to join a book club, but I know Mom can't. She won't be able to remember what she's read. Grandma doesn't want to hear that, so I don't say anything.

It didn't help my guilt that I got impatient with Mom tonight for giving me, essentially, a minute-by-minute update of how her Lean Cuisine peanut noodles were progressing in the microwave. Though Mom talks this way all the time these days—the attention-span problem again—I still want her to sound OK to assuage my guilt about not going down to visit more often. Truthfully, I want her to sound more than OK. I want every minute I talk with her to be meaningful, and, of course, it can't be.

Times like these I think Diana and I have that twin ESP thing. I called her right after talking to Mom. As soon as she heard my voice she said, "We have got to go to Florida." We made plans to go Labor Day weekend.

I'm going to turn into a fat-free Fudgsicle. Or at least a Fudgsicle. I can only wish I'd be fat-free.

I've been eating about four a night. Four are only 240 calories. But while the Fudgsicles are better than baby carrots or cherry tomatoes, they still don't quite cut it.

Spent forty-five minutes at the grocery store tonight looking for things I might want to eat—or at least things that aren't totally icky (brussels sprouts) but also don't make me want to eat all sorts of other (unhealthy) things. I was shocked to discover that my frozen food options are not actually limited to Healthy Choice and Weight Watchers. Stouffer's regular old chicken and dumplings has just 280 calories, the same as some candy bars and less than a couple of Boca Burgers. It's pathetic how excited I am by this discovery.

Hello from Camp Canyon Ranch, I feel like writing on postcards. *Please send Diet Coke.*

Shape has sent me to the spa as a reward for my first anniversary, and it's taken until now to schedule the trip.

The place reminds me of a summer camp. You're issued water bottles and tote bags, and it's not considered the least bit strange to walk around in big white terry cloth robes that are in endless supply.

Before I got here, I worried about all the fun things I'd be missing during my five days away, and I feared being lonely and depressed, watching all the mother-daughter pairs I was sure I'd find here. They are here, and sometimes I feel the pangs. But I'm busy. I've stopped caring about what's going on at home—stopped trying to check my e-mail on the one crappy connection—and am loving waking up and having nothing to do but focus on myself. No fear of food: I know it's there, I know it's going to be good, and I know it's going to be low-fat.

I wish I could come here every year, just to rejuvenate and to be reminded, as I have been, that I'm more athletic than I think I am. Yesterday I worked out for almost four hours straight. One of the classes I took was a stride class, a group workout on treadmills, where I won an actual athletic contest. I was the one who could hold the walk at the fastest speed (6.1 mph), which is an achievement because it's actually a lot harder—and a better calorie-burner—to try to walk very fast than to break into a run or a jog. And I did what Mary might call a buttload of squats—in kickboxing and then in boot camp—and my thighs aren't even sore. Guess I'm stronger than I think, too.

I'm halfway through my two-hour wait to have my blood taken again. I had it taken for the first time at 7:45 A.M., after two days of dreading the needle. I wasn't allowed to eat after 9:00 P.M. last night or to have breakfast this morning before I had the first sample taken. Then I was given a disgusting glucose drink.

This is Canyon Ranch's test for insulin resistance, a possible problem with my blood sugar levels that the doctor here thinks may be responsible for my inability to stop eating carbs. At first I wasn't too keen on meeting with a doctor to discuss my diet—after more than a year of dissecting every bite that goes into my mouth with a variety of experts, I figured I'd heard practically everything there was to hear. But now I'm feeling hopeful again—I almost want them to find what they're looking for, just because it will give me a road map. I'll know that if I follow their instructions, I'll definitely feel better—and I'll know for sure that if I eat a muffin (carbs) by itself, without any protein along with it, I'll be in trouble, and the trouble won't be just psychological. Years' worth of diet advice runs through my head here: why can't I just pretend I'm allergic—that I'll break out in monstrous fat cells if I eat certain things? Well, because I know perfectly well that I'm not. It's the same reason why setting my clock twenty minutes fast doesn't make me leap out of bed, thinking I'm late.

I won't get the results of the test for a few weeks. The last time I wished this badly for something to be medically wrong with me was when I got my thyroid tested when I was fifteen.

Went on a canoe trip yesterday—something I haven't done since summer camp—followed by a hike in the Berkshires. And I tried a Canyon Ranch ballet workout. I was self-conscious, especially because there were a few people wearing leotards and wrap skirts while I was in shorts and a grubby old frat-party T-shirt. But I've been reading since forever that ballet is supposed to do wonders for your muscles, and I figured better to try it here—where practically everyone is supportive—than back home. I didn't flail around nearly as much as I thought I would.

This morning—my last—I was supposed to have a manicure and pedicure. But I canceled them. Those I could get anywhere, and I wanted to go on one last hike.

I feel embarrassingly like a spa testimonial, but a week after I've left I'm still on a Canyon Ranch high. I've also lost two pounds. I feel smugly, nauseatingly healthy. I've been to the farmers' market and then to Fresh Fields and have not put a single processed thing in my body. I've drunk nothing but water—no Diet Coke, no after-work drinks. I've even cooked something from the Canyon Ranch cookbook—this banana nut French toast that seemed to have seventy-two ingredients and 437 steps. Don't know that I'll be doing that again anytime soon, but it was nice to realize that a break from the same old safe foods doesn't have to mean ice cream or nachos.

Is telling people what I'm feeling always going to make me regret it or otherwise make me feel crummier than I did before I decided to try to make myself feel better by getting the problem off my chest?

Today a message from one of my best friends from college—someone I've known for eight years—popped up in my e-mail box. I feel I hear from him only when he needs something or when he's stuck at work late waiting for his boss to sign off on something and has exhausted all other ways of filling time.

I haven't heard from him in several months. I'm sure I was being hypersensitive, but the e-mail felt like a classic "I'm e-mailing you so you can't say I never e-mail you." Nothing except a question about whether I'm on another continent this week.

So, buoyed by the Canyon Ranch high, I decided to take charge of at least one (nonfood) part of my life: I decided it was time to try working on my assertiveness. Except I didn't exactly go about it in the best way.

"Why, do you need something?" I asked, regretting the way the e-mail would sound from the moment I sent it.

"Not particularly," he wrote.

I told him he could call every once in a while, and I couldn't resist adding a zinger asking if this was something reserved for when the girlfriend wasn't around.

"Wow, you're way mean," he wrote.

I promptly apologized—always apologizing, it feels like—and said my feelings had been hurt because I seemed to hear from him only when he had nothing better to do.

"Oh, good God," he wrote, which just made me angrier and more defensive.

I wrote a long e-mail saying I was sorry I'd said anything about it at all, because while I didn't want things to continue as they had been, I didn't want him to feel obligated to talk to me, either.

Ugh. And I wonder why I avoid confrontation.

Actually, I know why. Because I'm terrible at it, because I feel like confrontation is yet another thing I should have learned how to do years ago but didn't because I was eating instead.

I've traded the uncomfortable feeling of wishing I could say something for the equally uncomfortable feeling of having made a mess of things. At least I don't want to eat anything—except my words.

Some days my life feels like one big struggle not to miss out on something really good. I'm happy to have options—Mary and the lawyers (where I am, the running joke goes, the token nonlawyer), the young-journalist crew, my old college friends, random people I've met—but sometimes I feel like I'm accumulating points or someone's taking attendance. A certain number of absences and I'll be out of the group—or at least out on all the inside jokes.

What to do on a Friday night is a small thing, but it's yet another reminder that I've been so consumed with food that I've never developed that unswerving internal compass that says this is what I want and points to something that isn't food or some other tangible. It goes back to the whole idea of being unable to trust my gut. Food has blotted out so much for so long that I'm rarely sure, on a most basic level, what I want.

Started tennis lessons with Alexy tonight, part of my unofficial plan to stop regretting and start doing. Unfortunately, I immediately hated the instructor, a guy in his late forties who has that kind of oozy, I'm-your-best-friend-though-I've-known-you-for-five-seconds manner. He's no best friend of mine. He told me loudly that playing tennis a couple of times a week would be great for me because I'd lose weight and be able to run faster.

It was just like the boxing instructor from last year, and once again I was too stung to say anything. Yes, I do a lot of things to lose weight, but at the same time I hate the assumption that that's the only reason I would try a sport.

I felt this urge to show Mr. Tennis Menace, to be the world's best beginner tennis player, which of course meant I made a crappy shot every time he looked in my direction.

Month 19 (July)

*A*fter a month of talking about it, my friend Cara and I have decided that if we're really going to run the marathon this year, we'd better start training. It's four months away, but if we don't start now, we won't have enough time to fit in even an eighteen-mile run—the bare minimum you need to be ready.

We ran ten miles today in the nasty, muggy heat, complaining all the way. What *are* we doing this for? Cara wants to do it once to be able to say she's done it. I'm not sure why I'm doing it. Because I'm hoping to regain some of that sense of peace I got on Saturday mornings from last year's training? Because I thought last year was a fluke, and I want to prove I really can do it?

Crazy stressed—have that boxed-in feeling where I'm pushing to see if there's even an inch of give anywhere. My "I am the master of my new, simplified, saying-no life" lasted, oh, about forty-five seconds. I've got a bunch of work to do for *Washingtonian* and *Shape*, and now I've got an article for *Mademoiselle* due in less than a week. I've got almost no time between now and then—I'm supposed to go to a baseball game tomorrow night, then play tennis, then the next night is a work party, all things I could give up but don't want to. Friday I'm off to North Carolina, and Erica's here Monday. And Tuesday I'm out of the office all day working on another story. Yikes. Must sit down tomorrow morning and map out how I'm going to get everything done, otherwise I will freak.

Meanwhile, got home tonight exhausted and starving and completely uninspired by everything in my refrigerator. Grumpy just at the thought of eating an (unsatisfying) frozen dinner, and figuring out something to make from a cookbook would mean (a) digging through some half-unpacked boxes to see if I still *have* a cookbook after the flood, (b) deciding what to make, and (c) schlepping to the grocery store to get the stuff, only to get home and realize I've forgotten something crucial and irreplaceable, like, say, the tomatoes needed for a marinara sauce.

So I called for Chinese takeout. And I wonder why I can't lose weight.

I haven't had a drink since before Canyon Ranch over a month ago, and now I just don't want to drink—well, get drunk—anymore. I don't want to drink all those calories, and I don't want to risk waking up the next morning feeling crummy. For most people, drinks make connections easier—alcohol as social lubricant. But these days drinks don't rid me of this terrible self-consciousness about being overweight. So I stand there with my Diet Coke, feeling like a buzzkill, a sentence I read a long time ago running through my head: "When you're fat, it all just kind of hangs out."

I don't know quite when and why the self-consciousness set in again.

Maybe because I was slowly, slowly becoming aware that my body was shrinking, and so now that it's expanding, it seems to take up more space than ever.

Mary has always said I wear my feelings on my face, and all I can do is hope that not everyone is as perceptive as she is. I hope not everybody can tell that I'm not having a blast.

My "invisible outsider" feelings came out tonight over the tiniest thing. I was at Tony & Joe's, a bar on the Georgetown waterfront, for an outing of a bunch of women—a big gang of us (this work friend of someone's, that old law school roommate of someone else's) that only recently has coalesced. Exactly the sort of outing that lately I've been finding less and less appealing: a let's-meet-new-people night (translation: male-type people). I don't want to meet anyone looking like this—don't even think I can. Instead I look at the women I know—smart, fun, pretty, and *thin*—and I envy them all.

I wasn't planning on drinking tonight, and I knew I had a *Shape* photo shoot tomorrow. When I showed up, everyone had been drinking for nearly two hours and was in full-on crazy, flirty mode—the opposite of how I felt. Hate summer, when there are no clothes to hide myself in.

There's also been this thing going on with one of the girls and me. Though we were pretty good friends last year, Alison doesn't speak to me unless absolutely necessary. She didn't look my way when I said hello tonight.

Not an auspicious beginning to the evening. Twenty minutes later, she didn't so much as offer to get me a drink when she headed to the bar. (The place was packed, and I loathe fighting my way to the bar for just a Diet Coke, because the bartenders are always annoyed—crummy tip.) Finally someone else from our group went over for a round and forgot my Diet Coke. I was pretty sure she wouldn't have forgotten anyone else's drink.

I ended up blinking back tears—yes, *again*—and muttering a lame excuse about allergies. Which Mary did not buy. I ended up nervously telling her that I hated feeling like I had to be drunk even to remotely belong in this group these days.

Her response surprised me.

"I sometimes feel that way, too," she said. But she always seems at the center of everything.

The key word: *seems*. There's the world as I imagine it in my mind, and there's this completely different reality I discover only when I say things—as I did today—that are hard to say.

Shape photo shoot—they were taking photos for two or three months' worth of columns. Exactly how many, I don't even want to know.

In what I was hoping wasn't going to be an omen for the shoot, the power went out on the whole street just before the shoot, so I couldn't blow-dry my hair. I had to wear it curly—Diana would say frizzy. Not attractive. At least I wasn't upset about the clothes this time: I did love the black bead-fringed capri pants the stylist had sent from the Gap.

Molly the photographer had an intern with her, who got a laugh out of the whole extravaganza. One shot of me hiking. Another of me hanging out. A third of me reading a book on the porch of Molly's friend's house. I once read that to keep her mind occupied during shoots, Cindy Crawford calculates how much money she's making per minute. Since for me that's a big fat zero (and let's not get started on how I'm not Cindy Crawford), I entertained myself with thoughts of which book I should pretend to read for my Cerebral Courtney shot that might get the most reaction out of readers. *Georgiana, Duchess of Devonshire*? Too dorky. *Bridget Jones's Diary*? Too obvious. *My Year of Meats* (my book-club book)? Sounds too much like a diet book, even though it's fiction. The cover of *Remembering Denny* is too dull for a photo. And the galleys from a book I'm reviewing—I think *Shape* would say that would make the photo unusable. There had been a handful of queries about where to buy a necklace I once wore—I'd bought it at a market in London—so I was supposed to be careful that anything visible in the picture could be purchased somewhere in the United States.

Talked to the Canyon Ranch doctor today, who says I don't have insulin resistance, though I may have a tendency toward low blood sugar, which makes it all the more important for me to eat every three hours. That might explain why I get so frantic and irritable when I don't and why I then make a mad dash for the sugar. To keep my sugar levels at an even keel, I'm supposed to eat more protein than carbohydrate at meals and eat my snack of fruit with some protein, such as nuts or string cheese. I've heard all these things from Dr. Peeke before, but I listened to them today as if they were some kind of breakthrough. The doctor suggested I go get my blood sugar tested at some point when I'm feeling cranky and irritable, but I'm sure I won't. Too much effort.

Crazy, isn't it? I'd go trekking all over town for some random snack food if someone told me it was low-fat and yummy, and I'd do any number of other inconvenient and/or embarrassing and/or unpleasant things to lose weight. But I won't go get a blood test. Probably because low blood sugar isn't the answer I'm looking for.

Another tentative stab at confrontation tonight. God, it is so much easier just to eat. But every time I have a negative feeling and I don't deal with it, I know my stomach will keep track.

Got annoyed with Mary that some of the things I told her were getting passed on to another friend of ours. It has caused a couple of sticky situations. So I took the proverbial deep breath and said, "I just wish you'd be careful what you tell Betsy."

And . . . it wasn't that bad. She agreed. She apologized. That was it.

So why can't I stop thinking about it? Why do I feel like it's I who's done something wrong?

Uncomfortable feelings versus feeling uncomfortably full. These are the choices.

For the amount of angst *Shape* causes me, occasionally I love it. Their travel editor has decided I should test my newfound athletic abilities by going hiking, rock climbing(!), and mountain biking in Colorado in September. And a classically trained chef who lost piles of weight when she took a chef's job at a spa has seen my weight-gain diary and told *Shape* she wants to fly out and rescue me.

She wants to come make over my kitchen—wait until she hears my kitchen is about the size of a phone booth and about as well equipped—and show me how to make quick, good food. For a story, of course.

I hope her idea of quick isn't two hours and seven pans.

Pants that didn't fit three weeks ago fit today. Hallelujah! Maybe I can dare to get on the scale this week?

On second thought, better not ruin my sense of triumph. You can "it's just a number" me all you want, but I know that when I see it, my weight will feel like a three-digit indictment. It will still be too far away from where I wish it were.

Month 20 (August)

*A*nother evening of flirtation—the third in two weeks—with a guy I've nicknamed Bacon Boy, because I know he's as bad for me as intravenous bacon.

Sometimes we're like best pals—or something more. Other times I feel like I might never hear from him again. He reminds me in so many ways—including looks—of an old boyfriend. Flirtatious. Funny and sarcastic, with an edge. But over the edge, you can fall.

It seems all I do is think and strategize about dealing with food, and yet somehow I still screw up so badly. I know perfectly well that I should not, say, show up at a dinner party starving, especially one that starts later than my usual dinner hour. I know I'll overeat, and yet I head on over there in denial, thinking that somehow this time I'll manage something I've never once managed in the past.

I go to the party hungry and I eat. That night or the next morning, I look at the way my jeans fit, and all I can think is: *What was I thinking?* Why, oh why, do I persist on hoping that somehow, as if by magic, this time will be different from all the others?

Anyone who's ever attempted to shed a pound has probably heard that losing weight—and keeping it off—is a lifelong process. But it's only now that I'm really beginning to understand what that means, even if I haven't totally accepted it yet. What it means is that every day, or at least every week, I have to think about what went right, what went wrong, and what I could have done differently—because almost every situation will repeat itself. It's constant refining—constant work.

I've spent much of the past few months ignoring everything I've just said, and I'm not pleased with the results. So I looked over my food journals—I haven't been managing to keep them every day, but four or five days a week gives me plenty to work with—and discovered that my number one determiner of a screwup day is breakfast. If I'm hungry at 10:00 A.M., I'm hungry (and grumpy and ready to grab anything) all day.

I'm hungry after breakfast, Shari thinks, because I'm eating too many carbs, which don't have staying power. Banana and Special K and milk—it's the protein, stupid. But besides bacon, which would make Shari cringe, the only protein I can think of that I'd eat for breakfast is egg-white omelets, and who has time to make those every morning? I've tried all the protein bars. They don't remotely taste like "chocolate chocolate chip" or "raspberry cheesecake," as the wrappers promise. They taste like dog food.

Shari, from the food-is-fuel school, wants to know why I think I deserve to eat food that tastes good. This questions a belief so basic—at least in the United States—that somehow it makes me furious.

"Why should I have to eat food that tastes bad?" I almost whined.

"What if someone told you you had to eat the same three meals for the rest of your life or you'd die?" she asked. "You'd do it and not look back."

"Right, but that's not the case," I said. OK, whined.

We reached an impasse on this. Stay tuned.

Kitchen makeover is scheduled for the end of this month, and I'm psyched. When I talked to Kathleen, the spa chef, last night, I admitted I had only two pots, one of which—a hand-me-down from my mother—probably dates from the Eisenhower administration. But Kathleen says she's helped clients who think pots are for washing out panty hose, so apparently the fact that I've made pasta in mine means I'm ahead of the game.

Shape is planning to bring a crew of nine—count 'em, nine—into my tiny studio apartment for this kitchen makeover session. A photographer, a food stylist, a prop stylist, a clothes stylist, a makeup artist, an editor, and I'm not even sure who else. They're also bringing a caterer, which cracks me up. Where are they going to put the food—in the bathroom?

Considering that *Shape* is sending someone to teach me how to make "yummy" (the word the editor keeps using) low-fat food, I've been pondering the deserving-food-that-tastes-good issue and why Shari's suggestion that this is not a right of mine annoys me so much.

There's the psychological explanation, about food being the thing I rely on for comfort and about food always having been the one thing I can rely on to be—to taste—good. But there's more to it than that. I think the food-tasting-good issue also points at choices I don't like to make or resent that I have to make. Food that tastes good (cheesecake, chocolate) versus being thinner.

And another set of choices: I don't mind cooking but am pressed for time and don't like to clean up. So I can decide to spare the time and suffer through the cleanup, and then I can make low-fat meals that taste good. Or I can decide I don't have the time and deal with the consequences: prepackaged or frozen low-fat things I don't like the taste of or other simple foods (egg-white omelets, grilled chicken) that I'm sick of. Have to pick one—can't have both. And I usually choose the latter.

Obviously, some compromises can be made, but essentially this is not an intellectual exercise, a logic problem to be solved. It's not something I can think my way out of. These are the choices. Period.

Alexy was coming over tonight, so I had to race through the Safeway. Remind me always to plan to be somewhere after the supermarket. I had to grab things with such speed that I didn't have time to so much as contemplate the cookie aisle.

When Alexy showed up, we fell into one of our usual discussions about dating, and I told her about Bacon Boy. Usually I think ambiguous situations involving men are Rorschach tests—a friend's opinion of it almost always says more about her than about the guy or the situation. Your friend who is secretly still clinging to hope that some guy from two months ago will call her will always look for the positive; the friend who can't tell her own boyfriend a thing will always give you detailed instructions for how to handle this particular guy; and so on.

But Alexy said the same thing both Mary and another friend had said: he's insecure. Why don't I look objectively at his hot-and-cold behavior and think that myself? I wondered as Alexy spoke. Then I realized I knew the answer: it's still a habit to look to myself for the cause of other people's behavior, wondering what *I've* done.

Mary doesn't like BB, the nickname for his nickname. She thinks he's bad for me. She says he's insecure—the perfect dance partner for my pathological minuet, I think wryly. BB flirts with me when he wants something and keeps me around because he needs to have someone think he's all that.

The books I've read suggest that compulsive overeaters should stay away from relationships while they're getting themselves sorted. I've been resisting the idea, though these days it makes more and more sense. It's hard enough to figure out what I want—the internal compass I never had—without adding someone else to change the direction.

So my kitchen has been reorganized, but not in front of the camera. Someone finally got the message that the nine people required for this shoot would barely fit into my apartment, much less my kitchen. So we borrowed a kitchen twice the size of my entire apartment. If I were a reader, I'd look at it and think: if she can afford a kitchen of that size, why doesn't she also hire a low-fat chef and a personal trainer?

For the camera I grated Parmesan cheese. I put berries on angel food cake. I cleaned the oven with a slightly bewildered expression on my face, probably because I'm not sure I've ever *used* my oven, much less cleaned it. Mary saw an outtake from the oven-cleaning shot and immediately requested a copy for her refrigerator so she could have something that would make her laugh every morning.

The day after the shoot, I actually cooked things. Kathleen, the size 6, five-star spa chef, really did completely make over my kitchen—cleaned and reorganized and stocked it. I love my kitchen now, even though the clutter we removed from it is now all over the rest of my apartment.

I got a ton of new stuff: a Microplane grater, a baby Cuisinart, a Teflon pan. I learned how to make granola and also jicama and apple slaw and a bunch of other things I probably won't remember how to do by tomorrow. I probably won't even remember what jicama looks like.

Tonight I cohosted a happy hour with this guy I've been bumping into in the laundry room of my building for at least a year and a half. We've been talking about getting all of our friends together for months—a summit between Capitol Hill staffers (what Mr. Clean is) and journalists. A summit that, we've been joking, will change life as we know it, like FDR meeting Stalin in 1944 or Nixon meeting Mao in Beijing in 1971. Only in Washington can you make jokes this geeky.

I stayed chatting with two "Team Rubin" members—as Mr. Clean referred to my half of the invite list—whom I don't know superwell. I still find it amazing how people think of you in ways you would never think of yourself. When they found out I had a twin sister, both said variations of the same thing: that Diana and I must be so different because I'm "*so* social."

Then I went home and made a Kathleen recipe: two pieces of ginger lime chicken, one for tonight and one for lunch tomorrow.

I'm dreading going to Miami next week. I wish I could see Mom and Grandma without the obligatory weekend of shopping (translation: talking about weight), eating out (translation: talking about food and weight and how much so-and-so has left over on her plate, if anything), and talking about the evils of diets in general and bread in particular.

I'm so sick of thinking about how to spend my calories so as to get the most bang for my buck. The thought that I'm going to have to do this daily sounds about as appealing as a steady diet of iceberg lettuce with no dressing. Will I ever be able to put something in my mouth again without thinking about whether it's worth the calories?

Once upon a time, I thought I'd be willing to pay the price of admission to the thin club, no matter how high. Now I'm not always sure. Peeke refers to my current situation—having lost some weight but still with plenty to go—as mile 21 of the marathon, but here's the difference between the two: the marathon had a definite ending.

Month 21 (September)

IN MIAMI

I used to call my mother Mom, but on this visit she has become Mother. As in "Not until you eat something, Mother" or "Take your medicine, Mother."

I want to tell the whole rest of the world to be nice to her—that she's sick—but I'm not very kind to her myself. Every time I snap at her I swear I'll be patient with her for the entire rest of the visit, but my resolve never lasts long.

I've never seen her this bad. I can barely make eye contact with her. The circles under her eyes are huge, and the color of her skin looks terrible. She's so thin. She's so proud that she's so thin, but Diana and I are horrified.

She seems to enjoy everyone's making a fuss about her eating. I can hardly stand to watch her eat. I want to do everything for her, because I can't bear to watch her do it herself. It seems to take forever for her to scoop the inside out of her bagel.

"Mother," I want to yell, "you do not need to save calories by scooping out the inside of the bagel." It takes even longer for her to slice leftover steak for a sandwich. Then she eats three bites and leaves it.

"I'm just not hungry anymore," she says proudly.

Neither am I. I think this is the only time in my life I haven't been able to eat. There's a lump in my throat so huge even ice cream seems too much to swallow.

The world shrinks away here, and not in that vacation bubble way. Instead it just seems like nothing else exists except the hour-by-hour of getting through the day—of arguing with Mom to eat, of making doctors' appointments, of wondering what's next.

As we were packing up to leave, I realized this was the first time Mom hadn't asked before we got here: "What are you eating now?" She's slipping more and more into her own world.

But still we talked about food, because there's not much else to talk about. We talked about what the forty ingredients might be in the dipping sauce of an Outback Steakhouse Bloomin' Onion, which my mother loves. We talked about mayonnaise and how much Diana hates it. We talked about how Mom hated fish as a kid.

Food as connection. Again.

Mom didn't want to eat. On the morning we left, she wanted to fuss about giving us disposable razors, the way she usually fusses over giving us coupons she's clipped. I don't use disposables and told her I didn't want them.

"So you'll have extra," she snapped, which made me suddenly, inexplicably, very angry. I went into the other room and fumed to Diana that I didn't want the damn razors. I just want her to be normal and fine for five minutes.

"She can't help it," Diana said.

Of course she can't, but I was angry anyway. I hate this—hate all of it. Hate that she's here but not here. Hate that she wants to give us things but they're the wrong things. Hate feeling guilty.

I went into the kitchen to get a drink, and when I came back, I saw Diana had left the razors on top of my suitcase. Defiantly, I hid them in the bathroom cabinet. Fifteen minutes later, I guiltily retrieved them and shoved them into my bag. When I got home, I put them in a drawer with all the other things I've gotten from Mom over the past year that I've been unable to make myself throw away: coupons that are expired before I've even received them because she forgets to mail them, little-girl-appropriate stationery I can't find a use for, a glittery butterfly barrette I would never wear.

I came back from Florida to find an e-mail from "Jerri Rubin"—Mom—in my in-box. Except it wasn't really from Mom. Diana had sent it while she was testing Mom's Internet connection, which we both know Mom will never use but busied ourselves with anyway. Like her VCR clock that we programmed, it was something we could point to that we had accomplished—something concrete we could do.

I cried over this e-mail—this reminder of something that will never be. It was a small thing, but I cried big, choking, snuffling sobs.

For two days I cried off and on—all the tears I hadn't cried over the weekend. I didn't overeat or not eat. I didn't try to stop crying or avoid crying. This, Shari says, is progress.

Sixteen-mile run with Cara that was, I think, the worst run I've ever had. We were both in poor spirits, especially when we got stopped on the trail by *Shape* readers. Cara was rolling her eyes, and I was slightly horrified. I like to hope I'm unrecognizable when I'm running—red-faced, slick with sweat, hair matted. I must look really charming in some of those magazine photos.

IN BOULDER, COLORADO

If I'd had a cell phone with me in the glider this afternoon, I would have called everyone I knew. I'm on another *Shape* assignment, though this one isn't column-related. This is an "adventure weekend" in Boulder—four days of doing things that scare the crap out of me. Today, Day 1, was gliding. I'd been wavering about doing it all day—I was terrified. It requires no athletic ability—a plane tows your glider up a mile high, then leaves you to float back to earth—but there was my little fear-of-heights problem. Even though the guy said I could come down after ten minutes if I didn't like it, to get down you still have to be released from the plane—which is the part I was most afraid of.

Actually, I was afraid of all of it.

I watched two guys go up—I didn't want to go until one of them came down safely. And even then I couldn't help thinking that even if they were fine, my time up in the air could be the one time when something went wrong. But I knew I'd be really upset with myself if I were here, watched two people go up, and then didn't go.

So I took a deep breath and strapped myself into the plane. It took twenty minutes before every slight bump didn't convince me of my impending doom, but the bird's-eye view of Boulder—with the jagged peaks of the Rockies close enough to touch—was a reward that trumped any CD or lipstick I've ever tried to bribe myself to exercise with. The glide became something of a visual mantra for the weekend. When something frightened me, I thought about the views—and better yet, the feeling of accomplishment—I would have missed by not trying.

I'm totally exhausted and a bit sore, though I'm not sure from what. The hike we did today in Gregory Canyon was hard, but not *that* hard. Maybe it was the dodgy footing, something I'm not used to. This was about the fourth hike I'd ever gone on, since growing up in below-sea-level Florida didn't offer much opportunity for mountain climbing.

After lunch we went fly-fishing, which at first I found infuriating. I just felt so bad at it—couldn't cast the reel the right way, couldn't see the fly, couldn't see the fish. I felt so conspicuous standing on the banks of Boulder Creek—overweight and clumsy in these hip-high waders.

I cannot understand how people fly-fish to relax. The forearm motion you need to master seems impossibly elusive. I would have bailed after forty-five minutes—the wading boots were rubbing uncomfortably—but quitting seemed out of the spirit of this, the Can-Do Weekend. Nearly three hours and no trout later, I was relieved it was time to go.

Up at dawn this morning, already panicking about the rock climbing on the schedule for this afternoon. But first up was mountain biking. As I reached the top of Boulder Canyon, I was shocked to realize I'd biked uphill for an hour without stopping—and without feeling like a Mack truck had hit me. It's one thing to know I can run five miles for a workout—or even run a marathon—but it's still awe-inspiring when I see how fitness translates to the rest of my life.

During lunch I rationalized eating more than my share of a fried-apple-with-custard appetizer, seeing as it might be my last meal.

Time for rock climbing.

After a steep hike up Gregory Canyon to Boulder's Flatirons, I put on my harness.

"If you fall, you've got the rope," the guides said repeatedly.

How comforting.

Am I the heaviest person ever to do this? I thought. What if they're wondering if I'll break the rope? What if I *do* break the rope? My arms shook with fear.

Coaxed by the guides, who yelled suggestions for footholds, I climbed at the pace of an anemic turtle, and I didn't make it to the top.

But the point is that I climbed—and at one point I even deliberately let go, savoring the feeling of hanging in midair, facing down this mountain of rock.

Back home, and back down to earth. The battle against weight, it seems, is fought in an endless series of tiny struggles, like choosing a snack of low-fat crackers instead of a couple of cookies. I won't say you coast along—it's definitely not that easy—but you do sort of trudge.

I'm tired of trudging, so I've been doing a little sprint. Back on the Peeke diet for three days. No cooking—I don't want any more interaction with food than I have to have. And in structure, at least for me, there is freedom.

I've been hungry for the whole three days—one of which included a phone appointment with Nancy Clark. I told her I literally felt like all I was doing all day was drinking Diet Coke and trying to hang on until the next time I was "supposed" to eat. I told her I thought this was why I was having such trouble getting back on the wagon for more than a week—because I dreaded this kind of hunger. Because now that I've eaten the old Boca-Burgers-and-egg-white-omelets way for three days, it seems like I'm always hungry.

"Maybe you are," she said. "Are you eating enough?"

Of course I laughed. The idea that someone like me might have to eat more just sounded insane. Counting calories makes me miserable, but Nancy calculated the calories of everything I'd eaten in the past two days and suggested that for my weight (I estimated 185, though I was fearing it might be closer to 200) and activity level I could probably eat twenty-one to twenty-two hundred calories. In other words, another three or four hundred calories a day. That's a couple of chocolate-chip cookies or a peanut butter sandwich.

I found this hard to believe, and the addict in me thought, "Well, I really just want to get done with losing weight, so I'm not going to eat the extra." Finally Nancy said, "If you exercise and you're starving, your body goes into a famine state. It thinks it needs to hold on to every last calorie."

Famine is something I've associated with eight-hundred-calorie diets, not the eighteen hundred or so I've been eating. But there was a real-life expert telling me this was applicable, so you can guess what I'll be doing this week. I've already calculated that even if my body doesn't need the extra four hundred calories per day—that they're extra—that's twenty-eight hundred, or a gain of less than a pound. Which, sadly, is probably a better outcome than that of an awful lot of weeks of this year.

E-mail from an editor who wants to know if, for an article, I want to test ways to make sex more fun. I write back: "Is the magazine providing the person with whom I test this?"

I got on the scale this morning, because I can't test Nancy's eat-an-extra-four-hundred if I don't know where I've started from. Somehow I've dieted myself up to 190 pounds—just 16 away from where I started twenty months ago. I couldn't stop thinking: *That's just 10 away from 200.*

So I found myself eating today—and a lot more than four hundred calories. I can't get on the scale tomorrow—no weighing two days in a row. Every good dieter knows that—and also knows not to get on the scale after a lot of eating.

Now I won't be able to tell if Nancy's plan has worked, since I've probably gained weight from today. I raged at myself for eating and ruining the plan for the week. Tried to throw the piece of paper with my grocery shopping list across the room. But paper doesn't absorb violence. It flutters delicately. So unsatisfying.

I've been eating the extra four hundred calories for four days. I'm definitely not full but not quite hungry enough to be on a diet. It feels wrong. It feels like I'm cheating. It feels dangerous.

What also feels dangerous is all the calculating and plotting and bargaining (could I save two hundred calories for tomorrow?) I'm already doing. The addict in me picking at the edges of this, wondering if I can make it three hundred fifty calories per day next week and then three hundred the week after.

And the scale hasn't budged: 190 again. But I'm not as frustrated by this as usual, maybe because I didn't feel hungry every moment of this week. I wouldn't say I was so full I didn't deserve a reward on the scale, but I definitely wasn't so hungry that I felt like the scale inching downward was the only thing that would make the hunger worth it.

I'm trying four hundred extra calories a day again this week.

Talked to Mom and then Dad tonight and decided I didn't want to choose where I was going for Thanksgiving this year—or worse, deal with a joint affair, which they're still threatening. I'm going away—opting out entirely.

Month 22 (October)

I'm road testing tips from the "Does Your Environment Make You Fat?" story, and they're freaking me out. I feel like I should or could be moving something at every moment to make up for all the calories I'm apparently saving by not having to churn my own butter, by having a suitcase on wheels, and by sending e-mails.

One tip is to set an alarm at work and get up from your desk once an hour—not, of course, to hit the vending machine but to walk around for five minutes. By the end of an eight-hour workday you'll have forty extra minutes of activity to show for it.

Except if you're me. By the end of an eight-hour workday you'll have an obsessive person who thinks, *Hmmm, if I add an extra half minute to each of those intervals, how many calories will that burn in the long run? An extra minute?*

The process of burning off all the calories I'm supposedly saving by living in the twenty-first century—I always suspected I had been born in the wrong century—seems so huge and insurmountable it makes me want to do nothing.

I've given up on the four hundred extra calories a day. The constant calculating and recalculating of options is making me crazy. My compromise is to eat another snack if I'm feeling hungry, but the snack has to be relatively healthy. Fruit. Yogurt. A handful of nuts. A small bag of pretzels. Limited choices. Nothing too exciting.

Erica and I are going to Costa Rica for Thanksgiving. Hiking, sailing, whitewater rafting, the whole works. Pause for a moment of silence: I am actually *choosing* to spend a vacation doing things that burn a whole lot more calories than lying on a couch.

Ran eighteen miles today. My last big training run before the marathon, and I feel anything but ready. I've barely thought about it and barely planned for it. The weekends have rolled around, and I've thought about where to squeeze in the run, as opposed to last year, when I planned my weekends around the run.

Tonight—after someone announced I had run eighteen miles this morning—what feels like the gazillionth woman said to me, "How much weight have you lost with all that running?"

And the gazillionth woman was disappointed by my answer: "Not much."

It's the same disappointed response I get when I tell them I don't have a simple answer to dieting, like don't eat carbs, clap your hands four times after each meal, don't eat potatoes, don't eat anything purple, don't eat after 8:17 P.M. People seem to hate hearing that you can't just add a marathon to your life and watch the weight fall away no matter what you eat. If you could, wouldn't there be a book by now called *The Marathon Diet: The Six-Month Plan to Stuff Your Face and Still Lose Weight*?

Sounds like a bestseller to me.

Today I ran the Army Eleven and a Half Miler. Its official name is the Army Ten Miler, but I got stuck in major traffic and ended up having to jump out of the cab and run about a mile and a half just to make it to the starting line on time. It wasn't the best race I've ever done, but I think I'm the proudest of it because I almost didn't do it at all.

Last night I hopped from a party to disco bowling and didn't have so much as a cocktail at either one because I had to get up early and run. (I'm back to having a couple of drinks at parties.) Cara—my race buddy—and I left when everyone was going to Polly Esthers, this cheesier-than-a-pot-of-fondue dance place I happen to love. But as she has before—and though she, too, chose to train for the marathon—Cara seemed to treat me like it was my fault that she had to run, had to get up early, couldn't have a few drinks. I told her that if she didn't want to run, she didn't have to, but that I wanted to get in one more good run before the marathon.

It was late, and we'd have to get up in four and a half or five hours, but I'd already not drunk any alcohol all night in preparation and had schlepped out to Alexandria to pick up my race packet. Besides, I knew it was going to be hot today, and if we didn't do the race, we'd still have to do a decently long run. I didn't want to end up doing it in the middle of the afternoon, the sun glazing us with sweat.

Just as the cab we were sharing dropped her at her door, Cara bailed. She decided she wasn't getting up in four hours and running ten miles. As the cab pulled away, I almost told the driver to turn around and take me to Polly Esthers, because if I wasn't going to have to get up early, I might as well have some fun.

That's when I got angry.

Not so much at Cara, but at myself. Why did I immediately assume that because my friend wasn't running the race, I couldn't? Why was I allowing somebody else to prevent me from doing what I knew I should do? It was like my not speaking up about restaurants (voting, say, for the one with healthier food). I knew I should do the race—I knew I'd feel more confident about the marathon if I did it, and that's important, because the marathon is at least 50 percent mental. Besides, I'd never run a race by myself—was I even capable of doing one without someone to get me through it?

I couldn't sleep last night. The longest I'd ever run by myself was seven miles or so, and that had always been with music, which isn't allowed at races. I worried about feeling like a loser, running a race alone. I prayed for rain, aka a legitimate excuse to bail myself, but the day dawned bright and sunny. Traffic almost kept me away, but by that point I was so determined I hopped out of the cab and ran to the starting line, arriving just as the gun went off.

The race seemed long and lonely, but I never wondered—as I occasionally have in races past—why I was doing it. I was doing it for myself.

Something in me snapped this week. I was talking with Shari about how when I started losing weight last year I was so rigid about it—eating the same things over and over. That was too strict, but what I'm doing now—following Peeke's diet halfheartedly, making "substitutions" that I know are not calorically equivalent (giant chocolate-chip cookie for a nonfat yogurt and a fruit)—is obviously too lax. So I've got to do something in the middle. But what is that—and how can I keep the search for the middle from becoming another obsession?

That's something I'm still figuring out—and probably will be for a while. For now, I've decided that the middle is going to be that I follow Peeke's diet five days a week and try to figure out what I really *want* to eat the other two days. I know chances are I won't lose weight this way, but for now the sense of control seems reward enough.

OK, that's a lie. It's not enough, but it will have to do.

For the past four days I haven't eaten a single thing that feels anything but safe. No low-fat desserts. No restaurant salads that probably have as many calories as fettuccine Alfredo (if not quite as much fat). I've also gotten up for the past four mornings and done my entire fifty minutes of cardio.

Next week's project: to get back to lifting weights religiously.

Depressing fifty-years-ago-versus-today calorie-burning list, courtesy of more research for my "Does Your Environment Make You Fat?" story:

climbing the stairs (18 calories per minute) vs.
taking the elevator, aka standing (1.8 calories per minute)

grocery shopping (3.5 calories per minute) vs.
ordering groceries online, aka typing (1.5 calories per minute)

washing dishes (2.5 calories per minute) vs.
watching TV while the dishwasher runs (.9 calorie per minute)

chopping wood for fire (6 calories per minute) vs.
turning up the thermostat (1 calorie per minute)

mowing the lawn with a hand mower (6 calories per minute) vs.
riding the lawn mower (2.5 calories per minute)

washing the car (4.5 calories per minute) vs.
hitting the automatic car wash (1 calorie per minute)

The timer on my phone says I've talked to Mom for fifty-three seconds. I think I've talked to telemarketers for longer than that.

I couldn't think of anything to say, and she didn't seem to want to talk about the TV or whatever was in her direct line of vision. I hung up the phone and wondered whom I could call to talk about her. Not Diana—these days we feed off each other's grief, escalating into a crescendo of tears.

I couldn't think of a single person who would make me feel better—or who wouldn't make me feel any worse. Not because they wouldn't try to help, but what is there to say? People always try to solve the problem. But they can't. Nobody can.

I want my friends to tell me how to deal with this, like it's a lesson I can learn somewhere. It is like losing weight in that I want someone to tell me what to do, preferably simple and concrete things. But losing weight and dealing with Mom's illness aren't secrets to be passed along. They're things I have to figure out for myself.

I finished marathon number two, though I probably had no business running it with my lack of training. Definitely proof that if you want to do something badly enough, you can get yourself through it.

This year was much less fun than last year—none of the thrill of doing something new and the joy of discovering I could—and much hotter. My favorite runners' T-shirt: "Caution, This Runner Makes Frequent Stops."

Now I have done a marathon not once but twice. It is not a fluke.

Passed a store where I used to buy bingeables and thought to myself that it's been a while since I've done that. I've eaten loads of things I shouldn't have, but not in that rapid, panicky, doomed succession. It's been a messy, painful, teary couple of months, but Shari has a cleaning-the-chicken-pan theory of life: things get really icky just before they get really clean.

For Halloween this year Mary and Abby and I are going as teenyboppers. Mary's wearing a pink T-shirt that says "I love boys" and even dug out her old retainer. Abby has a tiny clear plastic backpack. I'm wearing a Backstreet Boys T-shirt and some cheesy jewelry we bought at the mall. Unfortunately, I also seem to have extremely authentic zits.

Month 23 (November)

*T*his has been one of the longest weeks of my life. Fighting with Diana over so many things, the very tiniest of which is that she borrowed a black dress of mine and it had a hole in it and was crumpled when I needed to wear it. From that point on, every fight we've ever had in the past twenty-five years seems to have been replayed.

There's so much crap flying—so many old resentments that flare up so easily—that I don't know how we're ever going to get through them.

It always comes down to the same question: why do we each treat our friends better than we treat each other?

Dad is coming to D.C. next week, and this week has left Diana and me beyond the point where we can be polite to each other for an evening. I called Dad to suggest that I see him one day and Diana see him the next, so he wouldn't have to be in the middle. Ended up crying as I tried to explain the whole thing, which, as a way of coping, is better than eating, but still I'm not thrilled with the idea of this becoming a regular thing.

Dad said something about how he'd known for a while that Diana and I had "issues" with each other, but he's been denying that it was this bad.

Called Diana to discuss plans for Dad's visit, and the conversation went downhill fast. It ended with her slamming down the phone and sending me an e-mail that said: "I just called Dad and asked him if he was sorry that he was coming to visit (I would be). Aren't we great kids? Not that you care, but I will be doing nothing for Thanksgiving."

No matter how angry I get with her, that last line still makes me feel guilty.

I gave up on the separate-nights idea with Dad. I felt, as always, like I was being the difficult child and immediately backed off. I have the backbone of an éclair.

Dinner on Diana and Dad time, which is usually about ninety minutes later than planned and indeed was this evening. They were busy dealing with a problem with Diana's computer—and there were more than a few comments from Dad about why I wasn't at all interested in the specifics of what was wrong with it. I considered asking him if my being fascinated by motherboards and memory would be better use of the intelligence he and my sister seem to think is wasted on what I do now, but I didn't. Instead I sat on Diana's futon reading a magazine and trying not to think about how hungry I was and how annoyed I was with myself for bothering to arrive on time.

Dinner was perfectly pleasant, mostly because I didn't say much and wasn't asked much. They talked about a load of Internet-related things that I didn't care much about. For a while I tried to pay attention, but since they both appeared to have forgotten I was there, eventually I gave up and let the words sail over my head. I didn't feel left out, as I usually do, because I wasn't trying to join in. I just sat there, apart but content, watching people and eating my salmon. As a method of coping, not engaging with Diana or Dad definitely beats crying, but it's pretty lame as a long-term solution.

Diana and I had a fight this morning about the whereabouts of my pink twin-set—basically, whether she had ever given it back to me—which quickly degenerated into the usual name-calling.

Have decided not to speak to her until I get back from Costa Rica. It's scary how easy that will probably be, because we're both so busy.

I'm so desperate not to feel guilty and not to overeat over her that I'm becoming positively granola: I'm trying breathing. When I'm obsessing, I've been breathing in for four counts, holding it for seven, and exhaling for eight counts. It's actually hard to think about anything else when I'm concentrating on that.

And I signed up for a lunchtime yoga class.

Caitlin from my fiction group sent around an e-mail to everyone she knew about an apartment for rent. Upon seeing my name, someone else on the list sent Caitlin an e-mail that said: "You know Courtney Rubin??? Personally? I am a huge fan."

Caitlin forwarded this to me, and I of course forwarded it to Mary, because I knew she'd make me laugh about the whole thing.

Mary promptly e-mailed back, threatening to dig out things I've left at her house to auction off on eBay. "I'll make a mint off Courtney stuff! Authentic skanky running socks worn by Courtney Rubin on July 7, 1999." At least I'll never have to worry about her giving out my cell phone number—she can never remember it.

Today I fixed a cabinet door that was coming unhinged. Went out, got a screwdriver, and fixed it. I'm feeling smug—like the love child of Martha Stewart and Bob Vila. Fixing the cabinet is such a small thing, but to me it's significant.

I once read a description of alcoholism as "fear of life." It's equally apt for compulsive overeating. (In fact, much of the Overeaters Anonymous literature is Alcoholics Anonymous literature with the word *food* substituted for *alcohol.*) When you use food, you don't solve problems; you avoid them. Even if they're as small as screwing in a screw. You have no faith in your ability to solve them, so you leave them to fester into things so large all you can do is throw up your hands and eat—another way that the world is against you.

Dinner and a play with an acquaintance-probably-turning-friend—the cool person you always mean to get together with and somehow never do. Well, finally we did.

During dinner she made a comment about sometimes being unable to stop eating, and I thought it was one of those girly comments—the "I shouldn't eat this" statement women make because they feel they have to, because it's not OK just to eat.

We talked about other things for a while, then she speared a piece of chicken kebab on a fork, pointed it at me, and said, "You write about this stuff, don't you? I've read your stuff."

Then the bottom dropped out of the conversation. One of those crazy, mad, intensely personal conversations I usually associate with long train or plane trips, where you know you'll never see the person again.

She told me that lately she gets upset when she sees women she thinks are thinner or prettier. She's been comparing herself to other women so much more, and it makes her not want to leave the house.

I got a rush listening to this woman—who paints and cooks four-star dinners and will go turn cartwheels on the D.C. sidewalk just *because*. I watched her pick at her food, hands skittering like frightened animals. I thought about her possibly wondering what I would think of her for saying what she had just said, and I realized—as always, in that flash that comes when something has been so blindingly obvious that you've missed it entirely—that she wasn't thinking about me or what I had ordered or whether I had finished it. The world is not Courtney-centric, except in my mind.

Finally. I've lost weight for three weeks straight, for a total of six pounds. I love that the scale has gone down every week, but mostly I'm loving how totally in control I'm feeling. Working out. Eating right. Lifting. Without consulting anyone to tell me it's right or wrong, I've stuck with my plan of following Peeke's diet, but with the option of following it only five days a week, leaving two days a week for eating what I want. So far I haven't taken that option because I don't want to—but it helps to know the option is there. I hope it will keep me from repeating the Peeke's-diet-to-binge cycle of last year.

The success is especially sweet because these six pounds have been, to date, my hardest won—they've taken essentially a year. After all, it's been about a year since I had the momentum going to lose weight for more than a week or two at a time.

Now if only I could lose my food demons along with the weight. And then there's my glass-is-half-empty thinking. When I'm trying not to eat out so much and being vigilant about getting to the gym, the old worries resurface: I'm getting obsessive and being boring. Shari wrote me earlier this week after a particularly down-on-myself e-mail: "If you talked to a child the way you sometimes talk to yourself, I would have to call social services on you."

I've spent much of this past year working on myself, which—Nancy suggests—may be one of the reasons my weight loss most of this year has been so torturously slow to nonexistent. Even I know her mantra by now: it takes energy to lose weight, and mine has obviously been going other places.

I haven't binged in well over a month, but with prevacation nerves setting in, I called Erica to talk about it. We ended up drawing up a list of healthy snack food. Since she's been packed for at least a week, whereas it's two days before we leave and I have no idea where my shorts are, she even volunteered to go buy the stuff.

IN COSTA RICA

Two steps forward, one step back. We're in Costa Rica, and I am—as always—hating being overweight. Can't help noticing that I'm the only person around who is at all overweight. I wish I had checked our trip itinerary more carefully. I didn't realize there were so many times I'd have to get into a bathing suit.

Then again, I didn't let the bathing suit issue keep me from doing anything I wanted to do. (Forget that in the past I never would have been on a vacation that consisted solely of hiking and water sports.) In the past week I've gone hiking, kayaking, snorkeling, sailing, and white-water rafting. And there's still a week to go.

Forgot how much more forgiving Latin men are of any extra pounds (except if you're on South Beach in Miami).

I'm finding the attention sort of embarrassing, which Erica is finding amusing. She keeps poking me, saying, "He's checking you out," and giggling.

I speak Spanish, but Erica doesn't. So I can't talk to anyone for more than a minute without her asking what he's saying.

So much for a vacation fling.

Month 24 (December)

*J*ournalism conference in Boston. The fraud feelings again: I have such a hard time walking up to people I don't know. Who ever heard of a shy reporter? My gut reaction is still to deal with any discomfort by looking around for the food. Getting a drink and maybe a bit of cheese is something concrete to do.

Instead I walked up to another journalist standing by himself, and as we both stood there and tried to think of something to say, I made a joke about the awkwardness: who ever heard of a couple of reporters who draw complete blanks on something to say?

He just stared at me blankly. I felt like an idiot. But I'm still here. And anyway, someone else overheard—even laughed—and said something about how daunting he, too, found a roomful of journalists. (He also later told me that the first guy was usually about as fun to chat with as a piece of wood.) We talked about our jobs, and he said, matter-of-factly, that he has realized that as long as he works as a journalist, he'll have massive mood swings. Some weeks he's on a cool story and completely ecstatic about life. Other weeks he's not.

I am not alone.

Mom's birthday. For a moment she couldn't remember how old she was. Finally I asked her what year she was born, and she had to think about that, too.

The moment passed, and—as though it had never happened—she began telling me what she was watching on TV. If you don't really analyze what she's saying—you don't stop to consider that her words don't quite make a sentence—you could almost not know there was anything wrong with her.

That is what makes talking to her so difficult. Unless it's a really bad day for her, there's always a moment or two when I can be lulled into thinking she's not getting worse. And usually just as quickly that feeling is snatched away. It feels worse than if I'd never gotten it at all.

I didn't cry after I talked to her. Nor did I immediately look for something to distract myself, food or otherwise. Once upon a time I had two feelings: fat and angry. And fat is not a feeling. But tonight I sat with the anger and guilt and sadness and frustration and the whole range in between—emotions I can now name and distinguish, like the subtler points of fine wines.

Eventually I got up and found a notebook and pen. There's one thing Mom-related that upsets me and makes me feel guilty—and that I can actually do something about. That one thing is how little I know about her. So I started making a list of everything, no detail too small to be included. That she loves the color orange and pinball games and Italian food and hates coffee and peanut butter and cereal. The way, the night after she'd get her hair done, she would wrap toilet paper around her head when she slept so as not to ruin it. The way she would snap her fingers out of sync with the music as she drove. That she loved Picasso, though I couldn't recall ever going to a museum with her—or ever asking her why. I wrote down what I could remember about every story I've ever heard about her or from her: Mom at summer camp, Mom traveling around Europe, Mom as a caseworker in the Bronx. It was such a small list, filled with such seemingly insignificant details. I looked at it and couldn't help thinking that I know more about some people I've written articles about than I do about Mom. So I made a list of people I could ask for more stories about her.

I put the list in the drawer with the disposable razors and the butterfly barrette and the expired coupons she sent that I can't throw away.

My friend Richard from college came to town from New York for the weekend and so was here for the Christmas party crunch. We don't see each other often—until recently he was living in Tokyo and before that Madrid—but it never seems to matter. We always pick up where we left off.

People kept asking us this weekend how we knew each other, and he would say: "We had a child together." So deadpan. So unexpected. I love it.

Often I think Richard is the only person in the world I never put on a show for. He called me on my need always to be entertaining senior year of college, when we didn't even know each other *that* well, and since then I've been convinced he had some sort of supernatural power to see through me. Maybe it's that he's the child of two therapists.

Quite by accident at brunch Sunday, we ended up in this long conversation about how he makes me feel: comfortable with myself a lot of the time, but always with an undercurrent of pressure to maintain my slot on Richard's roster of friends. It was the sort of conversation I couldn't imagine having with anybody a year ago—just not a subject I would have dared broach. I would have wondered why I thought I had the right to bring this up and feared the consequences of doing so. I would have assumed it was all my problem or my fault. But today I thought: *I can't stand this anymore. And I don't have to. He's supposed to be one of my closest friends, and the way he makes me feel is making me not want to spend time with him.*

When he made a reference to yet another friend he'd cut out of his life because the friend wasn't up to par—a process Richard seems to manage with almost clinical ease—I finally said, in a voice I hoped was gentle: "You have incredibly high standards."

He asked what I meant.

"I love it when you're here or when I talk to you, but I worry about disappointing you," I said. "You seem to so suddenly decide certain people aren't worth your time, and it makes me wonder if I'm next."

"You've basically just summed up why my last relationship ended," he said. "We have to talk about this. You have to tell me where you get this feeling from."

We talked for more than two hours, and as we did, I could feel tension slowly draining out of my body. I felt this whole world of possibility opening up for myself—that I didn't have to take things as they came. That I didn't have to hide. I could tell people how I felt. Not all the time, but sometimes. And maybe some people would run, but some of them wouldn't. And the results had nothing to do with how much I weighed.

Later I realized that during that conversation I wasn't straining to play a role—funny, smart, sympathetic, whatever. I was just there in the moment, sometimes feeling uncomfortable, but feeling.

It felt good.

Holiday parties and cookie platters and that end-of-the-year urge to surrender to the madness—to get swept up in the current, holding on to the idea of January. In January I will do everything right. In January I will get everything in order. In January I will be perfect.

But this year I know I won't. Not because I have any less willpower or organization or whatever than I have had in any previous year. But because I know that I'll probably never have everything in my life in order. It's just not possible.

Without really discussing it, Diana and I have reached another of our uneasy truces. We're speaking, or at least exchanging e-mails and voice mails. But we're not discussing. It will have to do for now. Yet another thing I can't think (or eat) my way through. Just fumble.

Today I had a long lunch with a recently married friend. I asked Karen if it scared her at all that she'd met Jim when she was nineteen and—if all goes well—she'll be with him until she's ninety. She said that during the ten months she was planning the wedding, occasionally she thought about how she loved Jim but that she wished she'd met him five years later. It felt good to have that part of her life sorted, but scary at the same time—all these options now closed off.

She didn't sound sad about that—just matter-of-fact. We talked about the other options that had opened up to her now (she had found the person she wanted to sail around the world with and could plot to do it), and I didn't feel envious or even wistful. Instead I thought about my own options and reveled in the sense of possibility again—that rush I'd felt talking to Richard. The sense that anything could happen and just might.

Christmas, and what a very merry one it has been. In New York with Elizabeth, who's in town for a month. We saw two movies, had an hours-long chat over eggnog, went for a seafood dinner in Chinatown, then stayed up until 3:00 A.M. talking some more.

I looked at the levels in the two glasses of eggnog Elizabeth had poured, trying to nab the one that had more in it. That nagging feeling: what if there's not enough? What if I want more? It occurs to me—just briefly—that chances are Elizabeth wouldn't care.

Elizabeth's life seems like something you read about: living in London, boyfriend in Paris, popping back and forth among various countries and continents, always seeming to know what to say and wear and do. In the one suitcase she's brought to New York, she has a hair clip bought in Prague, bed linens from India, a hat from Ireland, a handbag from a Paris flea market—this tangible sense of having been places and done things.

I told her all of this, and she laughed.

"You've done other things," she said.

Elizabeth and I hit the Bloomingdale's after-Christmas sale. Through the din I heard endless talk about food: "I ate like a pig yesterday." "I shouldn't have eaten so much." And the old standby: "Do I look fat in this?"

I braved a full-length mirror—but only to wrap scarves around my neck. My body has shrunk and expanded and shrunk and expanded so much that I'm still never sure what I'm going to see.

I thought about the day after Christmas two years ago, when I started the *Shape* project—how hopeful I was, but oh, how naive.

I never did become the "after" picture.

The *Shape* project officially ended today, and I've still got plenty of pounds to go.

Still, now my weight is—I hope—not the first thing people notice when they meet me, although I know friends would insist that even at my heaviest, it never was.

I don't believe them. I wonder if I ever will.

These past two years I've learned a lot about carbs and cardio, weight lifting, and planning. But mostly I've learned how little of being overweight is really about food. It's about priorities and boundaries and fear and avoidance of anything you don't want to feel. It's about demands that are too high and resources that are too low.

I learned that I'm not alone in feeling alone.

I learned that if I sneak my food, it won't ruin the facade I've created, but it will rot me on the inside.

I learned a thousand other little things, some of which sound as cheerful and pat and homily-like as the fortunes in the cookies Elizabeth and I had yesterday. *The best exercise for you is the one you will do regularly. Stop thinking "I am not enough and there is not enough." You can't compare your inside to other people's outsides.*

Keeping a public journal about food and weight and body image has meant that I could never stop thinking about these things for very long. Now I'm hoping to work on letting go—letting food and weight fade to the background, where they belong, and filling that space in my life with other things.

I'm looking forward to it.

Epilogue

Christmas 2002 (Two Years Later)

IN MARRAKESH, MOROCCO

I'm traveling in Marrakesh over Christmas with Craig, a guy who, as of five days ago, I'm no longer dating. (Don't ask—this could be a book in itself.) I feel like the couple that calls off the wedding but goes on the honeymoon anyway because it's already paid for.

Traveling has always been difficult for me—the whole idea of anyone seeing what and how much I eat, meal after meal, day after day.

On this trip there's the added stress of whether we can really travel together for a week without either killing each other or ending up back in a relationship that's not going anywhere. Marrakesh is an incredibly romantic city—orange-pink sunsets that explode across the sky, candlelit restaurants with tiled waterfalls and half-hidden tables perfect for stolen kisses—and we've gone ahead with this trip for some awfully unromantic reasons. We've already paid for it, for one. We want to demonstrate that we are and can be friends. We both want to get out of gray and rainy London. And neither of us has anywhere better to be.

I met Craig in September, on my third night living in London. Nearly four years after I first planned to move, I finally took the leap.

I had been hearing about Craig for a couple of years. Not because anybody imagined we would necessarily hit it off but because he was a good friend of one of the only people I knew in London. Somehow I'd never managed to be in London when he was around.

We sat next to each other at a dinner. I wasn't feeling "on"—I'd gained some weight over the summer, and I was tired from running around dealing with a move to another continent. But halfway through dinner we ended up holding hands. I was still staying with Craig's friend until I could move into my flat, and we took the long way home. We walked around Notting Hill until 3:00 in the morning. He was leaving on vacation for a week the next day but said he'd call when he got back, and he did.

Dating him was a lot more of a cross-cultural experience than I'd expected. Usually we'd joke about misunderstandings. "I don't speak English very well," I'd say.

"I don't speak American very well," he'd answer. We'd laugh.

I had dated someone in the spring for five months, but that relationship had had the emotional weight of a handshake. Dan and I never discussed much, so it didn't occur to me to say anything to him about food. But with Craig it was different. I found myself wanting to say something. I wanted him to know why it mattered to me whether we'd eat dinner before or after the cinema—and why it sometimes made me cranky when his lateness meant we'd be forced into the latter—or why I cared more than another person might about the fact that he never had anything in his refrigerator besides butter.

I remember one particularly tense morning when I panicked because I had to borrow a shirt from him. He's thin—very thin—and I knew as he casually handed me the shirt that he couldn't possibly have any idea how *not* casual this was for me. My mind was racing. What excuse could I make up if the shirt didn't fit? Could I say I had just realized I had to be somewhere, grab my coat, and race off? (Luckily, the shirt fit.)

Dan never cared much about the things I wrote—he'd be happy for me if I was happy about something, but it ended there. But Craig would ask about the book, seeming frustrated that I was so vague about it. I didn't want to tell him about it, not just because it's very un-English to write anything so personal but because answering his questions about the book would bring us right up to the edge of discussing all kinds of things food and weight and body related that I didn't want to discuss.

It always felt too soon—our relationship still too fragile to bear that sort of weight.

So I hid, falling back into old, bad habits. Craig would disappear downstairs to practice piano for an hour, and I'd say I was heading out to get a newspaper or a Diet Coke. Along with them I'd usually buy a snack—sometimes healthy, sometimes not. It was insurance—something that would let me be with Craig all day and not worry, not obsess about when we might eat and whether at some point I was just going to have to announce that I was hungry.

I'm not a morning person, but in Marrakesh I would leap out of bed in the morning to be the first in the shower so I could go down to breakfast without him. Everything at the hotel was a buffet, and being alone in the morning—not feeling like anyone was watching or could tell that I was so unsure of how much to take—made it easier for me to handle the rest of the day.

On Christmas Eve we went to Chez Ali, a Moroccan palace that serves a family-style dinner and puts on a spectacle of music, camel riding, and fire. It was just Craig and me at a table meant for eight, and they served us as though the table were full.

Fear.

When a huge bowl of couscous arrived, he asked me to serve it. I muttered something about not being very good at it.

"Do you want to practice?" Craig snapped. "You don't have to be good at everything."

I sat there for a good thirty seconds, blinking furiously as I tried not to cry. I cast a glance around the dining room, looking for some clue as to how much to serve, like it was a pop quiz. Then I served—two ladles apiece. I put the ladle down slowly—*chink*—and looked at him warily.

Then I explained. I told him I was afraid to serve the couscous because I'm not sure what a normal portion is. I told him I'm not sure what a normal portion is because I've had problems with food all my life. I gave him the thirty-second version, testing the water.

"I should have known," he said and covered my hand with his. Then: "I'm glad you told me."

When the next course arrived, he served it. Was it my imagination, or was he beyond careful to serve us both exactly the same-size piece of pastry?

It never ends, but it gets easier.

The feelings cycle through faster, like a video on fast-forward. I didn't spend the whole evening brooding about having said anything to him. I didn't feel like I couldn't look him in the eye.

Instead I thought: *This is me. This is the real me.*

Food and my obsession with it are things I will always have to deal with. Some days the burden is heavy. Other days it isn't. But I know—the way I know I look terrible in the color yellow, the way I know I'm allergic to scallops—that this is mine to deal with, probably forever. That when I get stressed or frustrated or angry or upset I will immediately look to food, even if it's just for a second. It's a handicap I have to work around, and I'm working on it.

At Christmas lunch the next day, Craig and I talked about where we had been on Christmases past. As I told Craig about mine, I'd have a brief flash of what I had been wearing and what I ate or didn't eat.

A day later, as I wrote about Christmas lunch, I realized I didn't remember pacing myself during lunch so as not to finish my food before he did. I didn't remember what we ate or if I had left anything on my plate. I didn't remember what I was wearing and how it fit and whether I could feel the button on my jeans making an imprint on my stomach as I took another bite. I could remember only the conversation—the feeling of connection, the feeling of being lucky to be able to live in London for a while and to be traveling in Marrakesh, even though not under the most ideal of circumstances. I felt happy.

I felt lighter.

Acknowledgments

*A*cknowledgments always remind me of a cross between a yearbook message, where you strain for something unique and meaningful and not too sappy (but give up by the fifth book put in front of you), and a wedding invitation list, where each time you add another person, you think of about seventy-five others who then need to be added.

Thanks first to *Shape* magazine, which gave me an opportunity I couldn't begin to appreciate at the time and allowed me to take the column in directions they (and I) never expected. My editor, Maureen Healy, was unfailingly enthusiastic and encouraging. Dr. Pamela Peeke and Shari Frishett, LCSW, provided support that went well beyond what they originally signed on for. I am also indebted to Nancy Clark, M.S., R.D., and of course, to all the *Shape* readers whose heartfelt and heartening letters sustained me during the writing of both the column and the book.

For six years, Jack Limpert and *Washingtonian* magazine gave me the freedom to write about a lot of things that are important to me and to write in an office full of people who cheered me on. Special thanks to Sherri Dalphonse, Diane Granat, Leslie Milk, and, of course, Bill O'Sullivan, for his patient and careful reading of this book and so many of the stories that came before it.

Thank you to my agent, Ted Weinstein, and to my editors, Michele Pezzuti and Heidi Bresnahan, and everyone else at McGraw-Hill.

This book might never have left my daydreams without my amazing friends: Kate Ackley, Annemarie Borrego, Andrew Clark, Angie Fox, Sarah Gale, Josh Green, Cree Harry, David Hothersall, Jean Kalata, Cindy Kushner, Stephen Martin, Brent Mitchell, Mark Murray, Jon Spira, Jay Sumner, Ashley Wall, and Shawn Zeller. Thanks especially to some old and dear friends (lifelines throughout this project and so many others): Brian Hiatt, Adam Hill, Christie Kaefer, Erica Siegel, and Alexy Yoffie.

My family taught me to dream big dreams and to believe I could achieve them. The reassurance and enthusiasm of my father and grandmother helped give me the push I needed to write parts of this book. And I want to thank my mother for all she gave me. She missed seeing this book in print by just a few months, but I know she would have been happy for me that I wrote it.

In this book I have chronicled a lot of not-so-nice behavior on the part of my sister, Diana. I'm happy to say the rocky stage of our relationship seems to be ending as I write. Diana provided constant pep talks by phone and instant messenger and didn't try to stop me from being honest, even though she knew a lot of what I wrote might not be flattering to her. For all of that I am deeply grateful.

Finally, I am quite sure this book could not have been written without the wisdom and encouragement of two people I feel so lucky to know: Elizabeth Bard, my transatlantic cliff-jumping buddy, and my best friend, Mary Gardner, partner in crime, marathons (phone *and* running), and sushi.